THESE ISLES

THESE ISLES

THESE ISLES

A PEOPLE'S HISTORY OF ENGLAND, IRELAND, SCOTLAND AND WALES

BRIAN GROOM

Harper
North

HarperNorth
Windmill Green
24 Mount Street
Manchester M2 3NX

A division of
HarperCollins*Publishers*
1 London Bridge Street
London SE1 9GF

www.harpercollins.co.uk

HarperCollins*Publishers*
Macken House, 39/40 Mayor Street Upper
Dublin 1, D01 C9W8, Ireland

First published by HarperCollins*Publishers* 2026

1 3 5 7 9 10 8 6 4 2

A catalogue record of this book is available from the British Library

HB ISBN 978-0-00-860856-9

Printed and bound in the UK using 100% renewable electricity at CPI
Group (UK) Ltd

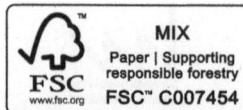

For my grandchildren
Oscar, Sidney, Iris and Nye

CONTENTS

INTRODUCTION

It is daunting to write about the history of the territory you call home, especially when that territory is so complex and when control of parts of it has been so bitterly disputed for centuries. The subject of this book is the people of a group of islands off continental Europe's north-west coast that encompasses the United Kingdom of Great Britain and Northern Ireland (including England, Scotland and Wales), along with the Republic of Ireland, the Isle of Man and the bailiwicks of Jersey and Guernsey (although the latter two are closer to the continental mainland than to the other islands).

A common term is the 'British Isles', though some understandably object that this implies a continued territorial claim or the political overlordship of the UK over the Republic of Ireland. Alternative terms include 'Britain and Ireland', the 'Atlantic Archipelago', the 'Anglo-Celtic Isles', the 'British-Irish Isles' and the 'Islands of the North Atlantic'. Diplomatic documents drawn up jointly by the UK and Irish governments refer simply to 'these islands'. I have opted for 'These Isles'.

I have attempted to tell the key parts of the story of the Isles' people from the first human footsteps to the present day. Wars have been fought within the Isles almost as long as there have been people. It has been a kaleidoscope of overlapping and conflicting identities.

Their inhabitants have made their mark in many fields of human endeavour, notably by pioneering the Industrial Revolution, which brought massive economic opportunities, wrenching social change and long-term environmental issues. They also managed to create history's largest Empire, covering almost a quarter of the globe, with consequences that remain with us today. Emigration and Empire have created a huge diaspora: the number who can claim descent from British or Irish emigrants has been estimated at about two hundred million, almost treble the Isles' current population of almost seventy-five million, with particular concentrations in Australia, Canada and the United States.

This book recounts the history of the Celts, Romans, Anglo-Saxons, Vikings and Normans along with more recent groups that have inhabited the Isles. As with my previous books, narrative history is interspersed with chapters on social and cultural themes including languages, emigrants' and immigrants' stories, women's fortunes, the smaller islands, popular culture and the arts, music and literature. High politics, monarchs and nobility all feature, but it is a people's history, and so I have foregrounded the average people and the quotidian parts of their lives wherever possible.

The relationship between England and the smaller nations is a tension that runs through the story. England conquered Wales in the Middle Ages and formed unions with Scotland in 1707 and Ireland in 1801. Wales and Ireland are often described as England's first colonies, yet eventually there were also Welsh and Irish people, as well as English and Scots, who became colonisers elsewhere in the world. Factors that fashioned the UK included the opportunities of Empire and a desire to defend Protestantism against a largely Catholic Europe. How far a common British identity was created in the process is much debated. Most of Ireland, with a Catholic majority, was never comfortable in the union and broke away in 1922 after a war of independence. Nationalism grew in Scotland and Wales, perhaps influenced in part by the crumbing of the Empire, helping to weaken bonds between the UK's nations. Northern

Ireland, which remained part of the UK, was wracked by a 30-year conflict known as the Troubles. Scotland voted against independence in a 2014 referendum, though in view of the Isles' volatile past it is hard to say with certainty whether the current alignment will endure. The history of the Isles is about much more than the smaller nations' relationship to England, however. I have done my best to give back to the peoples of Ireland, Wales, Scotland and the smaller isles their due part in the story.

For me, this project has been particularly rewarding as it has drawn on elements of my life experience. My previous books, *Northerners: A History, from the Ice Age to the Present Day* and *Made in Manchester: A People's History of the City that Shaped the Modern World*, drew on my north of England background. During my career as a journalist, for several years I led the *Financial Times'* coverage of the UK's regions and nations. In a spell as editor of the paper's Europe edition, coverage of the Republic of Ireland was part of my overall responsibilities. And in mid-career I spent 10 years in Scotland, where I launched and later edited *Scotland on Sunday*, *The Scotsman*'s Sunday paper.

It has been a pleasure to write the book, and I hope you find it interesting to read.

CHAPTER 1

ANCESTORS, CELTS AND ROMANS

A small group of adults and children walked along the mudflats of a river estuary, leaving a trail behind them. Who were they? Their footprints are the earliest evidence so far of humans in Britain, Ireland and the surrounding Isles. They are also the oldest human footprints outside Africa.[1]

These footprints were exposed briefly in 2013 on the beach at Happisburgh (pronounced Haysborough) in Norfolk. Using pollen in sediment layers, scientists were able to date the footprints – along with stone tools found in the area – to between 850,000 and 950,000 years ago. The age of the finds suggests they may have been made by *Homo antecessor*, a human species previously found only in Spain, thought to be the first of at least four types of human to have attempted to settle in Britain.[2]

Archaeology affords only glimpses of these Isles' early inhabitants, making it hard to be sure how far and quickly they spread. Later inhabitants would have a profound influence on the world through discovery, industry, wars, the slave trade and the most powerful empire ever known. All that, of course, is a brief pinprick in our story. More than 99 per cent of human history in Europe took place in the Stone Age. For much of that time, Britain was not an island. It was joined to the continent by a wide land bridge that we call Doggerland, now under the North Sea. Early humans came across in search of food in warmer spells during the last Ice Age. There are thought to have been at least 10 waves of occupation as people arrived, yet they were repeatedly driven out when the cold returned.

The climate fluctuated drastically. In colder periods, the landscape was a treeless tundra with ice sheets and glaciers covering Ireland, Scotland, Wales and northern England. Warmer spells could be Mediterranean-like, with birch trees, shrub, grasses and eventually oak woodland. There were exotic animals such as mammoths, rhinoceroses, straight-tusked elephants, hippopotamuses – and even cave lions in places such as London's Trafalgar Square.

Next came *Homo heidelbergensis* about 500,000 years ago. Tall, strong and with relatively large brains, they are the first human species for whom there is fossil evidence in Britain: a leg bone and two teeth found at Boxgrove in West Sussex. They used hand axes to butcher large animals and could plan and co-operate as a group. They probably reached northern England: hand axes found at Waverley Wood, Warwickshire, are made of andesite rock likely to have come from the Lake District about the same time.[3]

We know that *Homo neanderthalensis*, small and stocky, was in Britain as early as 400,000 years ago thanks to the discovery of a young woman's skull at Swanscombe, Kent. Neanderthals left and returned several times as the climate oscillated. Neanderthal teeth found at Pontnewydd Cave in Denbighshire, north Wales, date from about 230,000 years ago.[4]

Homo sapiens, or modern humans, are more recent: the earliest evidence is a jaw fragment found in Kents Cavern, Devon, estimated to be at least 40,000 years old. Their presence, initially sporadic, has been continuous since about 12,000 years ago. They were adaptable hunter-gatherers who moved over big distances in larger groups. The 'Red Lady of Paviland' – actually the skeleton of a man covered in red ochre, discovered in a cave in the Gower peninsula, Swansea, in 1823 – dates from about 33,000 years ago and is one of the earliest known ceremonial burials with grave goods.[5] In Ireland, analysis of a reindeer bone fragment in north Cork indicates human activity at a similar time.[6]

The earliest firm evidence in Scotland is a hunter-gatherer camp at Howburn Farm near Biggar, south Lanarkshire, dated to about 12000 BCE. They may have been chasing reindeer and other cold-adapted animals northwards as the climate warmed. Flints found at Biggar are similar to others from northern Germany and southern Denmark, suggesting cultural exchange across Doggerland.[7]

As the Ice Age ended, sea levels rose, cutting Britain off from continental Europe permanently, perhaps around 5500 BCE. Water had poured into the Irish Sea from about 10000 BCE, widening existing channels (it is unclear whether there was ever a land bridge between Ireland and Scotland). Humans began to settle. A site at Star Carr in Yorkshire, sometimes described as 'Britain's oldest house', dates from about 9000 BCE and may have been a seasonal hunting camp. Circular buildings at East Barns near Dunbar, Echline near South Queensferry, Howick in Northumberland and Mount Sandel in Northern Ireland are thought to have come slightly later.

The Neolithic period, roughly between 10000 and 2000 BCE, saw the start of farming. Stone axe heads made at Great Langdale in the Lake District have been found all over Britain and in Ireland, showing there was trading throughout the Isles. People began building tombs such as long barrows and cairns in eastern Britain or passage graves (burial chambers with a narrow access passage) in the west and Ireland. They also built ritual monuments such as stone circles and henges.

Orkney has a rich ritual landscape including the Standing Stones of Stenness, Maeshowe passage grave and the Ring of Brodgar. Skara Brae, Europe's best-preserved Neolithic settlement – exposed by a storm in 1850 – is believed to have been inhabited from about 3100 BCE. Many of these sites were abandoned about 600 years later, probably because the climate became colder. The Boyne Valley in County Meath, Ireland, has a complex ritual landscape including passage graves, henges, standing stones and wooden structures. Stonehenge in Wiltshire was probably constructed from about 3000 to 2000 BCE. A ring of igneous bluestones there is thought to have been transported 140 miles from Preseli, south-west Wales, possibly having already been used as a stone circle.[8]

The Bronze Age from about 2200 BCE saw mining of copper in Ireland and Wales, tin in Cornwall and gold in Ireland's Wicklow Mountains. The Iron Age from about 800 BCE was notable for hundreds of 'hill forts' or fortified sites of varying size around Britain, though these are rarer in Ireland. It is unclear whether they had a defensive purpose or were communal spaces used for ceremonial or trading purposes or keeping livestock. Tensions no doubt grew as the population expanded and competition for land intensified.

A highland–lowland divide in Britain was identified in the 1930s by archaeologist Cyril Fox. A ridge of Jurassic limestone runs through England from Dorset to the Yorkshire coast. To the north-west lies a highland zone, with harder rocks, suitable for hill farming such as raising sheep, occupied by isolated farmsteads or small hamlets. To the south-east is a lowland zone suitable for arable farming, creating larger villages. This division now tends to be seen as an over-simplification: Ireland, for example, though culturally and geographically linked with Scotland and Wales, was not in the highland zone. There is no doubt though that the south-east was wealthier, producing more decorated pottery. Coinage and markets developed there. A north–south divide was already in place in Britain.

The Indo-European languages that we call 'Celtic' took hold throughout the Isles in the Bronze Age or early Iron Age (what was spoken before is unclear; some words may have survived in Celtic languages). It used to be believed that Celts were an ethnic group that came from continental Europe in a wave of invasions, but a lack of evidence of large-scale arrivals has led to the view that the languages spread by a hazier process of cultural exchange and slow migration. They divided into two groups: Brythonic or Brittonic (which later developed into Breton, Cornish and Welsh) and Goidelic (Irish, Scottish Gaelic and Manx).

Britons speaking Celtic languages held sway across the Isles for centuries until the Romans and then the Anglo-Saxons came. Celtic culture and traditions still exert a compelling attraction. Celts produced art with abstract patterns of inimitable beauty, along with song, harp music and myths of gods, kings, heroines and heroes. Celtic religion involved the supernatural and a wide array of deities. Celts believed that spirits inhabited the natural world; they deposited offerings of treasured goods to them in sacred groves and streams. Ceremonies were overseen by priests known as druids, who were also judges, teachers and lore keepers. Greek and Roman writers accused them of human sacrifice, for which evidence appears uncertain. In Ireland, there were young warrior bands known as Fianna or 'Fenians'; legends in the Fianna Cycle recount heroic deeds by their leader Fionn mac Cumhaill or 'Finn MacCool'.

Greek explorer Pytheas circumnavigated Britain in about 320 BCE and was probably the source for writer Diodorus Siculus, who in the first century BCE called the island Pretannia (Greek Prettanike), or island of the Pretanī. 'Pretanī' is a Celtic word that probably meant 'the painted ones' or 'the tattooed folk'. It may well have been the name by which the people knew themselves. Pretannia evolved into Britannia, the Romans' name for England, Wales and southern Scotland throughout their occupation (Caledonia was roughly north of the Forth, while Ireland was Hibernia). A variant of the Celtic spelling is still used in Welsh, where the name for Britain is Prydain.[9] Britannia became the name of a Roman goddess, the personification of Britain, based on Minerva, goddess of trade and strategic warfare. The Old Irish name for Ireland was Ériu, also the name of a Gaelic goddess.

Julius Caesar, Roman general and future dictator, made two brief invasions of south-east Britain in 55 and 54 BCE as part of his Gallic wars, probably hoping it would strengthen him politically. Bad weather and hit-and-run resistance made things difficult.

Resistance to his second expedition was led by a chief called Caswallawn (in Welsh texts) or Cassivellaunus (in Latin), thought to have been king of the Catuvellauni tribe north of the Thames estuary. He has the distinction of being the first ancient Briton known by name. Caswallawn led an alliance of tribes but eventually surrendered when others submitted to Caesar and revealed his location. Caesar extracted a face-saving promise from Caswallawn to leave rival tribes in peace but ultimately gained little from his botched expeditions.[10]

Emperor Claudius, the club-footed stammerer, ordered an invasion in 43 CE with a large force and succeeded where Julius failed. Rome already had a major influence on British tribes through diplomacy and trade. Claudius, seeking a triumph, took advantage of squabbling over succession after the death of Cunobelin, another king of the Catuvellauni who controlled much of south-east England (and whom William Shakespeare called Cymbeline). Claudius arrived a few weeks after the invasion force, together with elephants, just in time to take part in the capture of Colchester.

Claudius stayed for 16 days and received the submission of 11 kings. According to fourth-century Roman historian Eutropius, these included the (unnamed) king of Orkney. This story appeared far-fetched until shards from Roman amphorae of a type that became obsolete by the end of the century were found at Broch of Gurness, lending weight to the tale. If this did happen, it must have taken considerable diplomatic effort and planning to persuade an Orkney king to make the 800-mile journey, timed for Claudius's arrival. Perhaps he was offered material rewards or some form of support against his enemies.[11]

After taking control of the south-east, the Romans headed north and west. The conquest period lasted 40 years. It has been estimated that between 100,000 and 250,000 Britons perished out of a British population of about two million.[12] The Romans came in order to exploit Britain's land, people and resources, yet it is an open question whether their occupation was ever profitable. For centuries, they needed to keep one-tenth of the legions there to control an area that comprised less than a thirtieth of the empire.[13] About eight emperors are thought to have visited Britain, plus others who served there before coming to power.

Cunobelin's son Caradog (in Welsh) or Caratacus (in Latin) led resistance in the south-east and then fled to Wales to fight alongside the Silures and Ordovices, ancient Celtic tribes. Publius Ostorius Scapula, governor of Britannia, finally defeated him in 51 CE in Snowdonia. Caradog's wife and daughter were captured, but he fled to Brigantia, the Pennine kingdom, where Cartimandua, queen of the Brigantes and an ally of Rome, handed him to the Romans. He was taken to Rome, where he made a speech so stirring that, according to historian Tacitus, Claudius pardoned him and let him live in exile there.[14]

A new governor, Gaius Suetonius Paulinus, attacked Anglesey, the druids' power centre, in 60 or 61, massacring druids and destroying their sacred groves. Meanwhile, the Iceni of eastern England rose in a ferocious revolt under their chief, Boudica. She was outraged after her territory had been annexed; she had been flogged and her two daughters raped. Thousands of Romans were slaughtered, and London was burned in the revolt, after which the Romans' revenge was even more ferocious, with tens of thousands of Britons killed. Boudica died by illness or suicide.[15]

Boudica has long been hailed, especially by Victorians, as a resistance heroine, whereas Cartimandua tends to be relegated to a few disparaging lines in history books. That is probably because she collaborated with the Romans, divorced her husband, married one of his aides and was overthrown by a revolt. Roman historians portrayed her, despite her loyalty, as an adulterous betrayer of British men. No Roman woman became emperor, so female rulers on the empire's fringes were seen as exotic. They tend to be stereotyped in Roman sources either as women of loose morals (Cartimandua, Cleopatra) or as fierce and unladylike (Boudica).

Cartimandua's former husband Venutius rebelled in 69 over her decision to marry a man called Vellocatus, formerly Venutius's armour-bearer. The Romans had to launch a rescue mission to extricate her, after which she vanished from the historical record. She had kept her territory free from annexation for up to 30 years, though in the end she was unable to halt the northward spread of Roman rule.

Gnaeus Julius Agricola, governor from 77 or 78, came as close as anyone to seizing Caledonia. Scotland has never been fully conquered by forces from the south: neither the Roman Empire, despite several campaigns, nor English medieval kings achieved it. Agricola remained in office for about six years, an exceptionally long term. The Roman army moved steadily north, building forts on the way. Agricola reached the Forth–Clyde isthmus and then the river Tay. According to Tacitus, his son-in-law, Agricola wanted to cross to Ireland, which he thought he could subdue with just one legion.[16] In fact, the Romans never attempted to occupy Ireland, though there were trading or raiding links evidenced by pottery and coinage.

In 83 or 84, according to Tacitus, Agricola defeated Caledonian tribes at Mons Graupius, an unknown highland mountain that many have attempted to identify. The tribes were led by a general called Calgacus, the first inhabitant of Scotland for whom we have a name. Tacitus portrays him as making a rousing speech (certainly invented) in which he excoriates Romans as 'robbers of the world': 'To robbery, slaughter, plunder, they give the lying name of empire; they make a solitude and call it peace.'[17] If Tacitus is to be believed, 10,000 Britons were killed but only 360 Romans. This was the high-water mark of Roman expansion. Agricola was soon recalled to Rome, and the Romans drew back to the Forth–Clyde. Troops were needed on the Danube.

The emphasis switched to consolidation. Emperor Hadrian arrived around 122 and started building his 74-mile wall, the most visible reminder of the Roman presence. Britons on either side were treated as potential enemies. Antoninus Pius, who succeeded Hadrian, had another wall built further north along the Forth–Clyde line. The Antonine Wall was shorter (37 miles) and simpler, but around 158 it in turn was abandoned, for unknown reasons.

Hadrian's Wall again became the frontier and remained so until Roman rule ended.

South-eastern Britain became the most Romanised and prosperous part of the Isles, with a fertile agricultural economy in which many villas developed, though its towns remained small compared with those on the continent. An elite native class embraced a Romanised lifestyle, bringing economic and social opportunities, but were a minority. Only the elite spoke and wrote in Latin, while the vast majority still spoke Celtic tongues. Highland areas such as north Wales and the Pennines were exploited more for their mineral resources.

Tantalising glimpses of life on the Roman frontier are provided by the Vindolanda tablets – letters and documents written in ink on wafer-thin slivers of wood, discovered around an early wooden fort just south of Hadrian's Wall. They date mostly from 90–105, when auxiliary troops from today's Netherlands and Belgium were based there. The best known was written by Claudia Severa, wife of the commander of a nearby fort, to Sulpicia Lepidina, wife of another commander, inviting her to a birthday party (translated from Latin): 'I shall expect you, sister. Farewell, sister, my dearest soul, as I hope to prosper, and hail.'[18] Soldiers from around the empire served at the fort and felt the northern winters. One anonymous letter reads: 'I have sent you ... pairs of socks from Sattua, two pairs of sandals and two pairs of underpants.'[19] Several artefacts and inscriptions clustered along Hadrian's Wall also record the presence of Africans.

Roman soldiers had a low opinion of native Britons, one tablet suggests. The author wrote: 'The Britons are unprotected by armour. There are very many cavalry. The cavalry do not use swords, nor do the wretched Britons [*Brittunculi*] mount in order to throw javelins.'[20] *Brittunculi* can alternatively be translated as 'little Britons'. It is unclear whether the writer meant Britons serving in the Roman forces or the natives he was fighting. Either way, the term appears derogatory.

A further attempt to conquer Caledonia was made by Septimius Severus, the 'African emperor', who was of mixed race from present-day

Libya. He came to Britain in 208 with his wife and his sons Caracalla and Geta, both designated as successors. He arrived possibly in response to a barbarian rebellion, though he may also have wanted to find a project to absorb his unruly sons. He made his base at Eboracum (York) and mounted campaigns in Caledonia in 209 and 210. Although the Caledonians fought a guerrilla war, Severus reached north-east Scotland. According to historian Cassius Dio, the tribes were forced to give up much of their territory. Severus proclaimed victory, but the Caledonians soon disavowed the terms and broke out again in revolt. Severus was preparing another invasion when he died at York in February 211. Caracalla and Geta became joint emperors, but Caracalla was ruthless even by Roman standards. He executed his father's household attendants at York, and on returning to Rome he killed Geta, who died clinging to his mother.[21]

Britain was split into two provinces in the third century: Britannia Inferior stretched from Hadrian's Wall to south of Lincoln, while Britannia Superior (so called because it was geographically closer to Rome) covered southern England and Wales. This was a turbulent period in the empire, with many soldier emperors, and Britannia Inferior was a military zone, so it benefited to an extent from imperial policy that poured money into the military. Britannia Superior's capital was at Londinium (London) while that of Britannia Inferior was Eboracum.

Exactly when or how Christianity came to Britain is unclear. A second-century 'word square' discovered in Mamucium, Roman Manchester, may be one of the earliest examples: the anagram spells *pater noster*, the opening of the Lord's Prayer in Latin.[22] Christianity became the empire's established religion during the fourth century. Although Hibernia and Caledonia were unconquered, there was a Romanising influence via Christian missionaries.

Caledonian tribes became labelled *Picti* or Picts by the Romans, taken to mean 'painted or tattooed people', though whether they were actually tattooed is uncertain. Frontier security deteriorated amid seaborne raiding by Picts, Attacotti and Scotti from Ireland

and Saxons from the east. The raids culminated in attacks in 367, which historian Ammianus Marcellinus labelled a 'barbarian conspiracy'. The invaders overwhelmed the northern regions, and cities were sacked before order was restored.

Roman troops frequently rebelled as the empire began to fragment. One imperial usurper based in Britain, a Spanish-born general called Magnus Maximus, crossed the Channel to Gaul in 383 and successfully seized control of the Western Empire, making himself emperor, before he was defeated and killed in 388. Some Welsh historians have called him father of the nation for allegedly transferring authority to local chiefs as he left.[23] Magnus Maximus became romanticised in Welsh legends as a mythical figure called *Macsen Wledig* who marries a British woman, while early Welsh genealogies portray him as the founding father of the dynasties of several medieval Welsh kingdoms.

Britannia became stripped of troops as instability grew in Rome. By 410, the Roman era was over, and Romano-British officials were left to fend for themselves. The Romans are often portrayed as having brought order and economic, social and cultural advance. They certainly brought useful innovations, including roads and towns, yet they were also colonisers who imposed their rule on others and killed and enslaved many. We do not know how most Britons viewed them. Their lasting legacy is perhaps less than might be expected for almost four centuries of rule. And they never conquered Ireland or most of Scotland.

CHAPTER 2

SHIFTING KINGDOMS

The Romans' withdrawal created a vacuum and set off a chain of migrations and resettlements, reshaping the Isles' populations. It was chaotic and complex, a kind of primordial soup from which our modern political geography eventually evolved.

Small kingdoms reasserted themselves and struggled against each other and Germanic incomers. Warfare was the norm. The Vikings' arrival at the end of the eighth century – first to plunder, then aiming to conquer and settle – further reshaped the map. Towards the end of the millennium, there was consolidation as the nations of England, Scotland, Ireland and Wales emerged. In the case of England and Scotland, the struggle against the Vikings played a big part in their creation.

After governance from Rome ended, Romano-British administrators hung on for decades, some perhaps hoping the Romans might return. However, their rule gradually weakened, and towns shrank or were abandoned. Migrants from northern Germany and southern Sweden – emboldened by the collapse of the Romans' Western Empire – began arriving on Britain's east coast with their mead halls, paganism and vengeful gods. Anglo-Saxons – a broad label for Germanic groups including Angles, Saxons, Jutes and Frisians – became established by the mid-fifth century and controlled large areas from the sixth.

For the Brythonic-speaking Celtic British, the Anglo-Saxons' arrival began a period of struggle and decline. Spirits were buoyed by a probably mythical king Arthur who resisted Anglo-Saxon expansion. A key battle was said to have been fought at Mount Badon, location unknown, where resistance may have been led by a Roman-style aristocrat called Ambrosius Aurelianus, another possibly mythical figure.

The 'Dark Ages' were not simply a Britons versus Anglo-Saxons struggle, however; Celts often fought Celts, and Anglo-Saxons fought Anglo-Saxons. In the past, scholars thought that Germanic incomers wiped out Britons or drove them westwards to Wales, but now it seems more likely that most of the existing population stayed and gradually adopted the arrivals' language and culture.[1] There was clearly some movement, though: many Britons fled to what became known as Brittany. Four broad cultural zones emerged: an Anglo-Saxon east; a British west and north; a Pictish north; and Gaelic Ireland, with enclaves in western Britain.

Christianity was reaching beyond former Roman boundaries by the fifth century. Patrick was the most famous of several missionaries to Ireland and northern Britain whose influence was both religious and political. Soon the Irish were bringing monastic Christianity back to Britain and the continent. The best-known Irish foundation is Columba or Colmcille's monastery at Iona, established in 563 or soon after. Over the sixth and seventh centuries, it became the greatest Christian centre in northern Britain, extending its influence to Northumbria via the monastery of Lindisfarne.

Ireland's conversion was complex and involved compromises with Celtic paganism, but it introduced literacy and monasteries, profoundly altering Irish society. Patrick was not the first pioneer to arrive, yet his all-embracing cult eclipsed others. Details of his life are far from clear. He was from a well-off Romanised family in western Britain (there are various candidates for where, including the Carlisle area) and was captured at age 16 by Irish raiders and shipped as a slave to Ireland, where he stayed, probably in north Connacht, for six years. He escaped and trained as a priest, then returned to Ireland to preach the gospel. There he won converts and penetrated parts of the country where no Christian missionary had gone before. Legends grew up, including one that he cleared the island of snakes and demons. By the seventh century, he was revered as Ireland's primary patron saint.[2]

Monasteries were initially ascetic but soon acquired wealthy patrons, creating a rich literary and artistic culture. Examples of Insular or Hiberno-Saxon art include the Book of Kells and Ardagh Chalice, while scholars excelled in Latin learning and theology. Ireland's myriad petty kingdoms were overtaken by five or six provincial overkings with real powers, notably the Uí Néill in the north and midlands and Eóganachta in Munster. It was a hierarchical society, with legal rights defined by status: kicking a bishop was a lot more expensive than kicking a peasant, according to an early Latin law tract. Marriage was unstable, and polygamy continued to be practised by the upper classes for centuries.[3]

Irish history, as written, is a largely male affair, though powerful women are a recurrent theme in legend, such as Mebh or Maeve, queen of Connacht in the Ulster Cycle of mythology. She had many husbands and lovers and led a raid to claim the most famous bull in Ireland. Brigid, one of three national saints along with Patrick and Columba, was said by medieval hagiographies to have been an abbess who founded the abbey of Kildare, though there is debate over whether she really existed. Brigid is also patroness of poetry, healing, blacksmithing and dairy farming.

The Irish established colonies in western Britain at Dál Riata, Man, Dyfed, the Llŷn Peninsula and even Cornwall. Only Dál Riata or Dalriada, which for a time straddled Scotland's western seaboard and north-eastern Ireland, endured. The hillfort of Dunadd in Argyll is believed to have been its capital. It was at its height under Áedán mac Gabráin, king from about 574 to 609, who campaigned to expand his territory, but he was defeated by Æthelfrith of Bernicia at the battle of Degsastan. Æthelfrith later also ruled Deira, roughly covering today's Yorkshire – thus uniting Northumbria's constituent parts.[4]

Columba (521–97), from what is now County Donegal, already had churches dedicated to him in Ireland. He turned Iona into a school for missionaries and spent most of the rest of his life in Scotland, presiding over the start of a vast chain of monasteries. His hagiographer Adomnán, a seventh-century Iona abbot, elevated the saint in his Life of Columba as a prophet, apostle and pilgrim. Other Christian pioneers in Scotland included Ninian of Whithorn, Donnán of Eigg and Kentigern of Strathclyde, also known as Mungo, founder and patron saint of the city of Glasgow.

Four main groups emerged in the area of north Britain, roughly corresponding to today's Scotland: the Picts in the east and north, with kingdoms between the river Forth and Shetland; the Gaels of Dál Riata in the west; the British kingdom of Strathclyde in the south-west, often called Alt Clut, the Brythonic name for their capital at Dumbarton Rock; and Northumbrians in Lothian and borders. These groups initially had little in common, but within 400 years a unified kingdom was being forged. The Northumbrians displaced two other British kingdoms of the *Hen Ogledd*, or Old North: Gododdin, in the south-east, and Rheged, thought to have straddled Galloway and Cumbria.

Irish missionaries from Dál Riata gradually introduced the previously pagan Picts to Christianity. The Picts are among the Isles' mysteries. Named by Roman sources at the end of the third century, they appear to have been an amalgam of tribes the Romans previously called Caledonians, yet their culture became erased by the mid-ninth century. Place names and personal names suggest they may have spoken a Brythonic language, but there is no literary evidence apart from hard-to-decipher symbols. They left behind monumental stones along with smaller objects of stone and bone and metalwork such as brooches. Alongside Christianity, the Picts gradually adopted Gaelic language and customs. The Picts defeated Northumbrian king Ecgfrith in 685 at Dun Nechtain or Nechtansmere (location in eastern Scotland debated), marking the disintegration of Northumbrian dominance over northern Britain.[5]

In Wales, several kingdoms emerged after the Romans departed, such as Gwynedd and Powys in north and mid Wales and Dyfed and Gwent in the south. The 'age of saints' saw monastic settlements created by religious leaders such as David, bishop of Mynyw (now St David's), who became Wales's patron saint. He was a renowned preacher who led an austere life in the Celtic monastic tradition that connected Wales with Ireland, Cornwall and western Scotland. Wales, however, became separated by Anglo-Saxons from what remained of the *Hen Ogledd*, symbolised by the defeat of Powys by Æthelfrith of Northumbria at the battle of Chester in 616. Powys also lost territory to Mercia, which built the earthwork known as Offa's Dyke, possibly marking an agreed border in the eighth century. Wales was not unified, though the term *Kymry* for the country was first recorded in a praise poem in about 633 (today *Cymru* for Wales and *Cymry* for the people). Anglo-Saxons used the term 'Welsh' to mean Romanised Britons.[6]

In what was to become England, the Anglo-Saxons created seven main kingdoms – Northumbria (uniting Bernicia and Deira), Mercia, East Anglia, Essex, Kent, Sussex and Wessex – plus a few smaller ones. Northumbria and Mercia dominated the seventh century, Mercia the eighth and Wessex the ninth. One of Northumbria's kings, Oswald, ruled for just eight years, from 634 to 642, yet he was the first English king to die a Christian martyr, and he became venerated as a saint. His cult spread around Europe and lasted for centuries. Mercia's kings included the powerful Offa, who reigned from 757 to 796. He extended Mercia's supremacy over most of the south.

Christianisation of Anglo-Saxon England began around 600, influenced by Celtic Christianity from the north-west and the Roman Catholic Church from the south-east. Augustine became the first Archbishop of Canterbury in 597, sent by Pope Gregory to convert King Æthelberht of Kent. Northumbria's Oswald, brought up on Iona, invited Bishop Aidan from there to establish a community of monks on Lindisfarne in 634.

Christianity brought literacy, enabling Northumbria to develop rapidly into northern Europe's leading intellectual and artistic centre. Its golden age produced scholars such as Bede and Alcuin. The growth of monasteries created opportunities for aristocratic women not destined to be queens, notably Hilda (or Hild), the illustrious first abbess of Whitby. She was 'the most religious handmaid of Christ', according to Bede, and her reputation for wisdom was such that 'not only meaner men in their need, but sometimes even kings and princes, sought and received her counsel'. At the Synod of Whitby in 664, Oswiu, Oswald's brother and successor as Northumbrian king, opted for Roman customs over Celtic ones. While the debate focused on doctrinal issues such as differing methods of calculating the date of Easter and the style of monastic tonsure (round for the Romans, horseshoe-shaped for the Celts), in reality the decision was more about jurisdiction and political influence.[7]

In 793 came a terrifying Viking attack on Lindisfarne, usually regarded as the start of the Viking age in Britain, though there had already been a raid at Portland on the south coast, and Vikings were almost certainly established in Orkney and Shetland by this time. 'The harrowing inroads of heathen men made lamentable havoc in the church of God in Holy-island, by rapine and slaughter,' wrote the later author of the *Anglo-Saxon Chronicle*.[8]

The Vikings' arrival changed the Isles' social and political geography. The raiders were probably driven abroad by competition for land in Scandinavia combined with awareness of treasures in vulnerable places such as coastal monasteries. They developed swift, shallow-bottomed vessels to mount lightning raids on coasts and up rivers. Broadly, those who raided the west came from what is now Norway, while those who attacked the east coast were from the area we call Denmark. Settlements were established on the coasts of Britain and Ireland as well as the Isle of Man, Shetland, Orkney and the Hebrides.

The Vikings' Great Army, led by Halfdan and Ivar the Boneless (his nickname is thought to refer to some kind of disability), captured York in 866, then overran Northumbria. Viking kings ruled an area between the Tees and Humber, known as the kingdom of Jorvik. They gained control over East Anglia and Mercia, leaving just Wessex resisting. Viking assaults must have been terrifying, but the Scandinavians soon became Christianised and integrated with local populations. Towns and trade developed. The term Viking – possibly from *víkingr*, Old Norse for an individual on a long-distance sea journey – was not common until Victorian times. Latin and Old English texts refer to Northmen, Danes, pirates, heathens, dark foreigners, fair foreigners, pagans and other terms. Areas where Viking laws and customs prevailed later became known as Danelaw, though it is doubtful whether there was ever an integrated realm covering the whole territory.[9]

Wessex's King Alfred, labelled 'the Great' in Tudor times, retreated to the island of Athelney on the Somerset Levels, from which he waged guerrilla war. He eventually defeated the Vikings at Edington in Wiltshire in 878, though the Danes continued to occupy much of England. In the tenth century, Viking rulers were evicted, and England became unified for the first time under Wessex kings, initially temporarily under Æthelstan, Alfred's grandson, then permanently under Æthelstan's half-brother Eadred.

By the end of the ninth century, Orkney was the centre of a powerful Norse earldom and a base for raiding the mainland, where the Vikings also controlled Caithness. What happened to the Picts is unclear: some think Pictish men were either slaughtered or forced to leave. Shetland and Orkney were to remain Norwegian until 1472. Pressure from Viking attacks was a factor behind a merger whereby Cináed mac Ailpin (Kenneth MacAlpin), king of Dál Riata, also became king of the Picts in 843, bringing to power the house of Alpin. Dublin Vikings sacked Strathclyde's capital Dumbarton in 870–71. Iona Abbey was attacked four times by Viking raiders, with 68 monks massacred there in 806. As in England, however, the incomers in some areas assimilated with the native population. In the Hebrides and south-west Scotland, a hybrid Gaelic–Norse population emerged, known to the Irish as Gall-Gaedhil ('foreign Gael').[10]

Dál Riata/Pictland became known as Alba, possibly a Gaelic translation of a Pictish name, by about 900. The term Scotia also became increasingly used, eventually becoming Scotland in English texts. Sometimes kings of Alba were able to play off Dublin Vikings against those from York. Causantín (Constantine II), who ruled 900–43, established control over much of what became modern Scotland and tried unsuccessfully to extend his reach to the Tyne and across Cumbria. After southern Alba was ravaged by Æthelstan, Causantín allied with the kings of Dublin and Strathclyde against the English king, but they were defeated in 937 at the battle of Brunanburh, an unknown location in northern England.[11]

Causantín was later buried at St Andrews, symbolising a shift in ecclesiastical power eastwards towards new holy places, Dunkeld and St Andrews, and away from Iona. A legend grew up that the relics of Andrew, one of Jesus's apostles, were brought to Scotland by a monk who had been told by an angel to carry them to the ends of the earth, and who was shipwrecked on the coast of Fife; but they were probably brought by St Augustine as part of his mission to Britain. By the fourteenth century, Andrew had become Scotland's patron saint.[12]

In the eleventh century, the Mac Alpin dynasty ran into trouble. Donnchad I (Duncan I), whose reign was marred by failed military adventures, was killed by troops belonging to a noble called Macbethad or Macbeth (rendered imaginatively by Shakespeare into an archetype of bloodthirsty treachery). Macbeth ruled for 17 years before he was killed by troops commanded by Donnchad's son, who soon became King Máel Coluim III (Malcolm III), better known as Malcolm Caenn Mór ('Great Chief'), whose dynasty would rule for 230 years.[13]

The Vikings' impact on Ireland was felt particularly around the coast and in the development of towns and a trading economy, though they never dominated the country. Their first raids were on the islands of Rathlin, Inishmurray and Inishbofin in 795. The Irish hit back, but attacks intensified, and Vikings started to overwinter in Ireland. During the ninth century, Viking trading posts were established at Dublin, Cork, Waterford and Limerick. The Isle of Man also became an important strategic focus. Dublin became a centre for trade in goods and especially slaves, and the Vikings began to build the town's infrastructure.[14]

In 902, the Vikings were expelled from Dublin by Irish lords. Survivors scattered across the North Sea and established communities in places such as the Wirral peninsula in north-west England. Dublin was retaken by the Vikings in 917; shortly afterwards, a leader called Rögnvaldr in Old Norse (Rægnald in English, Ragnall in Irish) invaded northern England and was acknowledged in 919 as king of York. This was the start of a 35-year period in which Irish Norse kings intermittently succeeded in creating a kingdom linking Dublin and York; but Æthelstan of Wessex annexed the kingdom from 924 until his death in 939, after which Dublin Vikings took it back again. Their last king, Eric (possibly Eric Bloodaxe, son of King Harald Finehair of Norway), was expelled in 954 and killed at Stainmore in the north Pennines.[15]

The tenth century's second half saw the swift rise of Brian Bóruma or Boru (c.941–1014), king of the southern Irish province of Munster, who ended the Uí Néill's dominance and came close to unifying Ireland for a short time. He styled himself 'Emperor of the Irish'. There was resistance to his rule, however. At the battle of Clontarf, near Dublin, his armies defeated a revolt by Leinstermen and the Dublin Norse, but Boru was killed. The battle has sometimes been portrayed as a struggle between the Irish and Vikings for the sovereignty of Ireland, though it was more complex: Irish were fighting Irish, with Norse allies on both sides. In the Victorian era, Irish nationalists nonetheless proclaimed Boru as a national hero, similar to the English cult of Alfred. The Vikings' political power was limited, though their towns and trade continued to grow.[16]

The Isle of Man came under Norse control, nominally under the sovereignty of the kings of Norway. While the native Christian Gaelic-speaking population was not wiped out, the distribution of Norse place-name elements suggests the settlers took the better, low-lying ground. A series of carved stone crosses incorporated Irish, English and Scandinavian motifs and both Christian and pagan imagery. A Norse–Gaelic ruler called Godred Crovan won control of the island in the eleventh century and made it part of a Norse 'Kingdom of the Isles' that also included the Hebrides. The Isle of Man remained under Norwegian sovereignty until 1266, when it was ceded to Scotland. Tynwald, the Isle of Man's parliament, claims to be the world's oldest continuous parliamentary assembly, with a tradition of more than 1,000 years of meetings and roots in the Celtic and Viking periods.[17]

The Dublin Vikings entered alliances with native Welsh rulers, Cornish princes and the Gaelic rulers of Scotia. The Vikings' presence was less marked in Wales than elsewhere in the Isles, though there were still consequences. Viking control of the Severn Sea (now Bristol Channel) – indicated by more than 40 Scandinavian place names in south Wales – along with the Dee estuary divided the Welsh from fellow Gaelic-speakers in Cornwall and Strathclyde. Some historians believe this helped to make Wales a distinct geographical area.[18]

A series of princes tried to unify Wales by extending their rule over other Welsh territories, though they met opposition. Unlike the English, the Welsh never succeeded in creating a united, enduring state. Rhodri ap Merfyn or Rhodri Mawr ('the Great'), king of Gwynedd in the ninth century, subjugated Powys and Ceredigion. His grandson Hywel ap Cadell or Hywel Dda ('the Good') formed the kingdom of Deheubarth by linking smaller kingdoms in the south-west and came to control most of Wales. He is credited with codifying Welsh laws with compassion, but his kingdom was divided when he died in 950. There were, though, only three kingdoms after that date compared with more than twice that number three centuries earlier.[19]

Gruffydd ap Llywelyn, originally king of Gwynedd, became the only Welsh king ever to rule over the entire territory of Wales, which he achieved for just six or seven years between 1056/7 and his death in 1063. He had a reputation for brutally killing opponents. He also annexed parts of England around the border, which was his undoing when he was defeated by Harold Godwinson, Earl of Wessex and soon-to-be king of England. Gruffydd was pursued and killed somewhere in Snowdonia, either by his own men or by the son of someone he had put to death. His territories were divided into traditional kingdoms.[20]

In England, Viking raids on the east coast started again in the 980s. King Æthelred II 'the Unready' (more accurately, 'the poorly advised') failed to buy them off, and Sweyn Forkbeard seized the throne in 1013. Sweyn died within weeks of becoming king. His son Cnut became king in 1017 and ruled England, Denmark, Norway and part of Sweden until his death in 1035. After Cnut died, his North Sea empire disintegrated during the short and turbulent reigns of his sons Harold Harefoot and Harthacnut. They were succeeded by Edward the Confessor, Æthelred's son.

Norwegian king Harald Hardrada ('Hard-Ruler') invaded to try to claim the English throne and was defeated at Stamford Bridge in 1066 by Harold, who had succeeded Edward. Harold was defeated 19 days later by William of Normandy at the battle of Hastings, shifting England's political focus from Scandinavia to western Europe. England would now be ruled by a Norman king descended from Scandinavians.

CHAPTER 3

SILENT TONGUES

The 'Welsh Not' has become notorious – a piece of wood, often bearing the letters 'WN', would be hung around the neck of any pupil caught speaking Welsh in some mid-nineteenth-century Welsh schools in order to encourage them to learn English. The offender could pass it on to any other schoolmate heard speaking Welsh, with the one wearing it at the end of the day being punished.[1]

There were variants elsewhere. In parts of Scotland, a 'hanging stick' might be placed round the neck of a child caught speaking Gaelic. The teacher at the end of the day beat all those who had worn it; examples were reported well into the twentieth century. In Ireland, children are said to have been forced to wear tally sticks and slates on cords around their necks. Each time they used an Irish word, the teacher would make a notch on the stick or write the word on the slate. The number of notches or words was counted and punishment administered accordingly.[2]

How widespread such practices were is unclear. This was, after all, a time when harsh physical punishment was commonly used to enforce obedience and manners. The Welsh Not – also known as the 'note', 'lump', 'stick', 'mark' or 'ticket' – was not state policy. Before 1870 in England and Wales, education was largely the realm of charities, religious bodies and private individuals. School attendance was voluntary until 1880, and Welsh parents sent children to school to learn English because they felt it would advance their chance of success in life. It is, though, symptomatic of pressures on several languages as English became dominant.

Celtic languages, part of the Indo-European family, were spoken throughout much of western Europe in Roman and pre-Roman times. Today, there are just four surviving – Irish, Scottish Gaelic, Welsh and Breton – and two revived ones, Cornish and Manx. All are spoken by a minority, though there are continuing efforts at revival.

These are not the only languages to have shrunk or disappeared. Pictish is believed to have been a Celtic language related to Brythonic (like Welsh, Cornish and Breton) rather than to Goidelic (Irish, Scottish Gaelic, Manx); scholars in the past thought it was pre-Indo-European. It was extinct by 1100, replaced by or subsumed into Gaelic. Cumbric, another Brythonic variant in north-west England and south-west Scotland, became extinct in the twelfth century. Norn, a Norse language, was spoken in Orkney and Shetland until the eighteenth or nineteenth centuries. Scots, a Germanic language related to English, suffered a steep decline, though efforts have been made in recent years to preserve it.

Over the centuries, while the Isles' inhabitants may not have forged a common British identity, the vast majority would come to speak English. The British Empire crumbled, yet a language originally spoken by a few thousand Anglo-Saxons is now used by about 1.5 billion people worldwide. In the process of assimilation, Celtic names were mangled to create English-style surnames. In Wales, for example, male Christian names were used to create a handful of anglicised surnames such as Jones, Davies and Williams. These became so common that nicknames such as 'Jones the milk' had to be adopted to tell them apart. In the Scottish highlands, surnames replaced patronymics after the clans were suppressed in 1746. The order to register led to the indiscriminate adoption of clan names as surnames such as Macdonald, Maclean and Macpherson.[3]

UNESCO, the United Nations' cultural agency, considers Cornish and Ulster Scots to be 'severely endangered', Irish, Scottish

Gaelic and Manx 'definitely endangered' and Welsh, Breton and Scots 'potentially vulnerable'.[4] For the most part, Celtic languages are not mutually intelligible, meaning that speakers of one are unlikely to understand the others automatically. There are similarities, however, and some are closer to each other than others.

International comparisons are fraught with difficulty. In Ireland, census data from 2022 suggests that 1.9 million, or 40.4 per cent, of people can speak Irish to some degree, though a significant proportion know only a little – fewer than 2 per cent use the language daily outside the education system. In Wales, 538,300, or 17.8 per cent, of people could speak some Welsh in 2021. In Scotland, just 58,000, or 1.1 per cent, of people could speak some Scottish Gaelic in 2011. Estimates of those who can speak some Breton in Brittany – which originated in Cornwall – range up to 20 per cent of the population, though the number of habitual speakers is thought to be far lower. In the Isle of Man, 2,200 or 2.6 per cent of people can speak, read or write Manx. In Cornwall, 3,000-plus, or below 1 per cent, have some Cornish words or phrases.[5]

Irish or *Gaeilge*, one of the world's oldest written languages, was seen first in the form of Ogham inscriptions from the fifth to seventh centuries – an alphabet of lines and notches cut on the edge of a stone and based on the Latin alphabet. Most are in Ireland, though others are found where the Irish settled in Cornwall, Devon, Wales and the Isle of Man. The Roman alphabet was adopted in Ireland from the early seventh century. With the arrival of the Vikings, a small number of Norse words entered Irish, such as *dorgha* (fishing line) and *pingin* (penny).[6]

The Anglo-Norman conquest from the late twelfth century started a period of multilingualism in Ireland, though gradually the Normans began to speak Irish outside the towns they founded. English eventually took over as the language of administration, however. Irish went into decline from the early seventeenth century when English power was consolidated first by military conquest and then by the planting of English-speaking colonists on a large scale.

Use of Irish was actively discouraged, and by 1800 it had ceased to be the language of anyone with power or wealth.[7]

During the nineteenth century, English became the dominant language, and Irish was restricted to poorer people in isolated areas, mainly on the west coast. Famine and emigration sharply reduced populations in Irish-speaking districts. Other factors driving the growth of English included the rise of the market economy, increased government centralisation, the education system and a widespread feeling that Irish was associated with poverty, ignorance and backwardness. By the time of the first census to record language use in 1851, 23 per cent of the population spoke Irish, but only 5 per cent spoke it exclusively.[8]

Later in the nineteenth century, there was a revival movement created by enthusiasts such as academic and linguist Douglas Hyde, son of a Church of Ireland rector, who led the establishment of the Gaelic League (Conradh na Gaeilge) in 1893 to encourage preservation of Irish culture, music, dance and language. This coincided with other cultural revivals, such as the creation of the Gaelic Athletic Association (GAA) and the performance of plays about Ireland in English by playwrights including W.B. Yeats, J.M. Synge, Seán O'Casey and Lady Gregory, along with the launch of the Abbey Theatre. Yeats, however, rejected Hyde's assertion that the Irish language should be the medium for cultural revival and instead aimed for a special brand of English with 'an indefinable Irish quality of rhythm and style'.[9]

To the dismay of some members, the Gaelic League became dominated by militant nationalists; Hyde resigned from its presidency in 1915 in protest after the league voted to affiliate with the separatist cause. When the independent Irish Free State was founded in 1922, some leaders had been committed language enthusiasts, but the government continued to use English as the language of administration even in regions where most people spoke Irish. While a qualification in Irish was required to apply for state jobs, this was set at a low level of fluency, and few used Irish in their work. Irish speakers had to use English to apply for things such as grants or to obtain an electricity supply. For many years, Irish was a compulsory subject in primary schools, and it became the first official language of the state in 1937, but numbers of native speakers continued to decline.[10]

In Northern Ireland, which remained part of the UK, the government saw Irish as a threat. Efforts were made to restrict teaching of Irish in schools, street names in Irish were banned and Irish could not be used for any official business. Official hostility to the Irish language and distrust of Irish speakers continued until the 1970s. Recently, however, there has been interest by some Protestants who recognise that Irish was not exclusively a Catholic language; in the past, Presbyterian ministers had to have knowledge of Irish because many of their rural congregants could not speak English.[11]

The Irish language has benefited from a global revival of interest in Irish culture in recent decades, including bars and folk music. In Ireland, while native speakers in the Gaeltacht – officially recognised Irish-speaking districts of the west coast – have declined, the number of second-language speakers has increased. Many are urban, upper class and educated in independent schools (called *gaelscoileanna* at primary level) that teach entirely through Irish and perform well academically. In 2023, *An Cailín Ciúin* (The Quiet Girl), a film about an introspective child packed off to distant relatives, became the first Irish-language movie to be shortlisted for an Oscar.[12]

Scottish Gaelic or *Gàidhlig* developed from the same roots as Old Irish and became a distinct spoken tongue, although the Gaels of Scotland and Ireland shared a common literary language until the seventeenth century. Gaelic was mostly confined to Dál Riata on the western seaboard until the eighth century, when it began expanding into Pictish areas to the east. The language reached its zenith in the eleventh century, when it was the language of the court and most of the country's population.[13]

Gaelic faced increasing competition from English and the emerging Scots language, however. An important juncture was the reign of

Malcolm Caenn Mór (Malcolm III) from 1058 to 1093. His wife, the pious Margaret of Wessex – Scotland's only royal saint – was an English princess brought up in exile in Hungary. She spoke no Gaelic, gave her children Anglo-Saxon names and brought English monks to Scotland. During the reigns of their sons Edgar, Alexander I and David I, Anglo-Norman culture spread.[14]

By the mid-fourteenth century, what eventually became Scots (initially termed Inglis) emerged as the official language of government and law. Gaelic continued to flourish in the highlands and islands, particularly in the heyday of the Lordship of the Isles in the fourteenth and fifteenth centuries, but its status weakened as the lordship's power declined. The Statutes of Iona, enacted under James VI in 1609, forced clan chiefs to have their eldest sons or daughters educated on the mainland, where they could be taught to 'speak, read and write in English', safely removed from 'barbarous' influences. These measures were ineffective, however, in changing the culture.[15]

Gaelic declined in the eighteenth and nineteenth centuries through anglicising measures and economic hardship. The Society in Scotland for Propagating Christian Knowledge, which taught the Church of Scotland catechism in its highland schools, aimed to 'extirpate the Irish Language'. Gaelic-speaking culture was damaged by reprisals against Jacobites after the battle of Culloden in 1746, when thousands of highlanders were killed, their property burned, their cattle stolen and the economy left in ruins. Highland clearances to make way for sheep, the 1840s potato famine and economic marginalisation meant that many Gaelic speakers left for the industrialising lowlands or emigrated to the New World. The number of Gaelic speakers in Canada increased.[16]

When Scotland moved in 1872 to a compulsory, state-funded system of education covering the entire country, no provision was made for Gaelic. In the First World War, losses of life at sea and in the armed forces took a heavy toll on the Gaelic population, and the interwar period saw further emigration, especially from the Hebrides.

The number of Gaelic speakers declined from 254,000 in 1891 to below 60,000 in 2001. Gaelic continues to decline in its traditional heartland, and internal migration has meant that almost half of Gaelic speakers now live in lowland, urban Scotland.[17]

The revival of interest in Celtic culture since the 1970s came none too soon. Now there are Gaelic playgroups, Gaelic-medium education at primary and secondary levels and a Gaelic-language college on Skye. There are bilingual road signs, Gaelic television and radio stations and growing interest in Gaelic music and arts. A development body, Bòrd na Gàidhlig, was created in 2005 and is required to prepare a National Gaelic Language Plan every five years. Despite these efforts, a team of Gaelic experts and socio-linguists at the University of the Highlands and Islands warned in 2020 that without radical action Gaelic could die out within a decade.[18]

Scots, a sister language of English, is sometimes called lowland Scots to distinguish it from Gaelic, or *braid* ('broad') Scots to distinguish it from Scottish Standard English. The Scots Language Centre, a Scottish government-backed body that promotes the language, describes it as 'the collective name for Scottish dialects known also as Doric, Lallans and Scotch or by more local names such as Buchan, Dundonian, Glesca or Shetland'. The 2011 Scottish census was the first to record the number of Scots speakers. It revealed that 1.5 million people spoke the language (30 per cent of the population). Another 267,000 said they could understand Scots but not read, write or speak the language.[19]

A variant called Ulster Scots has existed since colonists from lowland Scotland settled there in the seventeenth century. In the 2021 Northern Ireland census, 190,613 people (10.38 per cent of the population) reported having some knowledge of Ulster Scots, while 20,930 (1.14 per cent) said they could speak, read, write and understand it.[20]

Germanic settlers speaking a Northumbrian dialect of Old English established themselves in south-east Scotland up to the river Forth by the seventh century, when the region was part of the

Anglo-Saxon kingdom of Northumbria. As Gaelic's hold on Scotland weakened in the Middle Ages, use of English spread, and the variety of northern English spoken there began to diverge from that spoken in England. By the fourteenth century, it was the dominant speech of all ranks in Scottish society east and south of the Highland Line, except in Galloway. From the late fifteenth century, writers began to refer to it as 'Scots', a contraction of Scottis.[21]

South of the border, meanwhile, a process of standardising written English began in the late fifteenth century, followed later and less successfully by moves towards uniform spoken English. As London's power and prestige grew, so did belief that regional dialects were inferior. The death knell of northern and other regional dialects in England has been sounded regularly since the nineteenth century, yet still many survive despite English's growth into a global language.[22]

Written records of Scots began in 1375–6 with John Barbour's poem *The Bruce*, an account of the exploits of heroes Robert Bruce and James Douglas in the Wars of Independence. A strong group of Scots poets of the fifteenth and sixteenth centuries, including Robert Henryson and William Dunbar, have in the past been patronisingly dubbed the 'Scots Chaucerians' by English literary critics.

Scots, despite its separate development, was subject to anglicising pressures including the Reformation, the English Geneva Bible (an English-language version translated partly by English refugees in Geneva) and the increasing availability of printed books from England. Further pressure came from the Union of Crowns in 1603 and Union of Parliaments in 1707. James VI of Scotland and I of England declared in his first speech to the English parliament in March 1603: 'Hath not God first united these two Kingdomes both in Language, Religion, and similitude of maners?'[23] There were increased contacts between the upper classes of the two nations, resulting in most Scottish aristocrats gradually giving up their native speech for what one writer called the more 'elegant and perfect' English of the south. After 1707, intellectuals such as philosopher

David Hume and economist Adam Smith strove to keep Scotticisms out of their writings.

There was a revival of Scots as a literary language from the eighteenth century by writers such as Robert Burns and Allan Ramsay. The language had a tough time in the twentieth century despite efforts by Hugh MacDiarmid (Christopher Murray Grieve), whose poem *A Drunk Man Looks at the Thistle* (1926) was a major modernist work. In 1946, the Scottish Education Department declared that Scots was 'not the language of "educated" people anywhere, and could not be described as a suitable medium of education or culture'.[24]

Today, most people in Scotland speak somewhere on a continuum from Scots to Scottish Standard English. The Scottish government has included Scots in its national school curriculum and set its first Scots Language Policy in 2015, in which it pledged to support its preservation and encourage respect, recognition and use of Scots. Its future remains uncertain, though.[25]

Among smaller languages, Manx Gaelic or *Gaelg* dates back to the arrival of Irish missionaries in the Early Middle Ages. The island's Manx Gaelic name is *Ellan Vannin* or just *Mannin*, which may derive from a Celtic word for mountain or from Manannán, a mythical sea god. There has been a revival of interest in Manx Gaelic since the last native speaker, a fisherman called Ned Maddrell or 'Plucky Ned', died in 1974. The number of people learning the language has increased steadily, many street and office names are bilingual, there are radio broadcasts in Manx and there is a Manx-medium primary school.[26]

Cornish or *Kernewek* is closely related to Breton, which grew through emigration from south-west Britain to Armorica – a region of ancient Gaul between the Seine and the Loire – in the Early Middle Ages. There was a rebellion in Cornwall and Devon in 1549 against imposition of the English Book of Common Prayer as the sole legal form of worship, provoking a heavy-handed response from the government in which thousands died. Cornish gradually retreated westward in the face of English's dominance and is thought to have died out as a first language by the late eighteenth or early nineteenth centuries, though there has been a revival movement since the early twentieth.[27]

Some Cornish textbooks and works of literature have been published, and an increasing number of people speak the language. Cornish was recognised by the UK government under the European Charter for Regional or Minority Languages in 2002, giving it protected status alongside Welsh, Scottish Gaelic, Irish, Scots and Ulster Scots. A public body, the Cornish Language Partnership, was created in 2005. The need to reconstruct spelling and pronunciation of Cornish had led to the creation of competing systems, but a standard written form was agreed in 2008.

Welsh, or *Cymraeg*, evolved from Brythonic, which is thought to have been spoken throughout Britain south of the Firth of Forth from the Bronze or Iron Age. *Cymraeg* descends from the Brythonic *combrogi*, meaning compatriots. Advances westward by Germanic invaders led to Welsh developing separately from Cumbric and Cornish. It became a distinct language possibly by 600. The earliest Brythonic/Welsh literature, the poems of Taliesin and Aneirin, are thought to have been composed in the *Hen Ogledd*, or Old North, in southern Scotland around 600 but written down by Welsh scribes after 1250. The *Mabinogion*, prose stories of British legends featuring drama, philosophy, romance, tragedy, fantasy and humour, were compiled in Welsh in the twelfth or thirteenth centuries from earlier oral traditions.[28]

Norman invaders brought French to the valleys, and their followers introduced English. Henry VIII's English parliament in 1536 passed legislation that incorporated Wales into England in legal terms, abolished Welsh law, made English the only language of Welsh courts and banned the use of Welsh in public office. It would take two centuries or more, however, before English wholly ousted Welsh from the homes of the gentry. Bible translations into Welsh helped to maintain use of Welsh in daily life: the New Testament was translated by William Salesbury in 1567 and the complete Bible by William Morgan in 1588. The crown ordered that a Welsh Bible be put in every parish church, ensuring that Wales followed England's new Protestantism rather than Catholicism, and in doing so helped the language to fare better than Irish and Gaelic, which did not see their own versions of the Bible until 1690 and 1801.[29]

Welsh in the eighteenth century was boosted by the benevolence of Bridget Bevan from Carmarthenshire, a wealthy woman who supported a system of circulating schools created by Church of England clergyman Griffith Jones, which moved from village to village educating children and adults in the Welsh language. Almost half the population of Wales attended them, and Bevan continued the work after Jones died. By later in the century, Wales was one of the few countries with a literate majority. Russia's Catherine the Great commissioned a report on the schools. At the same time, Methodism and other forms of Nonconformism were growing, which encouraged reading of Welsh religious books. As the British Empire expanded, tens of thousands of Welsh people emigrated in search of better lives. Most destinations were English-speaking, but a group that wanted to create a Welsh-speaking colony settled in Patagonia in 1865 after negotiating rights to land with the Argentine government.[30]

Industrialisation in the nineteenth century led to a long-term decline in the use of Welsh. At first, English migrants into the coal-field learned Welsh. In time, however, the number of migrants became so large that the Welsh found themselves learning English, which became the language of education, the state, much of the press and popular entertainment. Even some chapels switched to it. In the 1891 census, the first time language was counted, 54.4 per cent of the Welsh population spoke Welsh, but that fell to 49.9 per cent in 1901 and 43.5 per cent in 1911; the biggest drop was in the Glamorgan coalfield. By 1931, just 36.8 per cent spoke Welsh.[31]

During the twentieth century, concern about the language's future grew in parallel with the rise of Welsh nationalism. In 1942, legislation was passed giving people the right to speak Welsh in court. Not everyone welcomed the idea of a stronger role for Welsh in government. Ebbw Vale Labour MP Aneurin Bevan, an opponent of any form of separate Welsh policy, warned the Commons in 1946 that some people in English-speaking parts of Wales feared becoming 'a vast majority tyrannised over by a few Welsh-speaking people in Cardiganshire'.[32]

By 1961, the proportion of Welsh speakers was down to 26 per cent. Plaid Cymru, the nationalist party, started to make electoral breakthroughs, and militant students took up Welsh issues, including language rights. A small group known as Mudiad Amddiffyn Cymru planted bombs around Wales in the late 1960s. The Labour government passed the Welsh Language Act 1967, which gave the nation's two languages equal validity and said use of Welsh in official and public business should be facilitated – but did not specify measures to achieve this.[33]

In 1980, Gwynfor Evans, Plaid Cymru president, threatened to go on hunger strike if Margaret Thatcher's Conservative government did not honour a commitment to provide a Welsh-language television service. S4C duly started broadcasting on 1 November 1982, the first television channel in Europe established to serve a minority language. Welsh was recognised as a core subject in the school curriculum for schools in Welsh-speaking areas in 1988. Another Welsh Language Act in 1993 declared that Welsh should have equal status with English, dependent on what was 'practical and expedient'. It also created a Welsh Language Board with power to require public bodies to prepare schemes to promote use of the language. The Welsh Assembly's Welsh Language (Wales) Measure 2011 required public bodies to provide services in Welsh; it also created a Welsh Language Commissioner with powers to enforce service users' rights and a tribunal to which people could appeal if their rights were denied.[34]

Wales's devolved Labour government has set a target of achieving one million Welsh speakers by 2050, but the 2021 census showed a decrease of 24,000 speakers to 538,300 in the past 10 years. This was despite measures to encourage it, such as the use of Welsh on public signage. Jeremy Miles, education and Welsh language minister, said there was 'more support than ever for the language' but acknowledged concerns including a drop in the number of 5- to 15-year-olds able to speak Welsh and a decline in traditional Welsh-speaking heartlands.[35]

Welsh remains among the most secure of the Isles' minority languages. All of these languages, nonetheless, face a continuing battle for survival.

CHAPTER 4

WARS AND MEDIEVAL CRUELTY

William the Conqueror was ruthless even for his times. His harrying of northern England, burning crops, herds and possessions to stamp out rebellions, caused devastation. His brutality can be traced to his childhood, when he became Duke of Normandy at age seven. Lords around him struggled for power, and guardians were murdered; his household steward's throat was cut while sleeping in the young duke's chamber. William's was not the only violence, however, as dynastic struggles marked the Middle Ages across the Isles.

Over three centuries, a French-speaking ascendancy spread through the archipelago, bringing social, political and economic change. Wales was turned into a virtual colony, while Anglo-Norman adventurers conquered eastern Ireland. It was not simply the French versus Anglo-Saxons and Celts; there were fights within the ruling elite. In Scotland, Normanisation happened from within as kings welcomed Anglo-Norman settlers and gave them land. That did not prevent almost 600 years of intermittent warfare between Scotland and England. In the first phase, Scottish kings sought to expand southwards; in the second, Scotland fought for its independence as English kings tried to impose overlordship.

William was descended from a Viking called Rollo, Normandy's first ruler, but by this time the Normans had become Frenchified in customs and language. The conquest shifted the Isles' strategic focus from Scandinavia to Franco-Latin Europe. England's kings became embroiled in Europe's affairs, either sharing in European crusades in the Holy Land or fighting for territory and titles in France. They spoke French. No post-conquest monarch of England had English as their mother tongue until Henry IV in 1399. Norman immigrants numbered perhaps 20,000, barely 1 per cent of England's population, but their impact was profound. Middle-ranking Anglo-Saxons were forced into servitude, and many that had formerly held land freely became rent-paying tenants, often on onerous terms.[1]

In due course, revolutionary changes spread around the Isles. Instruments of empire included the castle, church and borough. Normans built almost 1,000 castles in England and more than 300 in Wales, with others in Scotland and Ireland. They built cathedrals and abbeys and introduced French religious orders and colonies of monks. Boroughs were created with a degree of self-government. It was a two-class society with little intermarriage between Anglo-Norman aristocrats and natives until the Black Death changed the demography in the fourteenth century. Changes were particularly marked on either side of the Irish Sea, where social structures based on kinship were replaced by a hierarchical, feudal framework.[2]

William faced rebellions, notably in northern England. His harrying in 1069 took place after a couple of serious revolts and a Danish assault on York. William was trying to ensure that rebels had no place to hide and no resources to live on. Orderic Vitalis, a chronicler, wrote 50 years later:

In his anger he commanded that all crops and herds, chattels and food of every kind should be brought together and burned to ashes with consuming fire, so that the whole region north of the Humber might be stripped of all means of sustenance. As a consequence, so serious a scarcity was felt in England, and so terrible a famine fell upon the humble and defenceless people, that more than 100,000 Christian folk of both sexes, young and old alike, perished of hunger.[3]

It affected Yorkshire and parts of Durham, Cheshire, Shropshire and Staffordshire. Some historians argue that these accounts are exaggerated, but the combined evidence of a fall in land values and big drop in population does suggest significant devastation.

William had no intention of annexing Wales but sought to secure the border by giving lands in the Marches to faithful followers, who took every opportunity to add to their power and territory. Welsh rulers were fighting among themselves. In Scotland, Máel Coluim III (Malcolm Caenn Mór), no doubt encouraged by his English queen Margaret, raided Northumbria and gave refuge to royal Saxon refugees, notably Margaret's brother Edgar the Aetheling, the last male Wessex heir. That prompted the Conqueror to invade Scotland in 1072, forcing Máel Coluim to swear homage to William and become his vassal at Abernethy, near the Tay. Although later repudiated, it formed the basis of English kings' claims of overlordship. That did not deter Máel Coluim from raiding Northumbria again in 1079. The Conqueror sent his son Robert to reimpose the earlier peace terms; on his return journey, Robert built a 'new castle' on the Tyne. In 1093, Máel Coluim was ambushed and killed during yet another raid – his fifth – on Northumbria.[4]

Scottish kings' obsession with capturing, or recapturing, territory down to the Tees and beyond was to bring them only grief, while English kings were never able to translate claims of overlordship of Scotland into reality. When David I (Dauíd mac Maíl Choluim), who ruled Scotland 1124–53, became the third of Máel Coluim's sons to take the throne, it might be thought that he would serve Anglo-Norman interests well. He had spent his youth at the royal court in England and Normandy, he was schooled in Norman culture and had served as Henry I's virtual viceroy in northern England. David invited Norman families to settle in Scotland. Already middle-aged when he began, David reigned for almost three decades. He promoted commercial enterprise by creating royal burghs such as Berwick, Perth and Aberdeen as centres for trade. He introduced Scotland's first coinage. The four great border abbeys – Kelso, Melrose, Jedburgh and Dryburgh – were founded under David's auspices.[5]

When Henry I died, England was plunged into civil war as the throne was seized by the king's nephew Stephen. To the shock of English chroniclers, David launched successive invasions in support of the claims of Matilda, Henry's daughter and his own niece. One column attacked Clitheroe with ferocity. Unexpectedly, David's army was defeated by a smaller army in 1138 at the battle of the Standard near Northallerton, prompting a retreat. Despite this, David kept hold of territory down to the Ribble and Tees. However, Henry II of England forced David's successor, Malcolm IV, to cede Northumberland, Cumberland and Westmorland.

Matilda's son Henry II, a man of energy and foul temper, ruled 1154–89 and assembled what was later known as the Angevin empire, including Normandy, Aquitaine and Anjou. Some consider him the first 'Plantagenet' (his father was Geoffrey, Count of Anjou, whose family's heraldic badge depicted yellow broom, the *Planta Genista*). He sought to extend Angevin power to Scotland, Ireland and Wales. Wales remained divided, partly by its topography, into the 'Englishry' of Anglo-Norman lords who controlled the borders and south, and the *pura Walia* or 'Welshry' further west and north, comprising the kingdoms of Gwynedd, Powys and Deheubarth. Frustrated by the dominant Welsh ruler, Rhys ap Gruffydd of Deheubarth, some of Wales's Anglo-Normans sought another way to expand their influence by responding to appeals from the king of Leinster in Dublin, Diarmait Mac Murchada (Dermot MacMurrough), for help against Irish rebels.

A small company landed in 1169 in Waterford, followed a year later by a larger group led by Richard de Clare, Earl of Pembroke, later known as 'Strongbow'. Richard recovered Leinster and, after Diarmait died in 1171, became its king. Fearing Strongbow would have too much power, Henry II travelled to Ireland and received homage from Irish kings and Norman knights. After a pause, the Norman colonists drove west, halted only by Irish king Ruaidrí Ua Conchobair (Rory O'Connor). In a generation or two, within areas they controlled, Anglo-Normans created a feudal Ireland with castles, manors, monasteries and a French-speaking aristocracy.[6]

In Scotland, it was during Malcolm IV's reign that the phrases 'kingdom of Scots' or 'kingdom of Scotland' were first used by royal scribes in charters. A single kingdom was starting to emerge, though it would be a while before the north and west were subdued. Malcolm was succeeded by his brother William I (later dubbed 'the Lion' after his standard, a red lion rampant) who ruled 1165–1214. William rashly invaded Northumbria in 1174, was captured at Alnwick and thrown into the dungeon of Falaise castle in Normandy. In the humiliating Treaty of Falaise, William vowed homage to Henry II. Although its terms were abrogated by England's Richard the Lionheart in 1189 in return for 10,000 marks to fund his crusade, English kings renewed their claim of suzerainty (overlordship) over Scotland repeatedly over the next four centuries.[7]

England's Richard I was succeeded by his brother John, who had a genius for making enemies. Soon he had lost all his French lands except parts of Aquitaine. Barons, especially in northern England, were upset by John's schemes to extract taxes to fund his failing efforts to reconquer the empire. He also sought to extend authority over Scottish and Welsh rulers, especially Llywelyn ab Iorwerth of Gwynedd, known as Llywelyn the Great. John mounted expeditions in Scotland, Wales and Ireland. English barons forced him to agree to Magna Carta, a charter of rights, which John had no intention of sticking to. By his death in 1216, he was embroiled in a civil war. Rebels offered the throne to Prince Louis of France, who landed in Kent. Alexander II, Scotland's new king, marched to Dover to pay homage to Louis. Alexander showed that brutality was by no means confined to England. Earlier, in suppressing a revolt by the MacWilliams, he had ordered their leader's baby daughter's head to be smashed against Forfar's market cross.[8]

King John's infant son was quickly crowned Henry III, the barons' revolt fizzled out and Louis returned home. Alexander married Henry's sister Joan and, at the Treaty of York in 1237, accepted that the border counties were English. This established the border in a form that remains almost unchanged. The only modifications have been to the 'Debatable Land' north of Carlisle and to Berwick-upon-Tweed, retaken by England in 1482. Despite this, the borders were anything but stable: Anglo-Scottish wars destabilised frontier society and fuelled an upsurge in lawlessness from the fourteenth century that lasted for a couple of centuries or more. It could be brutal. In 1483, Northumbrian *heidsman* (family head) Robert Loraine was ambushed by a Scottish raiding party on his way home from church to his pele tower in Kirkharle, then butchered into pieces and packed into the saddlebags of his own horse.[9]

Edward I, England's king 1272–1307 and 'Hammer of the Scots' and the Welsh, tried to establish an English empire within the Isles. He did not wish, at least initially, to impose English institutions and law but wanted Irish, Welsh and Scottish rulers to acknowledge him as feudal overlord and provide men and money that he could use against the king of France. The dominant Welsh prince, Gwynedd's Llywelyn ap Gruffydd, grandson of Llywelyn the Great, angry that Welsh enemies were given refuge in England, prevaricated over pledging fealty to Edward. The king declared him a rebel and invaded in 1277 with the biggest army Wales had seen. Llywelyn capitulated and paid homage at Worcester, while his territories outside Gwynedd were stripped away.[10]

As Llywelyn became frustrated by English judges restricting his ability to rule, his younger brother, Dafydd, attacked an English garrison. Edward led another huge army into Wales. After initial successes, the offensive became bogged down. Llywelyn broke out of Snowdonia and marched south into Powys but was killed; his severed head was sent to Edward. Dafydd was captured and quadruply punished at Shrewsbury: dragged by horses to the scaffold (as a trai-tor), hanged alive (as a homicide), had his bowels burned out as a violator of religion (he had attacked at Easter) and had his body quartered (he had plotted the king's death). Londoners and Yorkshiremen brawled over who should get the prime body parts; the Londoners got the head.[11]

The Statute of Rhuddlan in 1284 incorporated Wales into England and gave it an English-style administrative system, policed by sheriffs (largely English). Welsh natives were forbidden to carry arms or have strangers stay overnight without permission. The Croes Naith, a holy relic held to be a fragment of the True Cross on which Jesus died, was taken to England along with Llywelyn's coronet. The king's son, Edward of Caernarfon, was invested as Prince of Wales – in Lincoln. Edward I began the biggest programme of castle-build-ing undertaken anywhere in medieval Europe, including castles at Beaumaris, Caernarfon, Conwy and Harlech.[12]

In 1290, Edward made England the first country to expel its Jews, uprooting 3,000 mainly in York, Lincoln and London. Jews had come to England after the conquest because early Norman kings needed to borrow money to build castles and secure their kingdom, and moneylending was forbidden to Christians, but hostility grew during the crusades. Stories were spread of Jews murdering Christian children, now known as the 'Blood Libel'. The Jews had been so stretched by forced loans and penal taxes that they were unable to yield much to Edward's coffers. Jews did not return until the 1650s, when Oliver Cromwell invited them to resettle.[13]

Also in 1290, seven-year-old Margaret, Maid of Norway, Scotland's queen designate, died at Kirkwall in Orkney, creating a succession crisis that would lead to more Anglo-Scottish wars. Margaret had been set to succeed her grandfather, Alexander III, the last Canmore king, who died unexpectedly by riding off a cliff in a storm. Alexander presided over a period of prosperity and kept Scotland out of conflicts. Margaret had been pledged to marry Edward I's infant son, Edward of Caernarfon.[14]

Edward I was invited to conduct proceedings to select a successor and administer the outcome, which he seized keenly. In return, he demanded acknowledgement by Scotland's Guardians of the Realm, a body of senior nobles and clerics, that he was their feudal overlord. After initial resistance, he got his way, while agreeing to maintain Scotland's 'laws and liberties' during his adjudication. In Berwick, 104 'auditors' heard the claims (40 each nominated by the two main competitors and 24 senior Scots chosen by Edward). They chose John Balliol, Earl of Galloway, over Robert Bruce of Annandale. Both had served in Edward's Welsh campaigns.[15]

Balliol was inaugurated at Scone, but Edward soon tested him. He humiliated Balliol at a hearing at Westminster in which the king judged an appeal in a Scottish legal case and also demanded that Scottish magnates provide military service against France. Instead, a council of 12 Scottish nobles in 1295 formed what was to be known as the Auld Alliance with France and launched an unsuccessful attack on Carlisle. They were encouraged by an uprising in Wales in which royal castles were seized before Edward led an army to subdue it (after which 500 Welshmen were slaughtered in their sleep). Edward responded by invading Scotland in 1296 and taking Berwick-upon-Tweed in a particularly bloody massacre of at least 11,000 people, including women and children. Scottish resistance ended at the battle of Dunbar, after which Edward removed the Stone of Destiny – Scotland's coronation stone – to Westminster, deposed Balliol and placed him in the Tower of London and installed Englishmen to govern the country.[16]

Resistance soon emerged led by Andrew de Moray in the north and William Wallace in the south. The enigmatic Wallace, a minor noble from Ayrshire, has been celebrated by nineteenth-century historians as a national hero, debunked by others as a self-serving outlaw and immortalised by Mel Gibson in the film *Braveheart*. The pair succeeded in defeating a larger English force in a river bottle-neck at the battle of Stirling Bridge in 1297. Next year, Wallace was defeated by Edward at Falkirk. Scots nobles fought a five-year war of attrition until most gave up and pledged allegiance to Edward. Wallace was betrayed to the English, who executed him in grisly fashion in London. His head was displayed on London Bridge, his corpse cut in four and the quarters displayed in Newcastle, Berwick, Stirling and Perth.[17]

Another patriot-avenger emerged – the wily and ruthless Robert the Bruce, Earl of Carrick. Bruce began by murdering his rival, John Comyn, at the altar of Greyfriars Abbey in Dumfries, after which he was inaugurated as King Robert I at Scone by Bishop Wishart of Glasgow. Robert was defeated by an English army and forced into hiding, travelling north and west, probably to the Hebrides and perhaps across the Irish Sea, before returning to fight an effective hit-and-run campaign. Two female supporters – his sister Mary and Isabella, Countess of Buchan, who had crowned him – were cruelly imprisoned in cages hung from turrets at Berwick and Roxburgh castles, in public view. Edward headed north but developed dysentery and died at Burgh by Sands, south of the Scottish border, in 1307. Robert then defeated rivals and controlled much of Scotland before beating a larger English army under Edward II at Bannockburn, near Stirling – the most celebrated victory in Scottish history.[18]

Robert sent his brother Edward to invade Ireland in 1315, to open a second front against the English and help Irish lords regain lands they had lost to the crown, which he portrayed as a pan-Gaelic alliance. Unfortunately, this coincided with a famine, leading famished Scots soldiers to take food by force from Irish villagers and (so it was said) dig up fresh graves and eat the cadavers. Civil war broke out, and Edward Bruce was killed in 1318.[19]

England's Edward II, meanwhile, refused to renounce his claim to be overlord of Scotland. Scottish nobles submitted the Declaration of Arbroath to Pope John XXII in 1320, declaring Robert as their rightful monarch and asserting Scotland's independence; it also made clear that if a king ever gave up that independence, magnates had the right to replace him. Edward II was deposed by his estranged wife and her lover in favour of his young son, Edward III; Edward II died at Berkeley Castle in Gloucestershire, probably murdered on orders of the new regime. Peace was reached between Scotland and England with the Treaty of Edinburgh–Northampton in 1328, by which Edward III renounced all claims to sovereignty over Scotland. Robert died in the following year.[20]

Edward III, who reigned for 50 years, did much in his early years to restore royal authority. He laid claim to the French throne in 1337, starting what would later be known as the Hundred Years' War (actually 116 years). After setbacks, the first phase went well for England with victories at Crécy, where Welsh and English longbowmen were effective, and Poitiers. The French called on their Scottish allies to attack England, so David II marched south, only to be defeated at Neville's Cross near Durham in 1346. David was captured and held prisoner for 11 years while he raised a large ransom.[21]

Hard times arrived, however, in the form of the Black Death, an outbreak of bubonic plague thought to have originated in central Asia or China, which spread through western Europe and hit England and Wales in 1348 and Scotland and Ireland in 1349. The plague is thought to have reduced England's population by almost half within 18 months. The result was labour shortages and rising wages, shifting economic power towards workers and helping to end serfdom. The plague returned in 1361 and continued to return intermittently for the next couple of centuries.[22]

Later phases of the Hundred Years' War went less well for England. Edward III's successor, Richard II, faced down a 'Peasants' Revolt' in south-east England in 1381 (the rebels were not peasants but yeomen or citizens of substance angry about a new poll tax). Yet as Richard fought an inconclusive campaign to assert his authority in Ireland, his throne was usurped by a rival, Henry Bolingbroke, who became Henry IV.

A Welsh nobleman, Owain Glyndŵr, revolted against Henry IV in 1400 and for a few years controlled most of Wales. His aims were grandiose, notably a document known as the Tripartite Indenture in which Glyndŵr, Henry Percy, Earl of Northumberland, and English noble Edmund Mortimer agreed to divide England and Wales between them. Glyndŵr was to get Wales and much of the west of England. Northumberland was to have the north, Northampton-shire, Norfolk, Warwickshire and Leicestershire. The Mortimers were to receive the rest of southern England. Henry IV defeated Percy at the battle of Shrewsbury. Glyndŵr's rebellion died out, but he was never captured. Henry's son, Henry V, achieved military victories, notably at Agincourt, but died after only nine years in power. By the time the Hundred Years' War ended in 1453, during the reign of the mentally unstable Henry VI, the English had lost all continental territories except the Pale of Calais.[23]

Scotland, meanwhile, had come under the control of the house of Stewart (later Stuart), which was to provide nine successive kings and queens of Scotland from 1371 to 1603, followed by seven kings and queens of England, Scotland and Ireland from 1603 to 1714. Their origins lay with Walter fitz Alan, who had been high steward running the royal household in the twelfth century. The first Stewart king was Robert II, grandson of Robert the Bruce. Unbroken Scottish succession contrasted with the English throne, frequently disrupted by childlessness and usurpation. Not that the Stewart line was problem-free. James I, who ruled 1406–37, spent 18 years as a hostage in England and ended by being stabbed to death in a sewer by Scottish conspirators. Three Stewarts – James II, III and IV – died in battle. Scotland assumed its modern frontiers in 1472 when Orkney and Shetland were annexed, having been promised as surety for a dowry when James III became engaged to Margaret of Denmark. James IV ended the quasi-independent rule of the Lord of the Isles, bringing the Western Isles under effective royal control for the first time.[24]

The English crown's hold on Ireland weakened from about 1300, partly because kings were distracted by wars elsewhere and also because shrinking populations after the Black Death meant some colonists migrated back to England. There was a Gaelic resurgence as Irish rulers enjoyed greater freedom of action and also a cultural revival as Bardic praise-poets, celebrating patrons in elaborate verse, came back into fashion. One notable noble was Mairgréag Ní Chearbhaill (Margaret O'Carroll), queen of the kingdom of Uí Failghe (Offaly). She was nicknamed 'Margaret of the Hospitality' for two feasts in 1433, a year of general shortage, to which she invited poets, historians, musicians, 'besides gamesters and poore men'. By the later Middle Ages, however, the main winners were Anglo-Irish magnates rather than the crown or native rulers. The area controlled by the royal administration shrank during the fifteenth century to the four eastern counties of Louth, Meath, Dublin and Kildare. To protect lives and property, a fortified earthen rampart known as the Pale was built to enclose it.[25]

The cost of the Hundred Years' War weakened the English monarchy and was among the underlying causes of the Wars of the Roses, a struggle between the houses of Lancaster and York, rival branches of the Plantagenets. These wars had a limited impact on most ordinary citizens, even while the aristocracy were slaughtering each other. Although the wars lasted more than 30 years, fighting is estimated to have occupied only 13 weeks.[26]

Both sides relied heavily on Welsh troops, and it was a man who was one-quarter Welsh, the Lancastrian claimant Henry Tudor (also a quarter-French and half-English), who ended the dynastic struggle. He landed at Mill Bay, Pembrokeshire, with a small French and Scottish force in August 1485, gathered support as he marched through Wales and defeated Yorkist king Richard III at the battle of Bosworth Field in Leicestershire on 22 August. His victory enabled him to be crowned as Henry VII of England and found the Tudor dynasty.

CHAPTER 5

REFORMATION AND REVOLUTION

Mary, Queen of Scots, vivacious, beautiful and frustrating, did not lack a sense of drama. 'Remember that the theatre of the whole world is wider than the kingdom of England,' she is said to have warned those trying her for treason at Fotheringhay Castle in Northamptonshire. Found guilty of endorsing a plot to murder her cousin, Elizabeth I of England, Mary wore a crimson petticoat, the colour of Catholic martyrdom, at her execution on 8 February 1587, aged 44. It took two axe blows to separate her head from her body, and even then the executioner had to use his axe to saw through a remaining tendon. According to one witness, her lips moved for some minutes after her head was cut off, and her lapdog emerged from hiding among her skirts. As the executioner tried to hold up her head, the auburn curls turned out to be a wig, and her skull fell to the ground, revealing a mat of grey stubble.[1]

If events had turned out differently, Mary might have been queen of Scotland, France and England. She ruled Scotland personally for just six years before she was forced to abdicate in favour of her one-year-old son James after being accused, among other things, of involvement in the murder of her husband, Lord Darnley (the evidence is circumstantial). Mary fled southward seeking Elizabeth's protection but was held captive for almost 19 years, perceived as a threat and a rallying point for Catholic rebels. She was undone when Francis Walsingham, Elizabeth's spymaster, set a trap that enabled him to read her coded letters. For centuries, historians have variously portrayed her as an adulterer and murderer, as the heroic victim of scheming noblemen or as a tragic failure. She certainly made some disastrous choices.

In the two centuries after the Wars of the Roses, all parts of the Isles became subordinated to some degree to the English crown, an empire that then extended overseas. Wales was legally unified with England. Henry VIII made himself king of Ireland (upgraded from a lordship). Rebellions in northern England were suppressed. The Scottish and English crowns became united under Mary's son James VI and I, though he failed in his aim to merge the kingdoms. All this happened against the background of a Protestant Reformation that created divisions across the archipelago.

The situation exploded in the seventeenth century in the Wars of the Three Kingdoms – civil wars sparked off by disputes over religion, power and money (plus some local score-settling). England and Wales executed their king and may have lost up to 4 per cent of population through fighting or disease, a higher proportion than in the First World War; deaths were higher still in Scotland and especially Ireland.[2] Cromwell, later England's Lord Protector (or military dictator), earned lasting enmity for a massacre at Drogheda. Colonisation of Ulster by 'plantation' of Scottish and English Protestants caused tensions that remain unresolved today. After the monarchy was restored in 1660, the Catholic James II was overthrown in the 1688 Protestant revolution (arguably more of a coup) and finally defeated at the battle of the Boyne in Ireland.

Two centuries earlier, Mary's great-grandfather, Henry VII of England, the Bosworth victor in 1485, had brought stability after seeing off plots in his early years. Lambert Simnel, a baker's son, was the figurehead of a rebellion in 1487 in which he was claimed to be the Yorkist Earl of Warwick, son of Edward IV's executed brother, George, Duke of Clarence. Simnel and his followers went to Ireland

and won support from the Earl of Kildare, Ireland's Lord Deputy. Simnel sailed from there with an army including European mercenaries to Piel of Fouldray castle in Morecambe Bay. Then he marched to defeat at the battle of Stoke Field, near Newark in Nottinghamshire. Simnel was given a job turning a spit in the royal kitchens.

There was a second rising by Perkin de Werbeque or Warbeck, who claimed to be Richard, Duke of York, second son of Edward IV and one of the supposedly murdered princes in the tower. For a time, Warbeck was welcomed by James IV of Scotland, who found him an aristocratic wife and saw him as a source of international leverage. Warbeck made several landings in England backed by small armies but met strong resistance and surrendered in 1497, after which he confessed to being an imposter from Tournai in Flanders. He was hanged two years later.

Henry gave his eldest daughter, Margaret, in marriage to James IV in 1503. All later holders of the English, Scottish and British thrones were either closely related to or descended from the partners of that Stewart–Tudor marriage. (French influence during the sixteenth century led to the spelling of Stewart becoming Stuart or Steuart, because of the lack of a 'w' in French.) James IV was a patron of the arts who also greatly expanded Scotland's royal navy. However, he fatefully chose to meet his obligations under the Auld Alliance when England's Henry VIII invaded France in 1513. James led a large army over the border into England, where he and many of his nobles were killed at the disastrous battle of Flodden, commemorated by the song 'Flowers of the Forest'.

The Tudors were centralisers who concentrated power where wealth was increasingly focused: London and south-east England. While England's wealth had trebled between 1334 and 1515, London's wealth increased fifteenfold.[3] London merchants' stranglehold over the cloth trade with Antwerp, the main continental entrepôt, helped to make it a formidable capital. Henry VIII is best known for his six marriages and for initiating the English Reformation as a result of his search for a male heir. He wanted to annul his first marriage to Catherine of Aragon, so when Pope Clement VII refused, Henry appointed himself supreme head of the Church of England in 1534.

The Reformation divided Ireland, which remained predominantly Catholic, from England, Wales and Scotland, which eventually came to accept Protestantism in differing forms. Opposition broke out however in the Pilgrimage of Grace in northern England in 1536–7, sparked by social and economic grievances combined with disgust at Henry's dissolution of smaller monasteries. Led by lawyer Robert Aske, the pilgrimage started in east Yorkshire and spread across most of the north except for central and southern Lancashire. It involved 30,000 rebels, the largest popular revolt in English history. Henry prevaricated and finally found a pretext to execute their leaders. Later, Elizabeth I saw off a rebellion by northern earls in 1569–70.

In Wales, Henry tightened his grip by having the English parliament pass laws in 1535 and 1542 that integrated Wales with England in legal terms, abolished the Welsh legal system and banned the Welsh language from any official role or status. The legislation did for the first time define the Wales–England border and allowed members representing Welsh constituencies into the English parliament. The kingdom of England was renamed 'the Kingdom of England and Wales'.[4]

In Ireland, the crown's authority had all but disappeared by the end of the fifteenth century as English kings were distracted by the Wars of the Roses. Power lay with the Fitzgerald earls of Kildare, who were increasingly asserting independence. In 1495, Henry VII's commissioner Sir Edward Poynings forced the Dublin parliament to pass an act invalidating all Irish legislation not previously approved in England. Gerald Fitzgerald, the eighth earl, who had backed the Lambert Simnel plot, was arrested and held in the Tower of London for several years. He eventually returned to his post as Lord Deputy, but his family remained a source of discontent for decades.[5]

Henry VIII, advised by chief minister Thomas Cromwell, aimed to overthrow the Kildare ascendancy in the 1530s and reassert crown rule so as to prevent Ireland from becoming a base for future rebellions or foreign invasions of England. Six Fitzgeralds were hanged at Tyburn in 1537 after rebelling against Henry's policies. In 1541, the Irish parliament passed an act making Ireland a sovereign kingdom, an essential step because Henry's Act of Supremacy had undermined Ireland's previous status as a lordship conferred by papal title. In effect, it created a personal union of crowns, parallel to that which would link England and Scotland after 1603, yet no Tudor monarch ever took the trouble to visit Ireland.[6]

Henry died in 1547 and was succeeded by his nine-year-old son Edward VI, who lived only until age 15. There was an uprising in Cornwall and Devon in 1549 against imposition of an English-language Book of Common Prayer in which 5,500 died, while in Norfolk a rebellion led by Robert Kett opposed enclosure of common land. Edward was succeeded by his Catholic half-sister Mary, who burned 220 men and 60 women at the stake in an attempt to revert to the old faith.[7]

Elizabeth I re-established the Church of England's independence from Rome after succeeding Mary in 1558 and sought to achieve a Protestant settlement that Catholics could live with. She was short-tempered and sometimes indecisive but enjoyed a fair amount of luck. As time went on, Elizabeth became celebrated as the 'Virgin queen'. Her reign saw a flourishing of drama, led by playwrights such as Shakespeare and Christopher Marlowe. It was notable for maritime adventurers such as Francis Drake and Walter Raleigh and for the defeat of the Spanish Armada. The English were slower to create New World colonies than the Spanish, Portuguese, Dutch and French, though Raleigh did return from Guiana with a strange plant for smoking, called tobacco. In Ireland, 'pirate queen' Grace O'Malley or Gráinne Mhaol, head of a dynasty renowned for piracy off the north and west coast, tussled with government officials but won a meeting with Elizabeth in which she secured the release of her son and brother.[8]

Henry VIII went to war against Scotland twice. In 1542, angered that the Scottish king had refused to follow him in breaking from

Rome, he defeated his nephew James V at Solway Moss on the English side of the border. James died shortly afterwards, leaving a baby daughter, the future Mary, Queen of Scots. In 1543, Henry began the Eight Years' War, later dubbed the 'Rough Wooing' by Sir Walter Scott, an unsuccessful attempt to force a marriage between Mary and his son Edward. It involved border skirmishing and English incursions. Mary was sent to France at age five as intended bride of the heir to the French throne. Her mother Marie de Guise, James V's French widow, stayed in Scotland to look after Mary's interests. Marie eventually became regent, which she used to advance French interests and influence. Opposition grew, and, after Marie died in 1560, the Auld Alliance ended with the Treaty of Edinburgh, which led to the removal of French and English troops from Scotland.

Scotland remained Catholic for 30 years after Henry VIII's break with Rome, but the Reformation gradually took hold and acquired a Calvinist or Presbyterian character, favouring governance by representative assemblies of elders rather than bishops. A key figure was John Knox, author of the *First Blast of the Trumpet against the Monstrous Regiment of Women* (1558) directed against two Catholic Marys, England's Queen Mary and Scotland's Marie de Guise. In 1560, Knox and allies persuaded the Scottish parliament to abolish the pope's jurisdiction, rule the Church of Scotland through a general assembly and introduce a Calvinist liturgy, though the reforms were not fully secured until Mary, Queen of Scots was driven into exile in 1567.

Mary had returned to Scotland in 1561 after her husband Francis, the French dauphin, died. She was pragmatic at first and governed as the Catholic monarch of a Protestant kingdom. Mary unwisely married her half-cousin, Henry Stuart, Lord Darnley, and they conceived a son, James. The handsome Darnley was often drunk, hunting or whoring. Their marriage soured after Darnley orchestrated the murder of Mary's Italian secretary and friend David Rizzio, suspected of being the child's father, in front of the pregnant

Mary in Holyrood Palace. Later, Darnley's residence was destroyed by an explosion, and he was found murdered in a nearby garden. James Hepburn, Earl of Bothwell, was suspected of arranging Darnley's death; he was acquitted of the charge and married Mary a month later. After an uprising against the couple, Mary was imprisoned in Lochleven Castle and forced to abdicate in favour of one-year-old James VI. She fled to England, though as things turned out, she might have been safer fleeing to France.[9]

James, baptised a Catholic, was crowned a Protestant. Described by one historian as 'one of the most complicated neurotics to sit … on the throne', he overcame his neuroses to bring a large measure of peace and concord to Scotland and England and was Scotland's longest-serving king (1567–1625). His early life was far from easy: three of the four regents who controlled his childhood were violently killed. An educated figure who wrote books, James was also obsessed by the witchcraft panic that swept Europe. He feared that he and his Danish bride, Anne, had been targeted by witches who conjured storms to try to kill them during voyages across the North Sea. James wrote *Daemonologie*, a book that explained witchcraft as a pact between humans and the devil. It inspired Shakespeare's witch scenes in *Macbeth*.[10]

After Elizabeth's death in 1603, James left Edinburgh for London to be crowned James I of England and Wales in addition to his Scottish title, promising to return every three years (in fact, he came back only once, in 1617). He styled himself 'King of Great Britain and Ireland', without legal force, while his aim of merging the kingdoms along with their laws and state churches was stymied by opposition in the English and Scottish parliaments. The Gunpowder Plot of 1605, a failed scheme to blow up the House of Lords and kill the king, showed there was still a threat from militant Catholics. One plotter, Guy Fawkes, interrogated about why he had so much gunpowder, allegedly replied that his intention was 'to blow you Scotch beggars back to your native mountains'.[11]

James became less popular as his reign went on, in part because he showered offices and money on Scottish companions and courtiers.

Apparently bisexual, James gave advancement to undistinguished male favourites, notably the handsome George Villiers, a knight's son from Leicestershire, whom he made Duke of Buckingham and called 'my sweet child and wife'. He also fathered eight children with his wife and conducted an ill-concealed affair with Anne Murray, daughter of the Earl of Tullibardine.[12] Among his reign's successes was commissioning the King James Bible, published in 1611, aimed at countering the influence of the Geneva Bible favoured by Puritan dissenters. Noted for its majesty of language, the Authorised Version helped to lay the foundation for English to become the world's dominant tongue.

In Scotland, James, who regarded the Hebridean population as barbarous, tried unsuccessfully to colonise the Western Isles with lowlanders before co-opting clan chiefs such as the Campbells, Mackenzies and Gordons with awards of status and lands in return for keeping their territories quiet – a decentralised system of government that Britain would later use repeatedly in its Empire from India to Nigeria. Instead, James sent lowland Protestants to colonise Ireland. Close to 100,000 Scots, Welsh and English immigrants were 'planted' there by the 1640s, most in Ulster and some in Munster.[13]

Charles I, who became king of England (incorporating Wales), Scotland and Ireland when his father James died in 1625, inherited his father's belief in the divine right of kings but was clumsier and more autocratic. His reign saw three English civil wars in a decade (1642–6, 1648–9, 1649–51), along with parallel conflicts in Scotland and Ireland, among the most destructive events in the Isles' history – not unlike Germany's Thirty Years' War. Charles lost his head in the process.

He had clashed with England's parliament, particularly over levying taxes without consent. His high church policies, coupled with marriage to a Catholic, generated antipathy from Puritans. Charles's conflicts began when he tried to introduce a high church English Book of Common Prayer to Scotland. This provoked orchestrated rioting (in myth it was initiated by a street stallholder called Jenny Geddes who threw a stool in Edinburgh's St Giles Cathedral). In 1638, various sections of Scottish society drew up a National Covenant, objecting to Charles's liturgical innovations, while a general assembly of the Kirk abolished bishops. Charles's forces were humiliatingly defeated in two Bishops' Wars (1639–40) in which a Scottish army captured Newcastle.

Desperate for money, Charles summoned what became known as the Long Parliament in 1640. It sought to force reforms on the king and condemned Thomas Wentworth, Earl of Strafford, his former Lord Deputy of Ireland, to death for 'high misdemeanours' there. Parliament feared that Strafford was encouraging the king to redeploy troops from Ireland to suppress opposition in England. Charles reluctantly signed Strafford's death warrant. Rebellion broke out in Ireland in 1641 involving not only Ulster Catholics seeking to overturn the effects of Protestant plantation but also leading members of the Catholic 'Old English' (descended from Anglo-Normans) – the start of 11 years of warfare. A Protestant Scots army sent by the Covenanters landed in Ulster to defend the embattled Protestant planters.

In January 1642, Charles unsuccessfully attempted to arrest five members of the Commons on a charge of treason. A few days later, he fled to York, set up court there and on 22 August raised his standard at Nottingham. At least a quarter of the adult male population is estimated to have borne arms at some stage in the subsequent conflict. Royalist support was strongest in rural areas of northern and western England, Wales, the Welsh marches and west midlands, while parliament drew support mainly from London and the south-east.[14]

At first, royalists had the upper hand, but things changed in 1644 after parliament allied with Scottish Covenanters, prompting 15,000 Scottish troops to invade northern England. A contingent again captured Newcastle, while the main force helped to besiege York. The northern royalist army was destroyed at Marston Moor, enhancing the career of Oliver Cromwell, who led the parliamentary cavalry. He was a Huntingdon-born MP who converted to radical

Puritanism after some kind of nervous breakdown. He believed that God was directing affairs through chosen people such as himself.

In Scotland, the Marquess of Montrose fought a campaign in support of the king with Irish help but was eventually defeated. In 1645, reorganisation of English parliamentary forces into the New Model Army under Sir Thomas Fairfax, with Cromwell as second-in-command, led to victories at Naseby in Northamptonshire and Langport in Somerset. The first civil war ended in May 1646 when Charles sought shelter with the Scottish army in Nottinghamshire and was handed over to parliament.

In a febrile time, the winning side was divided between the army, which championed independent religious views, and parliament, which favoured Presbyterianism. Charles agreed a treaty with Covenanters known as the Engagement to impose Presbyterianism in England for a three-year trial. In 1648, a poorly trained Engager army under James, Duke of Hamilton, marched into England. This second civil war was intended as a series of royalist risings, but other revolts were suppressed. Cromwell routed the Scots at Preston, and Hamilton was beheaded in London.

Parliament created a tribunal to try Charles for treason. Fairfax, a constitutional monarchist, declined to have anything to do with the trial and resigned as army head. This cleared Cromwell's road to power. The king was beheaded on 30 January 1649. Cromwell mounted a military campaign to regain control of parts of Ireland in 1649–50, where his troops carried out massacres in Drogheda and Wexford. It has been debated ever since whether his brutality was worse than that of the standards of the time. Estimates suggest that between 10 and 40 per cent of Ireland's population died between 1641 and 1653 through plague, famine or conflict.[15]

While England abolished the monarchy, the Scottish Covenanter government objected to Charles's execution and proclaimed his son as Charles II of Scotland, England and Ireland. He arrived in Scotland. Cromwell defeated a Scottish army at Dunbar, but that did not prevent Charles from marching south. He reached the west of England, though fewer supporters joined than he hoped. Cromwell defeated the new king at Worcester in September 1651, ending the third civil war. Charles II escaped via safe houses and a famous oak tree to France.

For the first time in history, England, Ireland, Scotland and Wales were all under Westminster's control, though difficult political tasks remained ahead. England was ruled by a republican government under the Commonwealth from 1649 to 1653. After infighting among factions in parliament, Cromwell became Lord Protector (in effect military dictator) until his death in 1658. Scotland, occupied by an English force under George Monck, was incorporated into the Commonwealth and lost its independent church government, parliament and legal system.

Cromwell's son Richard succeeded him, but he had no power base in parliament or the army and was forced to resign in May 1659, ending the Protectorate. The Commonwealth was restored, but parliament and the army were soon tearing each other to pieces again. Orderly government broke down, shops closed, trade stopped and duties went uncollected. In this chaos, Monck marched south with an army and organised a new Convention Parliament, which decided that Charles II had reigned as lawful monarch since his father's execution. Charles returned from exile in 1660 and was crowned in 1661.

Even parliamentarian Manchester was so war-weary that it celebrated Charles II's coronation heartily, and a public water conduit was made to run with claret so the crowd could drink from it.[16] Charles was affable and tolerant. Even royalists were shocked by his court's moral laxity; he acknowledged having at least a dozen illegitimate children by various mistresses. In 1665, Charles made war on the Dutch to please the Catholic French. Later, a furore of bigotry resulted from the so-called Popish Plot of 1678, in which one Titus Oates claimed to have evidence that English Catholics planned to kill the king, massacre Protestants and install a Catholic ministry. MPs believed this false story, and Catholics were arrested and tried, with several executed.

Scotland regained its system of law, parliament and Kirk. Legislation from the Covenant and Cromwell eras was repealed, and bishops returned. The restoration of episcopacy caused trouble in strongly Presbyterian south-west Scotland, where many inhabitants began to attend illegal field assemblies known as conventicles. Attempts to suppress these led to a rising in 1679, which was defeated at Bothwell Bridge. In Ireland, Catholics were relieved that the persecution of the Cromwell era had ended, but many were disappointed not to have their confiscated lands restored.

Charles died in 1685, and his younger brother succeeded as James II of England (incorporating Wales) and Ireland and VII of Scotland. James was a Catholic, and his reign was marked by struggles over religious tolerance and attempts to act without parliament's approval. Events in 1688 sparked a crisis. His son James Francis Edward was born, creating alarm among Protestants that this would create a Catholic dynasty. A group of seven nobles invited James's nephew and son-in-law William of Orange, stadtholder of the Dutch Republic and grandson of Charles I, to bring an army to England. After William landed at Brixham, James's army deserted, and he went into exile in France. William and his wife, James's eldest daughter Mary, became joint rulers in what became known to Protestants as the Glorious Revolution.

In Scotland, Presbyterianism was restored and bishops abolished yet again. There remained significant support for James in the highlands, a cause that became known as Jacobitism, from the Latin (Jacobus) for James. A Jacobite army led by John Graham, Viscount Dundee, defeated William's forces at Killiecrankie in 1689, but Dundee was killed in the fighting, and his army was soon defeated at Dunkeld. In 1692, almost 40 members of Clan MacDonald in Glencoe were killed by government forces for allegedly being slow to pledge allegiance to the new monarchs.

James landed in Ireland, where he had Catholic support, to try to recover his kingdoms. There was already conflict: in the siege of Derry, Protestant 'Apprentice Boys' bawled 'No Surrender' from the walls as they successfully resisted Catholic attackers – a cry that was to become the watchword of Ulster Protestantism.[17] At the battle of the Boyne in July 1690, James's outnumbered force of French regulars, German and Walloon mercenaries and Catholic Irish was defeated by William's – King Billy's – professional army of Dutchmen, Danes, Huguenots and English. The outcome ensured that for the next two centuries Ireland would be governed on the basis of a Protestant landowning ascendancy. James fled back to France. It was not the last time that Jacobites were to cause trouble.

CHAPTER 6

KINGDOMS UNITE

There was rejoicing and relief in London on 1 May 1707 when England and Scotland united in the new Kingdom of Great Britain. 'That whole day was spent in feastings, ringing of bells, and illuminations, and I have reasons to believe that at no time Scotsmen were more acceptable to the English than on that day,' recalled a Scottish delegate, Sir John Clerk of Penicuik.[1] Scotland's mood was more sombre. Many Presbyterian parishes held a day of fasting and humiliation, fearing the Church of England's influence might threaten their religious independence. There had been riots, protest meetings and petitions against the proposed union in the run-up to the Scottish parliament's decision to adopt the treaty, ending its own independent existence after almost five centuries.

This was to be a century bookended by unions, beginning with 1707 and ending with the creation of a United Kingdom of Great Britain and Ireland in 1801. England desperately wanted a constitutional union with Scotland to help secure a Protestant succession to childless Queen Anne. As long as Scotland was free to choose a different monarch such as a Stuart, it could have undermined the English government's plan to hand the crown to a member of the House of Hanover. Scotland, for its part, was simply broke, so the economic opportunities of union offered a potential lifeline. It had suffered failed harvests in 1692–8 known as the 'seven ill years', in which at least 5 per cent of the population died of hunger; its attempt to establish a colony at Darien on the Isthmus of Panama – led by William Paterson, Scottish co-founder of the Bank of England – ended in disaster, absorbing about a quarter of the nation's financial capital.[2]

Scots, despite their initial lack of enthusiasm for the union, were destined to play a huge part in the British Empire. Arguably, union opened the way for the Scottish Enlightenment as well as a great expansion of trade. As Linda Colley laid out in *Britons: Forging the Nation 1707–1837*, a British identity was created by factors including defence of Protestantism against a largely Catholic Europe, wars against France and the Isles' maritime prowess. In recent decades, however, the union has looked less secure as religion and Empire declined, causing many Scots to question its value.

Paterson, born in Dumfriesshire, conceived the Darien scheme to facilitate trade with east Asia while working as a young merchant in the West Indies. He tried and failed to persuade the governments of England, the Holy Roman Empire, Dutch Republic and Brandenburg to establish a colony in Panama. He went on to make his fortune in slavery-enabled trade at the Merchant Taylors' Company before co-founding the Bank of England (private sector banker to the English government) in 1694, after which he fell out with colleagues and devoted himself to Darien.[3]

Having failed elsewhere, Paterson won widespread support and investment in Scotland for the scheme. The English government opposed it: at war with France, it did not want to offend Spain, which claimed the territory. About 1,200 men, women and children set out for Panama in three ships in 1698, but disaster resulted. Poorly equipped, beset by incessant rain and disease, attacked by the Spanish and refused aid by the English, the colonists abandoned the project in 1700. Only one in four of the first settlers survived. Paterson's wife, daughter and maid died.[4]

Under economic pressure, Scotland depended heavily on cattle and linen sales to England. Its parliament passed an Act of Security in 1704, threatening to choose a different monarch unless England granted free trade. The English parliament responded with the Alien

Act 1705, labelling Scots as 'foreign nationals' and blocking about half of Scottish trade by impeding exports to England or its colonies unless Scotland negotiated a union. Presented with a take-it-or-leave-it offer, the Scottish parliament adopted the Treaty of Union by 110 votes to 69 in January 1707. Clerk, one of the negotiators, noted that it was 'contrary to the inclination of at least three-fourths of the kingdom'.[5]

Thus Scotland's parliament voted itself out of existence. Its government would survive only as a regional department of the London-based administration. Scotland would have free trade with England and be treated as 'home territory' under the Navigation Acts, which restricted foreign trade with England's colonies. Scotland would receive the 'Equivalent', a sum of £398,085 (more than £80 million in today's money) in return for taking on a share of England's national debt. The treaty was passed with the help of promised favours, offices and bribes. More than half of the Equivalent went to shareholders and creditors of the Darien scheme. The biggest beneficiaries were members of the ruling elite such as the Duke of Queensberry, the queen's commissioner in the Scottish parliament.[6]

The treaty replaced Scotland's systems of currency, taxation and trade laws with laws made in London. Scottish law remained separate from English law, and the religious system was unchanged. Forty-five Scots would be added to the 513 members of the House of Commons and 16 to the 190 members of the House of Lords. As historian Norman Davies put it: 'Henceforth, there would be a British state, a British monarchy, a British Parliament, a British Government, a British Empire, a British army, and a community of British subjects'; 1 May was 'the day when modern British history began'.[7]

Discontent grew in Scotland post-union as commercial benefits were slow to come through and taxes rose on items such as salt and malt, provoking a violent reaction. This helped create an opportunity for a Jacobite revival, exploited by the French. In 1708, James Francis Edward Stuart, the 'Old Pretender', son of James II and VII, tried to invade with a French fleet carrying 6,000 men, but the Royal

Navy prevented it from landing troops. A more serious attempt in 1715 failed when government arrests forestalled simultaneous risings in Wales and Devon. John Erskine, Earl of Mar, raised the Jacobite clans in Scotland but led the revolt poorly. An army fought its way into England before being defeated at Preston. James belatedly landed in Scotland but fled back to France.

In 1745, James's son Charles Edward Stuart, the 'Young Pretender', landed on Eriskay and began another rebellion. He took Edinburgh and defeated a government army at Prestonpans before marching into England, taking Carlisle and advancing as far south as Derby. Popular support was lacking, however. People were reluctant to put property and lives at risk in another civil war. In the face of poor support and the absence of a threatened French invasion, Charles's advisers persuaded him to turn back. He decided to fight at Culloden near Inverness on 16 April 1746, where his army lost heavily to Hanoverian forces under the Duke of Cumberland. The Jacobites were outnumbered, and the flat, open moor was perfect for Cumberland's canon and rifles.

Charles hid in the Outer Hebrides with the aid of highlanders before escaping back to France. He was helped by a woman called Flora (Fionnghal) Macdonald, who reluctantly agreed to take him by boat to Skye disguised as her Irish maid Betty Burke. Macdonald was arrested and imprisoned but later released under a general amnesty. In later life, she and her husband emigrated to North Carolina, where their support for Britain during the War of Independence meant the loss of their estates, and they returned to Scotland. She would be immortalised in Jacobite ballads and legends.[8]

Cumberland aimed to teach clan society a lesson that would prevent further Jacobite risings. Settlements were burned, plundered and laid waste. Cattle were confiscated. Military control was consolidated by extending a road system begun by Field Marshal George Wade and by building Fort George, east of Inverness. Highland dress was proscribed, and a Disarming Act stiffened legislation against carrying weapons. It was not these actions alone that destroyed Jacobitism, however. Deeper forces were already under-mining it. Clan leaders were turning into commercial landlords, and Scottish opposition to the union was fading by the 1740s.[9]

Meanwhile, access to London and the Empire opened up attractive career opportunities for ambitious middle- and upper-class Scots. Thousands, mainly lowlanders, gained positions of power in politics, civil service, the army and navy, trade and colonial enterprises. British officials liked to recruit Scottish soldiers, especially highlanders, because as Lord Barrington, secretary of war, told parliament in 1751: 'They are generally more hardy and less mutinous.'[10] The advance of Scots into senior civilian positions stirred resentment among the English, provoking violent diatribes by the radical John Wilkes, vulgar jokes and cartoons in the popular press and haughty ridicule by intellectuals such as Samuel Johnson, who defined oats in his dictionary as 'a grain, which in England is generally given to horses, but in Scotland supports the people'.

Scotland's economy was improving, and it avoided becoming a satellite agrarian economy supplying the English market, like Ireland. Landowners modernised their estates. Glasgow merchants undercut English rivals by smuggling imports of tobacco – and later captured a good part of the legal trade, turning the city into the tobacco metropolis of western Europe and generating profits that fed a range of industries. Several parts of British North America became, in effect, Scottish colonies, and Scots were prominent in the East India Company, a British joint-stock company that traded in the Indian Ocean region. Linen, Scotland's most important eighteenth-century industry, grew rapidly and nurtured skills for cotton manufacture when the Industrial Revolution began.

Scottish political affairs were firmly managed by Archibald Campbell, Earl of Islay and later Duke of Argyll, appointed by British Whig prime minister Robert Walpole to run Scotland. This gave Campbell great sources of patronage. Campbell's power from the 1720s until his death in 1761 was such that George II called him 'Vice Roy in Scotland'. In the latter part of the century, Henry

Dundas, lieutenant of British prime minister William Pitt the Younger, also dominated Scotland's politics through patronage. The political class was, however, hardly representative of the people as a whole. Only about 0.2 per cent of the population had the right to vote, a smaller elite even than in England and Ireland.[11]

Scotland's influence increased as prosperity grew. As historian Christopher Smout put it, the tail was 'beginning ever so slightly to wag the dog'. In 1750–1800, Scotland's overseas commerce grew by 300 per cent and that of England by 200 per cent. The proportion of Scots living in towns doubled, while England's larger urban population grew by only about a quarter. Boosted by imperial trade, Scottish towns developed broad streets, elegant houses and imposing public buildings. Edinburgh New Town was designed by James Craig in 1767 to celebrate British patriotism and showcase Scotland's, and the city's, place in the union.[12]

In the eighteenth century, Europe grew weary of the religious conflicts that had plagued it since the Reformation. An 'Age of Science and Reason' gradually took hold, also known as the Enlightenment. Some of this intellectual ferment of scientists, writers and philosophers took place in England. The Royal Society of London for Improving Natural Knowledge, founded in 1660, helped lead the way. Cambridge-educated mathematician Isaac Newton formulated laws of motion and gravity that dominated scientific thinking for centuries. Oxford philosopher John Locke wrote seminal works on religious practice, constitutional politics and psychology.

It was in Scotland, however, that the Enlightenment took particular hold. From the 1730s, it was building a reputation in fields such as philosophy, history, science, law and medicine. Its cities had developed a mutually supporting infrastructure of universities, reading societies, libraries, periodicals, museums and masonic lodges. The intolerance and puritan conformity of the later seventeenth century gave way to a spirit of open-minded enquiry. The issue was less Calvinism itself than the rigidity with which it had been applied. Factors that helped to shape a more liberal climate included: a

Patronage Act passed in 1711 by the Tory government in Westminster, which reasserted the right of lay patrons, rather than the local church community, to appoint ministers; growing liberalism in the universities where ministers were trained, encouraged by figures such as Francis Hutcheson, professor of moral philosophy at Glasgow; and the rise of a Moderate Party within the Church of Scotland, which dominated the General Assembly after about 1750. William Robert Scott later coined the term 'Scottish Enlightenment' in 1900 to describe the new era.[13]

Hutcheson, born in Ulster to a family of Scots Presbyterians, taught that a natural law existed that transcended the state's laws, and that man had an inalienable right to enjoy freedom of opinion and resist the tyranny of oppressive rulers. He influenced other thinkers, notably David Hume and Adam Smith. Hume concluded that all human knowledge derives solely from experience and denounced the evils that came from organised religion, a view that would have been considered blasphemous a few decades earlier. Smith, seen as the 'father of capitalism', was instrumental in the rise of classical liberalism. His master work *An Inquiry into the Nature and Causes of the Wealth of Nations* (1776) was the first analysis of political economy as a comprehensive system. Other figures included Adam Ferguson, William Robertson and James Hutton, pioneers in what became the disciplines respectively of sociology, history and geology. Chemist and physician Joseph Black discovered carbon dioxide and latent heat.

Despite these Enlightenment ideals, the general populace in parts of the Isles were not always as liberal-minded as the intellectual class. The Gordon Riots in 1780 saw several days of anti-Catholic rioting in London, the worst unrest in its history, in which several hundred died. It began as a protest against an attempt by parliament to repeal the harshest provisions of anti-Catholic legislation. Lord George Gordon, head of the Protestant Association, suggested the law would enable Catholics to join the British Army and plot treason. It took 12,000 troops to restore order, and about 25 rioters were later executed. In 1791, another mob burned down the Birmingham home and laboratory of chemist Joseph Priestley, along with the property of other prominent dissenters and several Nonconformist chapels. Priestley had dared to hold a dinner celebrating the anniversary of the fall of the Bastille. The mob linked religious dissent with political revolution. Priestley fled to London and then America.[14]

Arguably, the new religious fervour of Methodism was far more influential in popular appeal than Enlightenment rationalism. John Wesley, an Oxford tutor who had grown disillusioned with Church of England doctrines and practices, founded a revival movement within the church. He travelled widely and preached outdoors, establishing a network of preaching circuits and devotional societies. Wesley stressed the inner conviction of individual believers and the joy of redemption by God's grace. His followers, named Methodists because of the methodical way in which they pursued their faith, became a separate denomination after Wesley's death and grew strong in industrialising areas. Historian Élie Halévy argued that Methodism kept Britain immune from revolution.[15]

Methodism had a huge impact on Wales, particularly from the second half of the eighteenth century, where it turned the nation into a fortress of Nonconformity for two centuries. It took a different form from Wesleyan Methodism and was moderately Calvinist in doctrine as opposed to Wesley's Arminianism. The main difference was over predestination: Calvinists believed that God unconditionally elected some for salvation, whereas Dutch theologian Jacobus Arminius had argued that the choice depended on the strength of believers' faith. Welsh Methodism became particularly strong in Welsh-speaking north Wales, and its chapels and schools boosted the Welsh language. Welsh hymns and choirs became a great art form. The revival began within the Church of England in Wales and was promoted by figures such as evangelists Howell Harris and Daniel Rowland and hymn writer William Williams of Pantycelyn. The Methodists seceded from the established church in 1811 and established the Presbyterian Church of Wales in 1823.[16]

A Welsh educational and cultural revival was also under way. Literacy had been boosted by the system of circulating schools created by Griffith Jones and Bridget Bevan. A Welsh Romantic movement grew, reviving interest in things Welsh, in parallel with similar revivals in the Scottish lowlands and Ireland. Theophilus Evans, a curate in Breconshire, wrote *Drych y Prif Oesoedd* (Mirror of the Early Centuries) in 1716, mixing fact with myth in his effort to portray Welsh history as a glorious epic. Support for a Welsh revival was greatest among the Welsh in London, where the Honourable Society of Cymmrodorion (still in existence) was created in 1751 by Richard Morris, a clerk at the Admiralty. Edward Williams, better known by his self-created bardic name Iolo Morganwg, was an antiquarian renowned as an expert collector of medieval Welsh literature, though it emerged after his death that he had forged several manuscripts. He did, however, manage to revive the *eisteddfodau*, or poetry and music festivals, not seen since the mid-sixteenth century.[17]

In Ireland, most of the eighteenth century was more peaceful than the previous two centuries. The economy grew, and the population probably doubled to nearly five million, though there were periodic food shortages.[18] A serious famine in 1740–41, caused by the Great Frost across Europe, is estimated have killed 13–20 per cent of Ireland's people.[19] Foreign trade grew despite colonial restrictions on exports of Irish woollens, while turnpike roads and inland waterways expanded trading networks within the country. Fortunes were made by merchants, including many Catholics, in market towns and large ports such as Cork, Limerick and Waterford. The cattle market fed an increasingly insatiable English market, though in some areas small farmers became over-dependent on pigs and potatoes.

Jacobites' resistance in Ireland ended with their defeat at the battles of the Boyne and Aughrim in 1690–91. The Protestant 'Ascendancy', established by land redistributions of the seventeenth century, breathed a sigh of relief yet still felt insecure. A small group of Anglo-Irish families loyal to the Anglican Church of Ireland owned most farmland, where the work was done by Catholic peasants. By the early eighteenth century, Catholics, although about 75 per cent of the population, owned only 14 per cent of land.[20] Penal laws excluded Catholics from most areas of public life. Nonetheless, the Catholic Church managed gradually to assert a stronger role. Urban churches were being built by the 1720s. By the 1790s, Catholics could buy and sell land, and educational restrictions had been repealed.

The Protestant Ascendancy controlled the legal system and local government and held big majorities in both houses of the Irish parliament. They did not have full political control, however, because the London government had superior authority and treated Ireland as a colony, governed by viceroys. Irish patriots such as satirist Jonathan Swift sought more autonomy. In the *Drapier's Letters* (1724), he posed as a shopkeeper to attack a monopoly granted by the British government to William Wood to mint copper coinage for Ireland; it was widely believed he would need to flood Ireland with debased coinage to make a profit. The letters had such an impact that the government offered a reward to anyone disclosing the author's identity. After an outcry, Wood's patent was rescinded, and the coins were kept out of circulation.

Tensions grew in Ireland towards the century's end, heightened by the American War of Independence. The government tried to contain them by removing restrictions on Irish commerce and giving Ireland's parliament greater powers to initiate legislation. In Belfast, a group of Presbyterians, frustrated about being excluded from power, formed the Society of United Irishmen, inspired by the American and French revolutions. They sought to make common cause with the Catholic majority, seeking Catholic emancipation and parliamentary reform. Despairing of progress, they linked with other disgruntled people in Dublin and around Ireland and became an underground republican movement.

A government crackdown and arrests forced the conspirators into the open, leading to the Irish Rebellion of 1798, a series of uncoordinated risings in counties Carlow and Wexford in the south-east, in Antrim and Down in the north and closer to Dublin in Meath and

Kildare. The risings were swiftly put down. A French expeditionary force landed too late in County Mayo and surrendered. A second French force was defeated in a naval action off Donegal, leading to the capture of Theobald Wolfe Tone, the United Irish leader who had arranged the French intervention. Sentenced to be hanged, he died from a reportedly self-inflicted wound. Irish nationalists later hailed him as a hero.[21]

Largely because of these events, Irish self-government was ended when the Irish and British parliaments enacted the Acts of Union 1800, creating the United Kingdom of Great Britain and Ireland from 1 January 1801. The intention was that the Test Act would be repealed to remove remaining discrimination against Catholics, Presbyterians, Baptists and other dissenters in the UK, but George III controversially blocked it. Pitt the Younger resigned in protest, but his successor Henry Addington failed to change the situation. Ireland's status was set to become an even bigger issue over the coming century.

CHAPTER 7

BRITAIN INDUSTRIALISES

The Industrial Revolution got under way in England's midlands and north, yet before long spread to other parts of the Isles, notably the west of Scotland, Ulster and south Wales. It enabled populations to grow and eventually allowed living standards to rise. For those living through it, it brought both new opportunities and wrenching social change.

Conditions could be appalling. In one Scottish coal mine, a government commission found a six-year-old girl, Margaret Leveston, who carried half a hundredweight of coal (56 pounds or 25 kilos) on her back from the main shaft to the pithead up to 14 times every working day. Each journey was the equivalent of climbing to the top of St Paul's Cathedral.[1] In the cotton industry, children worked 15-hour days and were often beaten to keep them awake. Sometimes they lost fingers and limbs or were even decapitated or crushed.

Yet not all lives were blighted by industrialisation. Charles Campbell, for example, spent his childhood working in a cotton mill in Johnstone, Renfrewshire, after which he sought adventure at sea. Later, after medical training at Glasgow University, he established a small medical practice in a west highland village, but when it failed to pay, Campbell sought a 'more congenial situation'.

He became a spinner in a Glasgow cotton factory, where he earned a hefty 40 shillings a week.[2] For many, factory work was preferable to rural poverty.

The Industrial Revolution provokes much debate. Was it really revolutionary? When did it begin and end? Many would say about 1760–1840. What was its human impact? The UK economy grew slowly in the eighteenth century before picking up speed in the nineteenth. Britain's reign as top manufacturing nation was to prove fairly short-lived. Its industrial output did not overtake that of China until almost 1860, according to economic historian Paul Bairoch, and before 1900 Britain had been overtaken by the US.[3]

Argument rages about why the revolution first happened in Britain. Victorians liked to attribute it to the genius of British inventors. Underlying causes often cited today include: plentiful coal and iron ore; tolerance of religious dissenters; colonial resource extraction; profits from the slave trade; expansion of the navy to protect world trade; an agrarian revolution that enabled population and consumer demand to increase; navigable rivers; and a framework of social and political institutions favouring entrepreneurship, encouraged by economic liberalism.

The revolution's dominant early industry was cotton textiles. A nation that was a marginal producer in 1760 – and lies thousands of miles from where raw cotton is grown – was by 1860 home to two-thirds of the world's cotton spindles, notably in Lancashire.[4] The north-west benefited from having rivers to provide water power, coal for steam engines, connections to Liverpool giving access to slave-grown cotton and easy access to sources of iron and chemicals. It already had the experience of its cottage-based textile industry.

Scotland's union with England and Wales offered free trade within Britain and access to colonial markets. Scotland remained a poor, agricultural economy in the eighteenth century but began to industrialise after about 1790, when its strength in linen helped it to create a significant cotton-spinning and weaving industry. Industrialisation developed rapidly after 1830, particularly in the century's second half when coal, iron, steel and shipbuilding transformed the nation into a global manufacturer. 'Clyde-built' became a source of pride for a new, skilled working class.

Scotland's population doubled to almost 4.8 million between 1831 and 1911, particularly in and around Glasgow, heavy industry's heartland.[5] Migrants arrived from Ireland in the decades after the Great Famine, attracted by job opportunities in Scottish industry, though Scots themselves also migrated in large numbers to north America, Australia and England in search of more reliable and better-paid work.

At first, there was significant technology transfer from England to Scotland. English methods were widely adopted in iron-manufacturing, pottery, wool and glass-making. Richard Arkwright's cotton-spinning technology became the basis of the Scottish cotton industry. Arkwright and others invested in Scotland, attracted by lower wage costs. Yet Scottish innovators were also important, notably James Watt, father of steam engine technology.[6] In 1776, he developed an engine that improved on Thomas Newcomen's 1712 version and became a key driver of the Industrial Revolution.

Watt (1736–1819) was born in Greenock, Renfrewshire, where his father ran a successful ship- and house-building business. While working as a maker of mathematical instruments at the University of Glasgow, Watt found himself repairing a Newcomen engine and saw it was wasting energy by cooling and reheating the cylinder. His solution was a separate condenser, in which the steam cylinder remained hot while a separate condensing vessel was cold. He eventually adapted his engine to produce rotary motion, broadening its use beyond pumping water.

Watt formed a partnership with John Roebuck, founder of the Carron Iron Works near Falkirk. When Roebuck went bankrupt, his patent rights were acquired by Matthew Boulton, who owned the Soho Works in Birmingham. Watt moved to Birmingham, where he and Boulton began a 25-year partnership in which Boulton's financial support enabled rapid progress. Demands for Watt's engines came from paper mills, flour mills, cotton mills, iron mills, distilleries, canals and waterworks, making him wealthy despite his personal nervousness about business dealings.

Other Scottish innovators and scientists included: Henry Bell, whose paddle steamer *Comet* pioneered steam propulsion for ships; James Beaumont Neilson, whose hot-blast process slashed the cost of smelting iron; civil engineers such as Dumfriesshire-born Thomas Telford, the 'Colossus of Roads' who also built bridges such as the Menai Bridge, and Sir William Arrol, builder of the Forth Bridge, Tay Bridge and London's Tower Bridge; James 'Paraffin' Young, who pioneered exploitation of shale oil deposits in west Lothian; chemist and physicist Joseph Black, whose discoveries included carbon dioxide, magnesium and latent heat; physicist William Thomson, Lord Kelvin, who helped to formulate the first and second laws of thermodynamics and determined the correct value of absolute zero; and mathematical physicist James Clerk Maxwell, whose theory of electromagnetism was fundamental to the development of radio and other applications. Multi-millionaires included: ironmaster William Baird; Sir Charles Tennant, owner of the St Rollox chemicals works; Sir James and Peter Coats of the thread-making dynasty; and William Weir, colliery owner and iron-manufacturer.

The growth of a flexible and dynamic banking sector helped to finance industrialisation and economic development. Scotland's social elite were energetic in founding banks such as the Bank of Scotland, the Royal Bank of Scotland and the British Linen Bank. The Royal Bank developed the 'cash accompt', the world's first overdraft facility, in 1728 when it allowed Edinburgh merchant William Hog to temporarily take more money from his account than he held in it.[7]

Scottish cotton-spinning declined sharply after 1850, facing competition from abroad and Lancashire at the finer end of the trade, but other textile sectors bloomed. Coats of Paisley merged with Patons in 1896 to create the world's biggest thread-making producer. Dundee became 'Juteopolis', making cheap, tough fabrics for products such as sacking and canvas by importing fibre from

Bengal. Cox Brothers' Camperdown Works in Lochee in the 1880s employed 14,000 (mainly women) workers, making it the world's biggest jute complex.[8] Among other towns, Kirkcaldy specialised in linoleum; Galashiels, Hawick and Selkirk in the Borders in tartans, tweeds and knitwear; Kilmarnock and Glasgow in carpets; and Darvel and Galston in Ayrshire in lace curtains. Whisky distilling took place in many locations. At Clydebank, Singer of the US created the world's largest sewing machine-manufacturing complex, employing more than 10,000.

The result was rapid urbanisation, driven particularly by expansion of Glasgow, Edinburgh, Dundee and Aberdeen. Queen Victoria opened Glasgow's lavish City Chambers in 1888, a step towards Glasgow seeing itself as the 'second city of Empire', a vague accolade to which Dublin and Calcutta also aspired. A small number of families made fortunes, while elegant suburbs bloomed in places such as Glasgow's West End, Broughty Ferry near Dundee and Edinburgh's Newington and Corstorphine. There was huge inequality, however, and economic volatility brought sharp periods of unemployment. Average wages were lower than in England, while living costs were higher. There were occasional disputes such as strikes by Glasgow weavers in 1787 and 1812 and spinners in 1837, though Scotland was relatively slow to organise effective trade unionism.

Scottish cities developed majestic buildings, yet many were also squalid. Glasgow slum districts included the High Street, Gallowgate and Saltmarket areas. The reporter of the West of Scotland Handloom Weavers Commission noted:

> I have seen degradation in some of its worst phases, both in England and abroad, but I can advisedly say that I do not believe until I visited the wynds of Glasgow that so large an amount of filth, crime, misery and disease existed in one spot in any civilised country.[9]

Cholera visited Scotland in 1832, leaving 10,000 dead, with further outbreaks in 1848, 1853 and 1866. Housing in Scottish cities was severely overcrowded. Dundee, like Glasgow, suffered acute problems of health, sanitation and poverty. More than half its workforce was employed in textiles, and increasingly these were low-paid women in the heavy linen and jute industries.

In England, the Industrial Revolution accelerated rapidly, first in the midlands and then in the north. In 1709, at Coalbrookdale, Shropshire, Abraham Darby I established the first blast furnace to smelt iron with coke successfully, ensuring the availability of inexpensive iron. Birmingham's population quadrupled between 1700 and 1750, and the city emerged at the forefront of developments in science, technology, medicine, philosophy and natural history as part of a cultural transformation now labelled the Midlands Enlightenment. The Lunar Society of Birmingham, which met between 1765 and 1813, discussed natural philosophy and how it applied to manufacturing. Members included chemist Joseph Priestley and physician Erasmus Darwin alongside Watt and Boulton.

Lewis Paul and John Wyatt invented roller spinning, which enabled cotton to be spun without the aid of human fingers, and in 1741 opened the world's first cotton mill in Birmingham's Upper Priory. In 1765, Boulton opened his Soho Manufactory, pioneering mechanisation of previously separate manufacturing activities under one roof through a system known as 'rational manufacture'. John Roebuck invented the lead chamber process to manufacture sulphuric acid in 1746, and James Keir pioneered the manufacture of alkali, which together marked the birth of the modern chemical industry.

Cotton textiles took off mainly in the north through inventors such as John Kay (flying shuttle), James Hargreaves (spinning jenny), Richard Arkwright (water frame) and Samuel Crompton (spinning mule). Preston-born Arkwright played a big part in creating the factory system, starting with his water-powered mill at Cromford in Derbyshire in 1771. Benjamin Huntsman in Sheffield invented crucible, or cast, steel in the 1740s. Britain's first proper canal, the Bridgewater, opened in 1761 between Worsley and Manchester.

George Stephenson and his son Robert built the first steam locomotive to haul passengers on a public railway, the Stockton and Darlington, opened in 1825. Joseph Whitworth, a Manchester-based pioneer of machine tools, created a standard for screw threads, laying the foundation of modern mass production. William Armstrong, an artillery and warship manufacturer, turned Tyneside into the arsenal of the British Empire.

By 1871, more than half of Britain's 30 largest towns were in northern England. Manchester's population grew from 10,000 in 1700 to 303,000 in 1851. Liverpool, Leeds and Sheffield also saw strong increases. Middlesbrough, lauded by William Gladstone as 'an infant Hercules', had just 25 inhabitants in 1801; by 1891, it had more than 75,000.[10]

As in Scotland, industrialisation brought opportunities but also tough conditions. In one cotton factory, 14 pounds in cast-iron weights were attached to the back and shoulders of a nine-year-old throstle spinner to stop her running away.[11] There was slum housing, smoke and filth in explosively growing towns and cities into which workers crowded. Industrialisation caused alarm among intellectuals. Thomas Carlyle, Scottish essayist and historian, coined the expression the 'Condition of England' in 1839, warning that the 'working body of this rich English Nation has sunk or is fast sinking into a state, to which, all sides of it considered, there was literally never any parallel'.[12] But Edwin Chadwick, whose pioneering research into urban slums formed the basis for the earliest public health measures, believed that 'wages, or the means of obtaining the necessaries of life for the whole mass of the labouring community, have advanced, and the comforts within the reach of the labouring classes have increased with the late increase of population'.[13]

In Ireland, the only large-scale industrialisation was in east Ulster, where Belfast's population soared on the back of its linen and then shipbuilding industries. At the start of the century, it had just 20,000 inhabitants, but by 1851 there were 98,000 and by 1901 almost 350,000, overtaking Dublin in 1891. The city's Presbyterian bourgeoisie had made Belfast into Ireland's most important cotton town before the removal of protective duties in the 1820s and competition from Manchester killed the sector. It then successfully developed its linen-spinning industry by mass-producing linen of improving quality at falling cost. Steam-powered mills clustered in Belfast – 'Linenopolis' – with easy access to the docks for imported coal and additional supplies of flax brought in mainly from Russia. The York Street Flax Spinning and Weaving Company, the largest of its kind in the world, employed 4,000 workers, not including embroiderers and other outworkers, and had branches and agencies in New York, Riga, St Petersburg and Melbourne.[14]

The emergence of Belfast's River Lagan as a shipbuilding centre to rival Clydeside came about in part through a fortuitous accident. A debt-laden ironworks hired a young engineer, Scarborough-born Edward Harland, to build ships with its iron. Harland turned out to be a genius – he stayed in Belfast only because Liverpool City Council rejected his application to open a new shipyard, citing his inexperience. Harland & Wolff was formed in 1861 when Harland took over the small Belfast shipyard where he was general manager and made his assistant, Hamburg-born Gustav Wolff, a partner. Harland secured the financial backing of Wolff's uncle, Gustav Schwabe, a partner in the Bibby Line, and the first three ships he built were for that line. Harland made several innovations, notably replacing the wooden upper decks of ships with iron ones, which increased their strength; and giving the hulls a flatter bottom and squarer cross-section, which increased their capacity. From 1880, Harland & Wolff was building its own marine engines, and in 1899 the firm launched the *Oceanic*, the largest ship ever built up to then. A vigorous engineering industry also emerged to meet the needs of linen and shipbuilding firms.

In 1888, Belfast was awarded city status by Queen Victoria. As historian Jonathan Bardon puts it: 'Belfast was at the zenith of its importance in the years running up to the Great War. It then had the world's largest shipyard, launching the world's biggest ships, and the largest rope works, tobacco factory, linen-spinning mill, tea machinery works, dry dock and aerated water factory.'[15] That war was, however, to create a far more hostile environment for Belfast's export-oriented businesses.

The rest of Ireland was less industrialised, though there were hotspots. The Malcomson family, corn and cotton magnates, turned Portlaw in Waterford into a model spinning and weaving village. A brewery created at St James's Gate, Dublin, by Arthur Guinness in 1759 became the world's largest by 1880.[16] The Jacob's biscuit and cracker brand began in 1851 when William Beale Jacob and his brother Robert opened a small bakery in Waterford before moving to Dublin the following year. Industries that were based on agriculture and well adapted to exporting to Britain, such as linen and brewing, continued to prosper in the free market established by the late 1820s after Ireland's union with Great Britain. Others struggled against competition from British factories, however, leading to unemployment and industrial decline.[17]

Ireland had far less coal and iron than Britain. It remained largely a backward agrarian economy, exposing it to the Great Famine of 1845–9, caused by potato blight, when about one million people died and another million were forced to emigrate (see chapter 10). There was no industrial take-off afterwards. Recently, however, there has been renewed interest in the country's industrial past, with some historians arguing that Ireland, while less industrialised than Britain, saw development comparable to countries such as the Netherlands and Belgium. The Industrial Heritage Association of Ireland has been developing an archive of bridges, canals, railways, derelict mills, despoiled landscapes and rusting machinery that mark the sites of former industries.[18]

The Industrial Revolution took hold in Wales from the end of the eighteenth century, notably in the south-east, where the presence of iron ore, limestone and large coal deposits led to the creation of ironworks and coal mines. Wales's population doubled to more than one million between 1801 and 1851, with most of the increase occurring in coal-mining districts, notably Glamorganshire.[19] The rise was partly down to falling death rates, as in most industrialising countries, but there was also much immigration – mainly from England, but also substantial numbers from Ireland. While a number of Welsh people emigrated to America or England, this was less than it might have been because industry provided jobs for many at home.

While a few cotton mills were established in Wales, its main development was in metals and coal. Wales embraced the Steam Age. Its ironworks were among the first to adopt the steam engine; the first experiments with locomotion were made in Wales, and many of the world's railways used tracks manufactured there. It became a global supplier of coal to fuel steam trains and ships.

Flintshire in the north-east, with links to Merseyside, had the greatest variety of industries. The town of Buckley had 14 potteries, while Holywell had 14 metal works. The metal industry encouraged growth of coal mining around Wrexham. Bersham Ironworks near Wrexham, managed by John Wilkinson from 1753, became one of Europe's leading ironworks and produced almost all the cylinders used in Watt's steam engines along with cannon for several countries' armies. Copper mines were developed using rich veins discovered at Mynydd near Amlwch. Their chief agent was Thomas Williams, an entrepreneurial solicitor from Llanidan, who also built smelting works in Swansea and Lancashire. His empire grew to control half the world's copper production, and he was dubbed the 'copper king'.[20]

In north-west Wales, the slate industry was developed by local landowners, notably Richard Pennant, who drew on wealth amassed by his family from their Jamaican slave plantations. He established Port Penrhyn near Bangor to serve the slate industry. The creation of such small ports was crucial. Having previously depended largely on trade with England, Wales now embraced maritime trade with the rest of the world. Flannel and other woollen goods were also exported, largely to America.

In south-east Wales, there was rapid growth both in established towns such as Swansea, Neath and Pontypool and in new communities such as Merthyr Tydfil, Ebbw Vale and Blaenavon, hitherto virtually uninhabited. Swansea, Wales's most populous town at the start of the nineteenth century, strengthened its role as the centre of Britain's leading copper-producing area. Industry in the south Wales coalfield was centred on a narrow strip from Hirwaun to Blaenavon, with Merthyr at its centre. Merthyr had iron ore, coal, timber, limestone and water. 'The whole district,' said one commentator, 'seems to have been intended to be one great ironwork.' It embraced the 'puddling' or stirring of iron discovered by Hampshire-based Henry Cort in 1784, which became known as the 'Welsh method'. Many ironworks were established in the area, notably Dowlais and Cyfarthfa. The latter was taken over by Yorkshire-born Richard Crawshay, who ran it so successfully that he became one of Britain's first millionaires. Canals were built linking the iron districts to Swansea, Neath, Cardiff and Newport.[21]

Migrants flooded into industrial districts despite their mountainous environment and rainy climate, lethal dangers of furnaces and collieries, lack of sewerage and pure drinking water, high infant mortality and frequent outbreaks of disease. These areas still offered a better standard of living to most than was possible in the countryside. Despite unstable employment in the iron industry, with sudden dismissals and wage cuts, an ordinary worker in Dowlais earned at least three times as much as the shilling a day earned by a farm servant. Iron output soared, and new markets were found. The chains of the Menai Bridge were manufactured in Penydarren and those of Brighton Pier at Pontypridd. Trains on the Stockton and Darlington Railway ran on rails produced at Ebbw Vale. Foreign markets were developed.[22]

Iron's growth led to increased coal output. By the 1820s, enough coal was being produced not only to meet iron's needs but to permit rapid growth in the coal trade, helped by the working of richer and deeper seams as a result of steam engines and the Davy safety lamp. Coal exports soared, notably from Newport and Cardiff. While the south Wales coalfield boomed, however, several industries in mid and north Wales, including copper and iron, experienced decline.

By the second quarter of the century, only the north's slate industry had substantial prospects.

The 1840s were an important period for south Wales. Demand rose for Welsh iron to build railway tracks in countries from Britain to the United States and Russia. Although iron output expanded greatly, it was overtaken as Wales's biggest industry by coal, which received even more of a boost from the transport revolution. Railways such as the Taff Vale, which linked Merthyr and Cardiff in 1841, slashed the time and cost involved in exporting coal compared with canals, and there was demand for coal to feed steam engines from every corner of the world. The Marquess of Bute spent £350,000 on building a large dock in Cardiff, opened in 1839, which helped propel Cardiff from the 25th largest town in Wales in 1801 to the largest by 1881.[23]

Among the era's intriguing figures was Lucy Thomas, who took over her husband's coal mine near Merthyr when he died in 1833, leading to her becoming known as the 'mother of the Welsh steam-coal trade'. That title derives from the business being an early (though not the first) supplier of steam-coal to London, although her husband may have negotiated the initial shipments and her agents did much of the work. Her legend has endured because she was a doughty widow engaging in a near-totally male-dominated industry and because the business grew tenfold under her hand in the 14 years after her husband's death.[24] Other notable female figures in Welsh industry include Lady Charlotte Guest, wife of the owner of Dowlais ironworks, who took over the business for three years after her husband died in 1852; and Amy Dillwyn, who inherited a heavily indebted spelter (zinc-lead alloy) business in Llansamlet, Swansea, when her father died in 1892 and succeeded in turning it round.[25]

Wales's population more than doubled again to 2.5 million between 1851 and 1914. By that time, almost 35 per cent of the male labour force were employed in collieries. Coal exports from south Wales grew from 450,000 tons in 1850 to 36,832,000 in

1913. Much of the world's economic development was fuelled by Welsh coal.[26]

By the early twentieth century, Britain appeared still in its industrial pomp, yet cracks were opening beneath the surface. It was over-dependent on industries such as textiles, iron, steel and ship-building, some of which had failed to innovate as fast as global competitors. Britain still led in trade, finance and shipping and had strong bases in manufacturing and mining, but its industrial growth had fallen behind those of its rivals. In 1910, Britain's share of world industrial capacity stood at 15 per cent, just behind Germany's 16 per cent and less than half the United States' 35 per cent.[27] The following decades were to prove much more difficult.

CHAPTER 8

EMPIRE ON WHICH THE SUN NEVER SETS

David Livingstone (1813–73), explorer and missionary, was in many ways the ultimate Victorian hero. Born in Blantyre, Lanarkshire, he began working life aged 10 as a piecer in a cotton mill, retying the broken threads of spinning machines for 14 hours a day. He managed to gain an education, became a devout Congregationalist and scraped together enough funds to study medicine in Glasgow before becoming a missionary in southern Africa.

He was not an archetypical colonist: his obsession was with ending slave trading within Africa, which he believed could be displaced by establishing routes for legitimate trade in manufactured goods as a precondition for spreading Christianity. His expeditions to open up the Zambezi as an artery into Africa's interior and to find the source of the River Nile were failures. Driven by duty to God, he could be tactless with others, and his family paid a price: his six children grew up missing their father; his wife Mary, who had joined him on a mission, died of malaria. His work did, however, enable large regions to be mapped and aided colonial settlement in the 'scramble for Africa' by European powers. (The story that Welsh-American adventurer Henry Stanley greeted him with the words 'Dr Livingstone, I presume?', after Livingstone had lost contact with the outside world for six years, may have been fabricated by Stanley, who later tore out the pages of this encounter in his diary.[1])

Livingstone was interred at Westminster Abbey and hailed as almost a Protestant saint. He represented Britain's Empire-builders as they would like to see themselves, fulfilling a civilising mission – though one that involved conquest, brutality and coercion. England had been late to colonialism compared with Spain and Portugal in the fifteenth and sixteenth centuries, but eventually the new political entity, Britain, was to build the largest empire in history; by the end of the nineteenth century, Britain ruled a quarter of the world's population and a fifth of its land surface. English people drove much of its creation and were responsible for many of its excesses. Scots were also to prove enthusiastic in seizing the opportunities created by Empire, even if access to it was initially slow after union with England in 1707. For Wales and Ireland, it was a more ambiguous experience. Both nations are often described as England's first colonies, yet there were also many Welsh and Irish people who became active colonisers.

John Dee, mathematician, astrologer, alchemist and adviser to Elizabeth I, advocated creating English colonies in the New World to form a 'British Empire', a term he is credited with coining. Dee was born in England to a Welsh family and constructed a pedigree purporting to show his descent from Rhodri Mawr ('the Great') in the ninth century.[2] Britain secured huge gains from the Seven Years' War (1756–63) in which, allied with Prussia, it fought France, Austria and Russia. As a result, Britain wrested colonial territory from France, including Canada, making it north America's dominant colonial power. It also controlled much of India after the British East India Company defeated the nawab of Bengal and his French allies at the battle of Plassey in 1757.

This larger empire required much greater investment in administration and military force, raising the question of whether this should be funded by British taxpayers or the colonists. Britain had hitherto been lax in enforcing taxation in America. New taxes were fiercely opposed by Americans – 'no taxation without representation' was the cry. The result was a war in 1775–83 in which the United States won independence. While retaining control of British North America (later Canada) and Caribbean territories, Britain's colonial expansion turned towards Asia, Africa and the Pacific. Naval power enabled it to dominate world trade. 'I contend that we are the first race in the world, and that the more of the world we inhabit the better it is for the human race,' wrote a young Cecil Rhodes, Hertfordshire-born and later founder of Rhodesia (today's Zimbabwe and Zambia).[3]

American independence did not put off Scots and others from seizing opportunities there. The largest number of emigrating Scots went to the United States, with Canada, Australia, New Zealand and South Africa also popular at various times. 'America would have been a poor show without the Scots,' said Andrew Carnegie from Dunfermline, whose corporation, Carnegie Steel, became the world's largest iron and steel producer.[4] Many Scots served in the British Army. Sons of the landed classes found employment as officers, doctors, missionaries or officials in the Indian civil service. Scottish merchants prospered in the transatlantic tobacco and Jamaican sugar trades, then spread their wings to India and Asia. India became, in the words of writer Sir Walter Scott, the 'corn chest for Scotland'.[5]

A third of colonial governors-general between 1850 and 1939 were Scottish. Glasgow-born Sir John A. MacDonald was the first prime minister of Canada (previously British North America), which became a partially self-governing dominion in 1867. Robert Stout, an Orkney teacher, became New Zealand's prime minister in 1884, while in Australia in 1908, Andrew Fisher, a miner from Ayrshire, became the world's first Labour prime minister.[6]

James Andrew Broun-Ramsay, First Marquess of Dalhousie – from Dalhousie Castle in Midlothian – served as governor-general of India 1848–56 and was a skilled administrator who seemed to personify the Empire's supposedly civilising mission. Seeking to improve Indian society in line with utilitarian ideals, he initiated a national system of education, laid the foundations for railway development and introduced the electric telegraph and uniform postage. Yet he was later accused of failing to foresee signs of the brewing Indian Mutiny of 1857 and of feeding discontent through heavy-handed policies including his enthusiastic application of the doctrine of lapse, whereby the British annexed any kingdom where a king lacked a male lineal heir. On these grounds, Satara was annexed in 1848 and Jhansi and Nagpur in 1854. Dalhousie also annexed the Punjab in 1849 after a local rebellion and in 1856 annexed Awadh (Oudh), a rich northern territory whose capital was Lucknow, where the nawab was accused of misgovernment.[7]

In 1876, Prime Minister Benjamin Disraeli arranged to buy the Khedive of Egypt's shares in the Suez Canal, gaining control of European access to India and thus improving the British Raj's strategic and economic prospects. He also had Queen Victoria proclaimed as Empress of India. However, India suffered frequent, devastating famines in which millions died and which the British did little to alleviate, as in Ireland in the 1840s, because officials saw them as a natural or providential occurrence. One indignant early Indian nationalist complained that the equivalent of almost the entire population of Ireland had died in a famine in 1877–8. To a growing number of critics, famine policy seemed always to be sacrificed to British economic self-interest. One critic was India's agriculture secretary Allan Octavian Hume – son of Scottish Radical MP Joseph Hume – who resigned when his plan for a progressive income tax to finance a relief fund was vetoed. He founded the Indian National Congress in 1885. In the twentieth century, under Mahatma Gandhi's leadership, it steered India to independence.[8]

Even as tensions in the Empire were beginning to show, Scots' involvement was deepening. Celebrated missionaries included Presbyterians Christina Forsyth from Glasgow and Aberdeen-born Mary Slessor. Slessor, from a poor family, had worked as a Dundee mill girl at age 11. As a missionary in Nigeria, she was best known for helping to end the practice of infanticide of twins among the

Efik people in Okoyong, who considered their birth an evil curse. Military heroes included Sir Colin Campbell, who with his 'thin red line of highlanders' repulsed the Russian attack on Balaclava during the Crimean War, and as commander-in-chief in India during the mutiny recaptured Lucknow. General Charles Gordon, born in England to a Scottish military family, disobeyed orders to evacuate Khartoum in the face of a Sudanese Muslim revolt and died a martyr's death after a siege lasting almost a year.

By 1860, much of Scotland's heavy industry was tied to Empire, leading Glasgow to see itself as an imperial city and the west of Scotland eventually to become celebrated as the 'work-shop of the Empire'. Scots dominated many economic areas in north America and elsewhere. George Stephen, son of a Banffshire carpenter, was the driving force behind the Canadian Pacific Railway, which linked Canada from east to west. Scots also contrib-uted to the making of Australia, though it was not always pretty. Scots pioneers in Victoria were often seen as ruthless land-grabbers. Scots, like the English, Welsh and Irish, shared in the harsh treat-ment of Aboriginal peoples.[9]

Many Scots, like counterparts elsewhere in the Isles, took part in the transatlantic slave trade or prospered from it before the UK abol-ished the trade in 1807 and slavery in most of the Empire in 1833. Research has identified just 27 slave trade voyages that left the ports of Greenock, Port Glasgow, Leith and Montrose between 1706 and 1766 – far lower than those from Liverpool, Bristol and other English ports. Liverpool alone recorded more than 1,000 slave voyages in that period. The contrast is misleading, however, because before the 1707 Act of Union, Scottish access to English ports was restricted by the Navigation Acts, which allowed English ports to establish a monopoly in the trade in enslaved people. Expatriate Scots in those ports were widely involved.[10]

Scots were directly implicated as investors, slave owners, over-seers on plantations and also in professions and trades that maintained the trade's infrastructure. A report by Stephen Mullen of the University of Glasgow found that 40 out of 79 lord provosts or mayors from the city were connected to the trade between 1636 and 1834, while 62 Glasgow streets were named after slave owners who built their fortunes on tobacco plantations. These include Buchanan Street and Glassford Street, named after 'tobacco lords' Andrew Buchanan and John Glassford. James Watt, whose improvements to the steam engine drove the Industrial Revolution, was personally involved in trafficking a black child for sale to a family in north-east Scotland.[11]

A number of Scots were also involved in the campaign to abolish slavery, however. Dundee-born Fanny Wright, reformer and utopian socialist, travelled to America in 1818 and 1824 and, during the second visit, published *A Plan for the Gradual Abolition of Slavery in the United States without Danger of Loss to the Citizens of the South*, which urged Congress to set aside land for emancipated slaves. She bought a 640-acre tract of land that she called Nashoba, purchased slaves, freed them and settled them there – though the project lasted only five years. She also advocated universal education, birth control, legal rights for married women and liberal divorce laws.[12]

Ireland's imperial legacy has been seen as a laboratory both for imperial rule and for resistance to that rule. Colonisation of Ireland is often dated to 1169, when groups of Anglo-Normans led by Richard de Clare arrived from Wales, which led Friedrich Engels to observe in an 1856 letter to Karl Marx that 'Ireland may be regarded as the first English colony.'[13] By the early eighteenth century, almost a third of Ireland's population was of immigrant stock, descendants of mostly Protestant settlers who had colonised Ireland. There was a large-scale transfer of land from Catholic to Protestant hands. Many Irish natives were condemned to subsistence farming and grinding poverty. Policies and government structures formulated in Ireland were later adopted elsewhere in the British Empire, including the promotion of English culture, language, religion and education. Indigenous north Americans were classed as racially inferior and, like the native Irish, prohibited from taking part in many institutions. Ireland's partition in 1920 was the template for later partitions of India and Pakistan, and Israel and Palestine.

However, some Irish people were also active colonists in the empires of Britain and other European powers. Philosopher George Berkeley owned slaves on his plantation in Rhode Island in the 1720s. Dublin-born statesman Edmund Burke was a fierce critic of the East India Company and suggested that Ireland and India were 'similarly victimised'; he perceived the evils of slavery yet proposed only gradual reform because sugar interests in the West Indies were important in underpinning Britain's global power. John Mitchel, nineteenth-century Irish nationalist writer, ended up in America as an enthusiastic pro-slavery partisan of the southern Confederacy.[14]

Considerable numbers of Irish people emigrated to America in the eighteenth century, notably 'Scots-Irish' from Ulster who lived on the frontiers and became the dominant culture of the Appalachians. Mary Jemison, a Scots-Irish frontierswoman in Pennsylvania and New York, was captured and adopted by a Seneca family at age 12 in 1755. She assimilated to their culture and married two Native American men in succession, having children with them. Several Irish-born people were among the founding fathers of the United States who signed the Declaration of Independence, including Charles Thomson from County Londonderry, patriot leader in Philadelphia; Dublin-born James Smith, another Pennsylvania lawyer; ironmaster George Taylor, also a Pennsylvania representative; and Matthew Thornton, a representative of New Hampshire.

Ireland's Great Famine of 1845–52 resulted in more than a million deaths from starvation and disease and a million refugees fleeing the country, mainly to America. Between 1801 and 1921, eight million people left Ireland, often for British dominions and territories such as Australia, New Zealand and Canada – an emigration larger in relative terms than any other in nineteenth-century Europe.[15] Most left willingly to seek a better life. Prominent Irish people in nineteenth-century America included Waterford-born Thomas Francis Meagher, a nationalist who had led the Young

Irelanders in an 1848 rebellion. Convicted of sedition, he was initially sentenced to death but transported to Van Diemen's Land (Tasmania), from where he escaped to the United States. He became a brigadier general during the American Civil War and recruited and led the Irish brigade. There were many in the Irish diaspora, especially in the US, who supported and financed various Irish independence movements.

Nellie Cashman, from County Cork, was a nurse, businesswoman and philanthropist who went prospecting for gold in Canada's Yukon during the Klondike Gold Rush. A devout Catholic, she raised funds for hospitals, schools and churches wherever she settled in north America. Thomas D'Arcy McGee, from County Louth, was a former Irish nationalist who became a Canadian politician and supported a self-governing Canada within the British Empire. He denounced the Fenian Brotherhood, a paramilitary secret society of Irish republicans, which responded by assassinating him in 1868.

In Australia, John O'Shanassy from County Tipperary was a wealthy businessman who became Victoria's second premier. After starting out as a draper in Melbourne, by the 1850s he was a major landowner and one of the colony's wealthiest men. Sir Charles Gavan Duffy, a poet and journalist from Monaghan Town, later became Victoria's eighth premier. Peter Fintan Lalor, from Raheen in Queen's County (later Laois) in Ireland, came to prominence in Victoria's Eureka Rebellion, in which gold diggers were militating for democratic rights. He lost an arm in a confrontation with troops and police but later became a conservative politician. Also in Victoria, outlaw Ned Kelly was the son of a transported convict from County Tipperary. Kelly's crimes included stock theft and murder, but in a manifesto letter he demanded justice for his family and the rural poor and inveighed against the police, the Victorian government and the British Empire. He and his gang evaded the police for two years before he was caught and hanged. Opinion remains divided as to whether he was an Australian Robin Hood or a murderous villain.

A few individuals with Irish connections participated in imperialism's worst excesses. General Reginald Dyer, born in India's Punjab in 1864, was the son of an Irish brewer and educated at Midleton College in Cork. On 13 April 1919, in what is now known as the Amritsar Massacre, Dyer gave the command at Jallianwala Bagh in the Punjab to open fire on a crowd of 20,000 civilians protesting against the extension of wartime laws. The official death toll was 379, though the Indian National Congress claimed it was nearer 1,000. Dyer's superior, the lieutenant governor of the Punjab, Michael O'Dwyer, was a Catholic from County Tipperary. The massacre angered many Indians and has been seen as a step towards the end of British rule.

Coming to terms with the Irish role in Empire has not been easy for Ireland. While most imperial statues have been removed or destroyed in the past 100 years, its legacy lives on in street names and buildings. Michael Higgins, Ireland's president, has held seminars to consider 'uncomfortable aspects of our shared history' in a 'journey of ethical remembering'. He added: 'The rewards for this will come in the form [of] restoring the connection between moral instinct and public policy. That is an authenticity for which so many of our citizens, on this shared, vulnerable planet, yearn.'[16]

Welsh people also helped to build the Empire, often in roles as district officers, missionaries, health workers and engineers. Several of the great Welsh industries grew with the Empire and declined with it. Among explorers, Sir Thomas Button, a Royal Navy officer from St Lythans in Glamorganshire, commanded an expedition in 1612–13 that unsuccessfully attempted to navigate the north-west passage via north America to India and China. He discovered and named Mansel Island after his uncle, Vice-Admiral Sir Robert Mansel, and named the west coast of Hudson's Bay New Wales. William Vaughan of Llangyndeyrn, Carmarthenshire, tried in vain to establish a Welsh colony in Newfoundland in 1616–32, around the time New England and Nova Scotia were created.[17]

We can probably discount claims that America was named after Richard Amerike (ap Meurig) of Glamorgan, a Bristol merchant and one of the sponsors of John Cabot's expeditions to seek the north-west passage, as lacking hard evidence. Similarly, there is little evidence for a legend that Madog ab Owain Gwynedd, a Welsh prince, sailed to the Americas in 1170. The story became prominent in Elizabethan times, when writers including John Dee employed it to claim sovereignty of the territories for Queen Elizabeth as successor to Welsh princes. Interest grew even more strongly in the late eighteenth century when there were rumours that Madog's voyagers had intermarried with Native Americans and that a tribe of Welsh-speaking natives, the Madogwys, dwelt in the heart of the continent. A book about the Madog story inspired a journey by John Evans of Waunfawr near Caernarfon, the first person to map the course of the Missouri river. He found no Welsh-speaking natives.[18]

By 1700, there was emigration by Quakers from central Wales to Pennsylvania, driven by persecution in Britain. They thrived there, although William Penn, author of the 'Holy Experiment', reneged on his promise that they would be granted a separate Welsh colony. Other groups of Nonconformists also set sail for America, including Baptists from Ilston, near Swansea, who settled in Swanzey, Massachusetts. There was a surge in Welsh emigration in the 1790s, driven by Madog fever and economic distress. They were welcomed and assisted by descendants of the previous century's Puritan exiles, who had played a notable role in Pennsylvania's development. Welsh books were published in Philadelphia from 1721 and a St David's Society established there in 1729.

Welsh-born founding fathers of the US who signed the Declaration of Independence included Francis Lewis, a merchant originally from Llandaff in Cardiff, who was a member of the New York Provincial Congress; Button Gwinnett, a representative from Georgia, who was born in Gloucestershire to a Welsh father (and later killed in a duel); and William Floyd, a wealthy farmer from New York, who came from a family of English and Welsh origins. Welsh immigration accelerated after the revolution, including coal miners to places such as Ohio. There were so many Welsh speakers in Minnesota by 1857 that the state constitution was translated into Welsh.[19] Businesspeople in America included David Thomas from Cadoxton near Neath, who built a furnace to produce anthracite iron in Pennsylvania, having devised a technique to produce it back home. Thomas Henry Blythe, from Mold in Flintshire, emigrated to California and became a successful capitalist, best known for buying the Palo Verde Valley in southern California and obtaining primary rights to Colorado river water to irrigate the valley. The city of Blythe is named after him.

In Canada, David Thompson, born in London to Welsh parents, was a fur trapper, explorer and mapmaker who charted almost half of north America in the late eighteenth and early nineteenth centuries. By horseback, canoe, dog sled and on foot, he travelled some 90,000 kilometres (55,000 miles), equivalent to circling the globe twice.[20] Richard Philipps, from Pembrokeshire, was governor of Nova Scotia 1717–49 but became so disillusioned with British neglect of the province that he returned home and spent his last years living on his allowances in London.

In Australia, Montgomeryshire-born Chartist John Basson Humffray was a vocal defender of aggrieved gold miners charged with high treason as a result of the Eureka Rebellion in Victoria. David Jones, from Carmarthenshire, was a retailer who founded early department stores. Samuel Griffith, a lawyer from Merthyr Tydfil, was premier of Queensland and later Australia's first chief justice. Thomas Price, from Brymbo near Wrexham, became South Australia's first United Labor Party premier.

There were Welsh people on both sides of the slavery issue. Richard Pennant, who owned Penrhyn Castle near Bangor, was a major figure in the slate industry, but he also owned six sugar plantations and slaves in Jamaica and opposed slave trade abolition in parliament. He was also a naturalist and friend of Joseph Banks, chief scientist on James Cook's second voyage; it is sometimes suggested that Banks' Welsh connection may have helped to influence Cook in naming Australia's east coast New South Wales.[21]

Sir Thomas Picton from Pembrokeshire displayed cruelty as governor of Trinidad and was initially convicted by an English court of approving the illegal torture of a 14-year-old girl, later overturned on the ground that Trinidad was subject to Spanish law, which permitted torture. In 2020, Cardiff Council voted to take down a statue of Picton at City Hall, and in 2022 the Museum of Wales moved his portrait to a side room. Anthony Bacon, owner of the Cyfarthfa ironworks in Merthyr, owned ships to transport enslaved people from Africa to the Caribbean.[22]

On the other side, William Williams of Pantycelyn in Carmarthenshire, a hymn writer, published a pamphlet in 1792 opposing the slave trade. He also translated the life stories of many slaves to draw attention to the trade's cruelty. Antiquarian and poet Iolo Morganwg had a shop in Cowbridge, Vale of Glamorgan, where he tried to avoid selling anything linked to slavery. However, his brothers were involved with a sugar plantation in Jamaica and owned slaves. When Morganwg faced a period of poverty, he initially refused money from his brothers to help him.[23]

Welsh people were involved from the early years in the East India Company. Major figures from this period include Thomas Parry of Welshpool, who established a merchant house in Madras (modern-day Chennai). Calcutta (Kolkata) judge and linguist William Jones founded the Asiatic Society of Bengal in 1784; he was an advocate of the common ancestry of European and Indian languages. Many Welsh people became missionaries, notably at the Welsh Calvinistic Methodist Mission in north-east India. An annual St David's Day dinner began in Calcutta in 1899. The first event included a menu of Welsh broth and leeks and Welsh rarebit. Toasts were made to 'Ein Frenhines ac Ymherodres' (Our Queen and Empress), 'Tywysog Cymru' (The Prince of Wales), St David and the land of Wales. The band played Welsh tunes and guests sang along heartily.[24]

The period 1815–1914 is sometimes described as Britain's 'imperial century' or 'Pax Britannica'. Having defeated Napoleon, the UK dominated the oceans and much of world trade. It was not always peaceful, though. In 1899–1902, the Empire fought the Boer War to assert control over the South African Republic and Orange Free State. It created concentration camps in which thousands died, mostly of starvation and disease. A young firebrand Welsh MP, David Lloyd George, made his name by vehemently opposing the war. Later he was prime minister during the First World War, which he saw as a just war to defend fellow small nations.

By the turn of the twentieth century, the UK's economy was falling behind Germany and the United States. Military, economic and colonial tensions were major causes of the First World War, in which Britain relied heavily on its Empire. After the war, it was no longer the world's pre-eminent industrial or military power. In the Second World War, British colonies in east Asia and south-east Asia were occupied by Japan. Britain and its allies won the war, but the damage to its prestige and economy helped to accelerate the Empire's decline. India gained independence in 1947. Subsequently, as part of a larger decolonisation movement, independence was granted to most of the Empire's territories. Many former colonies, along with most of the dominions, joined the Commonwealth of Nations, a free association of independent states.

CHAPTER 9

IMPERIAL CONFIDENCE, IRISH DISCOMFORT

Gerald Keegan, a village schoolteacher in County Sligo in the west of Ireland, left one of the most moving accounts of Ireland's Great Famine of 1845–52, caused by repeated failures of the potato crop, in which about one million people died and more than a million emigrated. 'We have come to the end of our rope. The twin spectres, famine and pestilence, hold sway over the land,' he wrote in his diary. 'People are dying so fast that their surviving relatives are unable to bury them all … Some have been found dead with grass in their mouth. Dogs and donkeys have become common items of diet. Scores of bodies lie along the roadsides.'

Cursing the English landlords who ruled their lives, Gerald and his wife Eileen took up the offer of a passage to Canada in return for paying off rent arrears. He reluctantly closed his school: 'Children have lost their normal youthful appearance. They look like old people. They do not laugh and play.' The couple endured a gruelling crossing of the Atlantic in a coffin ship, with fever rampant and bodies constantly thrown overboard. After arriving at the quarantine island of Grosse Île, Eileen died in Gerald's arms. 'I feel I have nothing to live for,' he wrote. Struck down himself at last by fever, Gerald was buried beside her in 1847 with a simple cross to mark the spot.[1]

The early nineteenth century in the Isles was a period of turbulence, marked by the Napoleonic wars, explosive population growth, food shortages caused by climatic disruption and poor harvests, radical protests in England's rural south as well as in the industrialising north and in Wales and Scotland. There were stresses of urbanisation and diseases such as tuberculosis, typhus and cholera. As the century progressed, industrial growth led to rising average incomes, while the expanding Empire fuelled a sense of Britishness among many, though this was far from universal. For the only time in history, a single parliament legislated for all four nations during most of the period 1801–1922, but the 'Irish question' was ever present. The UK government was blamed for a woeful response to the Great Famine, while politics later in the century was dominated by a vigorous campaign for Irish home rule.

During the French wars, William Pitt the Younger's government had clamped down on dissent in reaction to the French revolution by measures such as the Seditious Meetings Act, restricting the right of individuals to assemble, and suspension of *habeas corpus*, which protected citizens from unlawful detention. In the new century, protests of various kinds erupted, however. Machine-breaking by self-employed weavers and other textile workers who felt threatened by factories began in 1811 among Nottinghamshire hosiery workers, led by a probably mythical Ned Ludd, and spread to Yorkshire and Lancashire. It led to rioters being shot or hanged.

Britain ended the Napoleonic wars in 1815 with huge national debt; hasty demobilisation of the armed forces and spending cuts led to unemployment and a deeper slump. Pressure grew for democratic reforms such as universal male suffrage. At St Peter's Field, Manchester, on 16 August 1819, an estimated 18 people died and almost 700 were seriously injured when the yeomanry attempted to disperse a crowd waiting to hear Henry 'Orator' Hunt, a Wiltshire farmer and reformer. The name 'Peterloo' was coined by the editor of the radical *Manchester Observer*, comparing the attack on unarmed civilians to the brutality of the battle of Waterloo. Fearing armed rebellion, Lord Liverpool's Tory government passed the Six Acts to suppress radical meetings and publications.

A Whig government under Earl Grey passed the Reform Act 1832, which increased the electorate to about 20 per cent of adult males and enfranchised industrial towns including Manchester and Salford. It did not widen the social mix, however. The act created uniform voting qualifications based solely on ownership or occupation of property, strengthening the influence of landowners and the wealthy.[2] Chartism, a working-class movement, began in London in 1838 and gained strong support in the north. Its People's Charter demanded the vote for every male inhabitant of Britain and Ireland, a secret ballot, equal electoral districts, payment for MPs, abolition of the property qualification for MPs and annual parliaments. It had a charismatic Irish leader, Feargus O'Connor, who founded its newspaper, the *Northern Star*. The movement lost momentum in 1848 when leaders organised a rally on Kennington Common and decided not to defy a police ban on a procession to parliament. Several hundred Chartists were later arrested in London and the north. In the short term, it failed, though by 1918 all the charter's points had been achieved except annual general elections.

More successful was the Manchester-based Anti-Corn Law League, dominated by cotton manufacturers and merchants, also founded in 1839. It sought abolition of the corn laws, which barred imports of grain until the price reached near-famine levels, introduced in 1815 to protect landowners from loss of contracts to feed the armed forces. Campaigners led by Richard Cobden and John Bright saw cheaper bread and potentially cheaper labour as expanding world trade, to the benefit of British manufacturing. Sir Robert Peel, the Bury-born Conservative prime minister, repealed the corn laws in 1846 with Whig and Radical support, splitting his own party. Peel, son of a wealthy textile manufacturer and MP, was Britain's first prime minister from an industrial background.

In Wales, while some intellectuals were attracted by radical ideas of the French revolution, there was no equivalent of the United Irishmen's rebellion at the end of the eighteenth century. A landing by French troops at Fishguard, Pembrokeshire, in 1797 was resisted by British forces and the local population. However, industrialisation led to bitter social conflicts. The 1831 Merthyr Rising, one of the most serious events in Britain's industrial history, began when William Crawshay, owner of Cyfarthfa Ironworks, cut employees' wages. A huge crowd – already excited by agitation for political reform – seized control of the town, leading soldiers from the Argyll and Sutherland Highlanders to shoot dead about 20. More soldiers were sent and eventually regained control. One rebel leader, Richard Lewis (Dic Penderyn), was hanged after being found guilty of wounding a Scottish soldier, a crime to which another man later confessed.[3]

After that, many miners and steel workers in the area joined unions, but employers managed to stamp out unionism with dismissals and the help of military occupation. In Monmouthshire in 1832–4, a movement known as Scotch Cattle, incensed particularly by wages being paid in tokens that had to be exchanged in company shops, held mass meetings and destroyed employers' property. It was suppressed, and one protester was hanged. There was further unrest over the Poor Law Amendment Act 1834 in England and Wales, which restricted expenditure on relief of the poor by providing it only in workhouses.[4]

Chartism gained strong support in south Wales, where some of the most serious violence occurred. In an uprising in Newport in 1839, 5,000 men stormed a hotel where soldiers were stationed. In the struggle there and elsewhere in Newport, at least 20 Chartists were killed; three men were later exiled to Van Diemen's Land. Rural south-west Wales had the so-called Rebecca Riots in 1839–44, in which toll gates were destroyed in protest not only against high tolls on local turnpike roads but against dire poverty, which had increased with population growth. The rioters wore women's clothes and were known as Rebecca's Daughters, probably referring to Genesis 24:60, which claims that Rebecca's seed shall 'possess the gate of those which hate them'. In response, Peel's government created roads boards to take over the management of turnpike roads. Such protests died down by mid-century as industrial areas increasingly offered a livelihood to surplus rural workers.[5]

In Scotland, there were stirrings of radicalism in the early 1790s in response to the French revolution and Scotland's weak democracy, where an even smaller proportion of the population had the vote than in England and Ireland. However, France's declaration of war against Britain enabled the government to quash the threat. Several reformers were transported to Botany Bay, and a former government spy, Robert Watt, was executed for allegedly planning a coup in Edinburgh. Later in the decade, a secret society, the United Scotsmen, was formed, influenced by the United Irishmen. They were republicans committed to annual parliaments and universal suffrage but never posed a credible threat.[6]

Rapid industrialisation provoked unrest, as in England and Wales, including strikes by Glasgow weavers in 1787 and 1812. The aftermath of Peterloo and the Six Acts led to a growth in secret societies, some bent on overthrowing the government. The result was the so-called 'Radical War' of 1820, when leaders in south-west Scotland urged workers to strike. About 60,000 in Glasgow, Paisley and elsewhere responded. The government was alarmed at the prospect of armed revolt. The radicals' plan was for an uprising to be triggered by a popular revolt in England. The signal of rebellion in northern England was to be a halt in mail coaches to Scotland. Yet while there was some unrest in Yorkshire, there was no general rebellion. Mail coaches arrived from Manchester, and plans for Scottish insurrection were aborted. Three leaders were executed, and others sentenced to transportation. Mass political movements reappeared during the crisis before the 1832 Reform Bill and in the Chartist agitation, but this time the aims were peaceful.[7]

In Ireland, Daniel O'Connell, a lawyer who would become known as 'The Liberator', managed to rally the nation's Catholic majority behind a new campaign for emancipation. In 1823, he established the Catholic Association, which people could join for a 'Catholic rent' of a penny a month, typically paid through the local priest. Their investment enabled O'Connell to mount 'monster' rallies with crowds of more than 100,000.

In 1828, O'Connell won a parliamentary by-election against a British cabinet member. However, he could not take up his seat without taking the Oath of Supremacy, acknowledging the king as 'supreme governor' of the church and thus forswearing Catholicism. Fearing unrest, the government finally relented. The Duke of Wellington, Tory prime minister, persuaded George IV to give royal assent to the Roman Catholic Relief Act 1829 – threatening resignation if he did not do so. The act removed tests that barred Catholics in the UK from parliament and higher offices of the judiciary and state. O'Connell stood again for election and was returned unopposed. He achieved some reforms as an MP but formed a new movement in 1840 to press for repeal of the Act of Union and restoration of Irish self-government. This time, he was unsuccessful, and the campaign sputtered out with the onset of economic crisis.[8]

In the 1840s, western Europe was hit by potato blight, *Phytophthora infestans*, which led to deaths in countries such as the Netherlands, Germany and France and influenced unrest that culminated in the 1848 'year of revolutions'. The most serious human disaster by far was in Ireland, however. Its vulnerability was due partly to having small landholdings coupled with a large increase in population in the years before the famine. Land was routinely subdivided, with all sons inheriting equal shares, meaning that farms became so small that potatoes were the only crop that could feed a family. Many estates, from which small farmers rented, were poorly run by absentee landlords and often heavily mortgaged. There were plenty of warnings. There had been earlier famines and a series of commissions and special committees warned that Ireland was on the verge of starvation, with living standards barely at subsistence level.

After the blight hit Ireland in 1845, Peel ordered maize and corn-meal from America and set up a public works programme, but his government fell in 1846 when the Conservatives split over his repeal of the corn laws. The new Whig administration led by Lord John Russell took a laissez-faire approach, believing the market would solve the issue. It refused to interfere in the movement of food to England and halted Peel's food and relief works. In 1847, realising that its policies had failed, the government provided aid through workhouses and soup kitchens. Ulster and the east coast escaped lightly, but the west of Ireland suffered starvation, fever and death, leading to frantic emigration. Irish nationalists blamed British policy for the inadequate response, pointing particularly to the picture of Irish people starving as food was exported to England. Ireland had a population of almost 8.2 million in 1841 but lost almost a quarter of that during the next three decades; the decline bottomed out at 4.2 million in 1931, and even today the combined populations of the Irish republic and Northern Ireland, estimated at 7.2 million in 2024, have not yet reached the pre-famine total.[9]

The Scottish highlands were also hit by potato blight in 1846. The death rate rose, but a prompt relief effort averted mass starvation. Two vessels sold grain in Mull and Skye at controlled prices, and landowners could apply for loans to provide relief work. Charities were heavily involved, notably the Free Church of Scotland, which used a schooner to take emergency supplies to the neediest communities. The official effort was soon scaled back, however, for fear of encouraging dependency on aid. Some landlords provided 'assisted passages' for tenants to emigrate. More people became involved in seasonal migration to work in the lowlands.[10]

After turbulence in many parts of the Isles, the century's second half was calmer, helped by growing prosperity in which many working people shared. Victoria became queen in 1837 at age 18 after the death of her uncle, William IV. Her almost 64-year reign saw the United Kingdom grow in strength until it controlled the largest empire on earth. Though Victoria had occasional spells of unpopularity, she represented the UK at the peak of its international power and prestige, even though she was conceived in Germany, married a German and spoke German by preference. She saw out 10 prime ministers, of whom William Gladstone was the only one she detested. 'He speaks to me as if I was a public meeting,' she said. The growing self-confidence of the Victorian age was underlined when an average of 43,000 people flocked every day for six months to the 1851 Great Exhibition in London, seen as the embodiment of commercial, technological and political progress, in which Victoria's husband Albert was heavily involved. Historian Thomas Babington Macaulay concluded that 'there is as much chance of a revolution in England as of the falling of the moon'.[11]

The century was notable for its long tussle between Gladstone, a sombre Liberal, and Benjamin Disraeli, his flamboyant Conservative rival. Gladstone, born in Liverpool to Scottish parents, was prime minister for 12 years spread over four non-consecutive terms (the most of any British prime minister) between 1868 and 1894. He was also chancellor of the exchequer four times. He began as a High Tory, which became the Conservative Party under Peel, but joined the breakaway Peelite faction in 1846, which eventually merged into the new Liberal Party in 1859. Gladstone's doctrine, which emphasised equality of opportunity and opposition to trade protectionism, came to be known as Gladstonian liberalism. His popularity among the working class earned him the nickname 'The People's William'. Disraeli, born in Bloomsbury, Middlesex, was prime minister twice for a total of almost seven years and chancellor three times. He is the only British prime minister to have been born Jewish, but his father left Judaism after a dispute at his synagogue, and Benjamin became Anglican at age 12. He was known for one-nation Conservatism or 'Tory democracy' and made the Conservatives the party most identified with military action to expand the Empire.

It was an age of mutual self-help and respectability – friendly societies, trade unions and the co-operative movement, boosted by the Rochdale Pioneers in 1844, a group of 28 weavers and other tradesmen who banded together to open a shop selling food items they could not otherwise afford. Samuel Smiles – who was born in Haddington, east Lothian, and delivered evening classes for working people in Leeds – wrote the best-selling *Self-Help* (1859), which promoted thrift and claimed that poverty was caused largely by irresponsible habits.

A significant feature of the nineteenth century was religious revival among all Christian denominations and dramatic growth in Protestant Nonconformism, the latter particularly among industrialising communities of England's north and midlands and in Wales. Although half the population remained uninterested in organised religion, the number of religious activists rose sharply. Dissenters in England grew from a minority to numerical equality with the Anglican Church. This was arguably a bigger factor in the era's history than class conflict: class feelings, religious consciousness and ethnic rivalries all mingled to create tensions. There was a divide between the cultures of England's industrial north and rural south. Occasionally there was violence, such as when a parson in Newark, Nottinghamshire, ordered the fire engine to be wheeled out to hose down a dissenting preacher.[12]

Nonconformists included Presbyterians, Congregationalists, Baptists, Methodists, Quakers and Unitarians, all proclaiming devotion to hard work, temperance, frugality and upward mobility. They pressed for removal of barriers to civil and religious equality, leading in 1828 to repeal of the Test and Corporation Acts, which had restricted public employment to those who took communion in the Church of England. Other grievances included compulsory payment of tithes – rates to pay for the upkeep of the parish – along with a law that marriages had to be in an Anglican church to be legally recognised, and the continued exclusion of dissenters from Oxford and Cambridge universities.

Evangelicals and Nonconformists played a central role in the campaign to abolish the slave trade, a stance which stemmed from their moral and religious views. The abolitionist movement was formally born at a meeting in 1787 when 12 men – nine Quakers and three evangelical Anglicans – formed the Society for Effecting the Abolition of the Slave Trade.[13] The Slave Trade Act was passed in 1807, prohibiting the slave trade in the British Empire, after a dogged parliamentary campaign by William Wilberforce, an MP born in Kingston upon Hull and an evangelical Anglican. A renewed campaign led to the Slavery Abolition Act 1833, which abolished slavery in most of the Empire.

In Wales, the century's first half saw rapid growth in all Nonconformist denominations, notably Welsh Methodists. By 1851, there were 2,813 chapels, the result of a massive building programme. Nonconformism grew strongly in industrial areas as people flooded to work in furnaces, collieries and quarries, attracted to chapels partly because they had services in Welsh. Chapels had an atmosphere of equality and provided opportunities for laymen to play a prominent role. Nonconformity was more dominant in Wales than in England: in 1851, 52 per cent of seats available in places of worship in England were in Anglican churches; in Wales, the proportion was just 32 per cent.[14]

Members of the Anglican church in Wales responded to Nonconformism's growth by creating the National Society, a network of schools in which children of poor families would be educated in the established church's principles. St David's College, Lampeter, was created to train clergy. Church leaders became involved in organising provincial *eisteddfodau* and in Welsh literary and antiquarian studies. In the 1830s, reforms were made to the Church of England, helping to pave the way for revival: clerics were barred from holding multiple livings; the state acquired the authority to register births, marriages and deaths; and the church's duty to hold services in Welsh was underlined. Nonconformism became increasingly assertive, however, notably in forming temperance societies. At first, these urged moderation in drinking alcohol, but soon that became total abstinence, seen as a cause for moral self-improvement among the working class. Temperance also grew strongly in northern England.[15]

Many in the ruling class saw the Welsh language and culture as a curse, but there were also some champions of Welsh culture. The foundations of choral singing were laid in Merthyr by the musician John Thomas (Ieuan Dhu). Thomas Price (known by the bardic name Carnhaunawc), a clergyman who served in parishes around Crickhowell, Breconshire, was a historian who contributed to many journals and was prominent in the revival of the *eisteddfod*. He was also a pan-Celticist who learned the Breton language and encouraged the Welsh and Bretons to be aware of their ancient kinship. Augusta Hall, Lady Llanover, popularised what came to be seen as traditional Welsh costume and made her estate in Monmouthshire a centre for Welsh culture.

Uproar erupted in 1847 when a commission set up by the London government to examine the poor state of Welsh education – and look at opportunities for working-class people to learn English – was scathing about Nonconformism, the Welsh language and the morality of Welsh people. It accepted uncritically comments by Anglican clergy embittered by Nonconformity's successes, who suggested that the Welsh were uniquely lax in their sexual habits. The report inflamed sectarian tensions and became known as *Brad y Llyfrau Gleision*, the 'Treachery of the Blue Books'. Despite this outraged reaction, Nonconformist leaders campaigned in the following decades against wantonness, drunkenness and lawlessness.[16]

Meanwhile, religious tensions in Scotland led to a schism in the Church of Scotland known as the Great Disruption of 1843. A decade earlier, evangelicals had gained control of the General Assembly and passed the Veto Act, which allowed congregations to reject the choice of minister proposed by a patron, usually a landowner. However, years of wrangling led to defeat in the courts for the evangelicals. A breakaway was led by Thomas Chalmers, a minister and professor of theology, in which almost 40 per cent of ministers and a third of congregations, mainly from the north and highlands, formed the separate Free Church of Scotland. Chalmers sought to create a 'godly commonwealth' of small communities in which church and state were bound together in a society that conformed to the word of God.[17]

The Free Churches, which were more attuned to Gaelic language and culture, grew particularly strongly in the highlands and islands, where evangelicalism helped to give spiritual certainty amid the trauma of clearances and famine. This came after a period in which many landlords abandoned their old role as clan chiefs and displaced farmers in order to raise sheep. Many estates were sold to new land-owners, and evictions and forced removals were commonplace. Sometimes people were moved from inland glens to the coast to work in the fishing and kelp industry or to areas of moorland where new crofts were planted in waste ground and settlers encouraged to reclaim it by potato cultivation. Mass starvation was avoided in the potato famine, but about a third of the population is estimated to have migrated permanently to the lowlands or abroad between the early 1840s and late 1850s.[18] Sheep prices collapsed in the 1870s, accelerating the 'Balmoralisation' of Scotland, whereby large estates were dedicated to field sports such as deer stalking and grouse shooting.

Scottish Presbyterianism was deeply fragmented by the 1840s. By 1851, numbers attending the Free Churches and the Church of Scotland were almost equal. The Disruption accelerated shifting of some functions from church to state: for example, authority over poor relief was transferred from parish churches to elected boards. By 1849, the Free Church had erected 730 places of worship, supported 513 teachers instructing 44,000 children and founded a college on the Mound in Edinburgh to educate ministers.[19] The Church of Scotland also began to recover, with numbers rising from the 1860s. The Scottish Episcopal Church, which had seemed in terminal decline, also recovered rapidly. There was a resurgence of Catholicism created by an influx of Catholic Irish, leading to restoration of a Roman Catholic hierarchy in 1878. The Free Church itself split in 1893 when rigid Calvinists broke away to form the Free Presbyterian Church. Later there were moves towards reunion, however, notably in 1929 when the removal of legislation on lay patronage allowed the majority of the Free Church to re-join the Church of Scotland.[20]

Much of the nineteenth century's second half in Britain was taken up by the 'Irish question'. In 1848, Europe's year of revolutions, a breakaway group from O'Connell's Repeal Association known as the Young Irelanders launched a rebellion that was quickly suppressed by British military action. In 1858, the Irish Republican Brotherhood (IRB, also known as the Fenians, from *Fianna*, mythological warriors) was founded simultaneously in Ireland and the US as a secret society dedicated to armed rebellion. Their attempted rising in 1867 gathered little support, though there was one particularly memorable event. Fenians boldly attacked a police van in Manchester and rescued two prominent prisoners, IRB chief executive Thomas J. Kelly and his aide Timothy Deasy. Shots were fired, and a police officer, Sergeant Charles Brett, was killed. The prisoners escaped: Kelly hid in a water cistern and swapped clothes with a priest. They eventually reached New York. After a trial in Manchester, three men alleged to have been involved – William Allen, Michael Larkin and Michael O'Brien – were hanged. They shouted 'God save Ireland' in the dock and were commemorated for decades as the 'Manchester Martyrs'. In 1882, in what became known as the Phoenix Park Murders, Lord Frederick Cavendish, the newly appointed chief secretary for Ireland, and his under-secretary Thomas Burke were fatally stabbed in Dublin by an even more radical breakaway from the IRB, the Irish National Invincibles.[21]

After the famine, there was a long campaign for better rights for tenant farmers and ultimately for land redistribution, known in Ireland as the 'Land War', though a rise in farm prices brought a rise in living standards for all but the poorest farmers. One of Gladstone's first statements on becoming prime minister in 1868 concerned his intention to 'pacify Ireland'. His Landlord and Tenant (Ireland) Act 1870 compensated tenants for improvements made to a farm if they surrendered their lease or for 'disturbance' if evicted for causes other than non-payment of rent. It was criticised for not going far enough, but it was the first in a series of land acts that changed the balance between landlords and tenants.[22]

An Irish National Land League was formed in 1879 after poor harvests and an economic depression, with the aim of enabling tenant farmers to own the land they worked on. Among its tactics was the boycott, under which unpopular landlords were ostracised by the local community, named after Captain Charles Boycott, an agent of an absentee landlord against whom the tactic was employed. The league's president was Charles Stewart Parnell, a radical young Protestant landowner who was a Home Rule League MP, a party founded in 1873 by Isaac Butt. After Butt died, Parnell became the league's president and turned it into the Irish Parliamentary Party (IPP), seeking devolved home rule within the UK. It came to dominate Irish politics. Significant concessions were wrung from Gladstone's government: land courts were set up, and in 1882 the government agreed to pay rent in arrears on behalf of impoverished tenants. In the 1885 election, Parnell's party won four-fifths of the Irish MPs. Parnell's sisters, Anna and Fanny (a poet), formed a Ladies' Land League in 1880 to press for reform. While Fanny raised funds in America, Anna became its president in Ireland, travelling around the nation encouraging resistance to unjust rents. However, Anna became estranged from her brother when they fell out over strategy, leading to the Ladies' Land League being disbanded after bitter negotiations. They never spoke again, and Anna moved to England.[23]

Gladstone became converted to home rule and introduced bills to try to enact it in 1886 and 1893, though the first was defeated in the Commons and the second in the Lords. The issue split his party: a large group led by Joseph Chamberlain, who had been a notable mayor of Birmingham before becoming an MP, formed a unionist faction that supported the Conservative Party. Home Rule was also opposed in Ireland by a significant minority of unionists, mostly in Ulster. The Orange Order warned Protestants that a Dublin parliament dominated by Catholics and nationalists would discriminate against them and impose tariffs on trade with Britain. Rioting broke out in Belfast in 1886 as the first bill was debated.[24]

The 'Union of Hearts' between Gladstone and Parnell fell apart in 1890 when divorce proceedings by a fellow Irish MP, Captain William O'Shea, revealed that Parnell had been the long-term lover of O'Shea's long-separated wife Kitty and had fathered three of her children. An adverse reaction by Nonconformist Liberals forced Gladstone to demand that the IPP replace Parnell as leader; Catholic bishops in Ireland also turned against him. Parnell's party split; he was forced out and died in 1891. The Conservatives, who governed the UK largely continuously from 1885 to 1906, tried to neutralise support for home rule by a vigorous programme of reforms including several land acts, in which it became easier for tenants to buy out their landlords. The IPP was reunited in 1900 under the leadership of John Redmond.[25]

Ireland experienced a 'Gaelic revival' in the late nineteenth century, including Douglas Hyde's founding of the Gaelic League in 1893 to encourage preservation of Irish culture and language. The Gaelic Athletic Association (GAA), founded in 1884, revived and codified hurling, Gaelic football and other native sports. Protests against a visit by Queen Victoria in 1900 suggested that nationalists might not be content to remain within the Empire. In the same year, journalist Arthur Griffith founded Cumann na nGaedheal to try to unite disparate nationalist groups. He turned it into the Sinn Féin ('We Ourselves') party in 1905 – small at first but destined to be a rallying point after 1916.[26]

In Wales, the Liberals won a majority of MPs for the first time at the 1865 election, which increased in 1868. Their advance was driven not just by the growth of Nonconformism but also by the influence of Whig landowners, the attraction of the Liberals' free trade policy for new industrialists and the appeal to the rising middle class of the Liberals' emphasis on personal industriousness and prudence. Nonconformists were increasingly ready to challenge the Anglican Church's privileges. After Gladstone disestablished the Anglican Church in Ireland in 1869, calls grew for a similar step in Wales, though this did not happen until 1920. Meanwhile, an Anglican revival in Wales reached its height, with hundreds of new churches built in the century's second half. The Welsh Sunday Closing Act 1881, closing public houses on the sabbath, was seen as a step forward by prohibitionists but had limited impact on drunkenness because a host of unregulated clubs opened to fill the gap.[27]

In the 1885 election, Liberals won 30 out of 34 Welsh seats. Voters showed strong allegiance to Gladstone, who lived at Hawarden in Flintshire, his wife's family home. There was growing but unsuccessful pressure in the 1890s for Welsh home rule, championed by the young Liberal MP for Carnarvon Boroughs, David Lloyd George. The Liberal–Nonconformist consensus was weakening, however, partly the result of the franchise widening to more working-class men. Trade union militancy increased, and socialism developed in south Wales. James Keir Hardie, a Scottish miners' leader, co-founded the Scottish Labour Party in 1888, became MP for the English seat of West Ham South in 1892 and co-founded the Independent Labour Party the following year. He lost his seat in 1895 but was re-elected to parliament in 1900 for the Welsh constituency of Merthyr Tydfil and Aberdare. In the same year, he helped to form the union-based Labour Representation Committee (LRC), later renamed the Labour Party.[28]

In Scotland, the Scottish Reform Act 1832 increased the number of MPs and widened the franchise to include more middle-class men. After that, the Whigs and their Liberal successors won a majority of Scottish seats for the rest of the century, though at Westminster they were often outnumbered by English and Welsh Conservatives. They were seen as the party of progress, reform and liberty, though divided by factions. Few Scots held government office, but the English-educated Lord Aberdeen, a Peelite Conservative, led a coalition government in 1852–5. Gladstone, of Scottish parentage, became a cult figure, with engravings of his head and features adorning many Scottish homes. Things got harder from the 1880s when the Liberals split over Irish home rule and their share of the vote started falling, but they remained Scotland's main party until the First World War. A Conservative prime minister, Lord Salisbury, responded to pressure for Scottish home rule in 1885 by reviving the post of secretary of state for Scotland for the first time since 1746. The first Scottish Liberal prime minister was the Earl of Rosebery in 1894–5.[29]

Scots adapted to fears that urbanisation and industrialisation would erase their distinctive past, notably by embracing highland culture as part of the Romantic movement – ironic at a time when crofting society was enduring clearances and dispossession. The tartan and kilt became fashionable among the social elite across Europe, prompted by the popularity of James Macpherson's publication of the works of Ossian, a fictitious Gaelic poet, and by Walter Scott's Waverley novels. Scott was a master at inventing tradition. Invited to stage-manage the 1822 visit of George IV to Scotland, Scott dressed the king and many guests in tartan, prompting an upsurge in demand for kilts. Queen Victoria boosted highlandism by building a residence at Balmoral on Deeside and, after 1848, spending each autumn there on holiday. Aside from highland culture, Scotland's historic building tradition of castles, keeps and towers was revived in an architectural style known as Scotch Baronial. Above all, celebrating national heroes such as the poet Robert Burns and medieval independence leader William Wallace became popular.[30]

Victoria enjoyed a Golden Jubilee in 1887 and a Diamond Jubilee in 1897, both occasions for public celebration. In 1887, she marked the fiftieth anniversary of her accession with a banquet to which 50 kings and princes were invited, followed by a procession and thanksgiving service in Westminster Abbey. In 1897, her procession followed a route 6 miles long through London and included troops from across the Empire. Prime ministers of all the self-governing dominions were invited but not foreign heads of state – partly to avoid having to invite Victoria's grandson, the German emperor Wilhelm II, who, it was feared, might cause trouble.[31] She died in 1901, having reigned for 63 years and 216 days, longer than any predecessor. It had been a remarkable era of industrial, political and scientific change.

CHAPTER 10

MIGRANT TALES

People have migrated into, around and out of the Isles since the earliest times. Some travelled in order to conquer others or seek a better life, or because they were coerced, or simply to survive. It could be tough, as it was for example for John Gray, a Scottish eighteenth-century migrant in England who scraped a living for several years as a wandering musician after his father died, until justices of the peace in Yorkshire labelled him a vagrant and sent him back to Edinburgh.[1] People's lives sometimes ended in tragedy, as happened in the case of 40-year-old Bridget Callaghan, an Irish woman who migrated to England via Liverpool during the Great Famine in 1850. She set off to walk with her small children and young cousin to join a relative in Yorkshire but froze to death on the second night under a hedge in Bold, near St Helens.[2]

The nations' populations have been created entirely by waves of migration, including early humans, Romans, Anglo-Saxons, Norse people and Normans. Significant internal migration has taken place within the Isles too, particularly during the Industrial Revolution, with England the main recipient – notably the north and midlands. In 1801, England had roughly half the UK's population; by 1901, it had three-quarters.[3] A number of English emigrants were themselves drawn to south Wales and Ulster, while Scottish highlanders and Irish went to Glasgow and the west of Scotland, and Irish and Welsh went to places notably including the Liverpool area.

The story of emigration from the UK is if anything even more dramatic as Britain built an Empire that covered a fifth of the globe. It formed part of a vast migration of European and Asian peoples that began in the 1500s – the Age of Exploration – and peaked in the nineteenth and twentieth centuries. The consequences for indigenous populations were often disastrous as outsiders brought diseases for which they had no immunity, as well as occupying land and seizing resources. According to some estimates, British and Irish settlers totalled more than a third of some fifty million emigrants from Europe between 1815 and 1930.[4] By 1870, almost half as many natives of Ireland were living overseas as at home.[5] In the nineteenth century, about two-thirds of migrants from the Isles went to the United States, while after 1900 there was also a rising volume to Canada, Australia, New Zealand and southern Africa.[6] Some moved as a result of poverty or rural clearances, but many went simply to seek better opportunities. Male emigrants were often miners or agricultural workers, while women tended to be farm workers or domestic servants. Some emigrants were artisans, builders, mechanics, engineers, textile workers and, increasingly, shopkeepers, clerks and professional people.

The result is a huge diaspora. The number who can claim descent from British or Irish emigrants has been estimated at about two hundred million, almost treble the Isles' current population.[7] Those of Irish ancestry have been estimated at up to eighty million. Americans with Irish forebears have included former president Barack Obama (also with Scottish roots), Dublin-born actress Maureen O'Hara and boxer Muhammad Ali, who had a grandfather from County Clare. 'Most countries send out oil or iron, steel or gold, or some other crop, but Ireland has had only one export and that is its people,' said President John F. Kennedy, whose four grandparents were children of Irish immigrants.[8] The Scottish diaspora has been estimated by the Scottish government at between twenty-eight and forty million, while other estimates have ranged as high as eighty million, including US presidents Bill Clinton, George H.W. Bush, George W. Bush and Donald Trump.[9]

Immigration to the Isles has at various stages included Afro-Caribbeans, Africans, south Asians and Chinese, along with Jews from central and eastern Europe. It has often been difficult for ethnic minorities. In 1919, for example, riots started in Glasgow and spread to other seaports including Liverpool, South Shields, London, Hull, Newport, Barry and Cardiff. Five people were killed and hundreds injured as white soldiers returning from the war blamed blacks, Asians and Arabs for taking their jobs and homes. Amid a lack of jobs and an acute housing shortage, black men became scapegoats, even though many were themselves destitute, having been dismissed from ships to make way for demobilised white men.

Africans came to Britain with the Romans: an altar stone found in 1934 in the Cumbrian village of Beaumont records that, in mid-third century, a unit of north Africans was stationed at the fort of Aballava, at the western end of Hadrian's Wall – one of several artefacts and inscriptions clustered along the wall that record Africans' presence.[10] Ethnic minority migrants were rare between the end of the Western Roman Empire in the fifth century and Europe's Age of Exploration 1,000 years later. Romani travellers, who originated in northern India, have been in Britain since at least the early sixteenth century. Black people have been continuously present since around then.

There was a small group of African servants at the court of Scotland's James IV in the early sixteenth century, probably seized by Scottish privateers from a Portuguese slaving ship. The king particularly liked a drummer (*taubronar*) and choreographer, for whom he bought a horse, clothes, paid doctor's bills and gave money to his wife and child. There were several black young women in Edinburgh too. William Dunbar wrote a mockingly ribald poem, *Of Ane Blak-Moir*, depicting a tournament in which the king jousted to win the favour of a black lady, possibly Ellen or Elen More, a servant of James's daughter Margaret. Dunbar describes a lady like a monkey (*ane aep*), with thick lips (*mekle lippis*) and a short catlike nose (*schort catt nois up skippis*). The king was rewarded by the black lady's kiss and close embrace, while losers had to 'cum behind and kis hir hippis'.[11]

Black people have lived in Ireland in small numbers since the eighteenth century, mainly concentrated in cities and towns. Some married or had children with white Irish people. One child of an interracial marriage, 'Mulatto Jack', was abducted from Ireland in the early 1700s and sold as a slave in Antigua. After helping to plot a slave rebellion, he was deported back to Ireland.[12]

Empire and British seapower led to immigration, particularly in ports. From the seventeenth century, Indian servants and ayahs (nannies) arrived with English families returning from India, while Indian sailors crewed East India Company ships. Many settled in ports such as Liverpool, Hull and South Shields. There were a few thousand black people in Georgian England including domestic servants (or slaves), sailors, tavern workers, musicians and prostitutes; most lived in London, but an increasing number in Liverpool. Chinese seamen lodged in ports such as Liverpool and Cardiff after the East India Company's monopoly on trade with India ended in 1813 and with China in 1833. Groups of Muslim seamen in Britain included Somalis along with Yemenis from Aden, a British colony.[13]

Cardiff's coal exports and surging population drew in immigrants. Many settled in Tiger Bay, the dockland district, which became Wales's oldest multi-ethnic community. Sailors and workers from more than 50 countries settled there including Somalis, Yemenis and Greeks. It gained a reputation as tough and dangerous, but those who lived there describe a far friendlier place with a strong community spirit. Famous former residents include singer Shirley Bassey, who was born there. The 1960s saw wholesale destruction of large areas of the Bay and displacement of the community. Since the 1990s, it has become a leisure and business hot spot known as Cardiff Bay.[14]

With the dawn of the Industrial Revolution, there was massive internal migration to England's north and midlands, notably from Ireland but also from Scotland, Wales and other English regions. It was a chance to escape rural poverty, though working in factories was a shock for many: long hours, bad conditions and irksome discipline.

Workers faced slum housing, smoke and disease as they crowded into explosively growing towns and cities. Manchester also drew in Germans (both Jewish and gentile), French, Russians, Italians, Greeks, Dutch, Spanish, Armenians, Danes, Swiss, Turkish, Portuguese, Swedes and Moroccans.[15]

Scotland saw Glasgow and surrounding towns grow rapidly as centres of industry and mining. Wales experienced immigration into the mining and industrial districts of Glamorgan and Monmouthshire, an influx that was to turn into a flood at the start of the twentieth century. The English were the most numerous group, followed by the Irish, with smaller numbers of Italians as well as Russian and Polish Jews.[16]

Manchester saw an influx of German Jews in the early nineteenth century to engage in the Industrial Revolution; its Jewish community became the largest outside London. Later there was Jewish immigration from tsarist Russia and Poland, giving the community in Britain a poorer cast until the mid-twentieth century. They came to escape pogroms and lack of access to the tsarist empire's industrialising cities and regions. Glasgow also acquired a significant Jewish community. By the end of the 1880s, the city's main centre of Jewish settlement had shifted from prosperous Garnethill in the West End to the Gorbals, south of the Clyde.

Waves of Irish, Lithuanian, Polish, Asian and English people also settled in Scotland during the nineteenth and twentieth centuries. The Irish were by far the largest group, more significant even than in England: the Irish formed 7.2 per cent of Scotland's population in 1851, compared with 2.9 per cent in England and Wales.[17] They were attracted by jobs in booming parts of the western lowlands such as Airdrie, Coatbridge and Motherwell. They came largely from Ulster, and most were Catholic, though up to a quarter were Protestant, descendants of Presbyterian Scots who had settled in Ulster in the seventeenth century. Ulster's tribal conflicts were imported to some communities in Lanarkshire and Ayrshire.

Irish migrants in England suffered a backlash in a nation already unnerved by urbanisation and social unrest. The idea took hold that the Irish were to blame for their own misfortune. Engels, in Manchester, wrote that the Irish were at home with filth and drunkenness, lacked furniture and shared their domestic space with pigs. He held that view even though he had set up home with Mary Burns, a second-generation Irish mill worker, and her sister Lizzie. Engels' analysis later became more sophisticated after visiting Ireland with the sisters.[18] Anti-Catholic rioting in Stockport, near Manchester, in 1852 led to one dead, 51 injured and the ransacking of a Catholic church. 'No popery' lecturers such as William Murphy toured towns and villages denouncing Irish Catholics.

Britain's industrial expansion was achieved on the back of slavery, notably by importing cotton from the West Indies and the United States. Between 1780 and 1807, ships departing from Liverpool accounted for half of all slaving voyages originating in Europe.[19] Even after abolition of the slave trade in 1807 and slavery in most of the British Empire in 1833, Britain imported slave-grown cotton from the US up to the civil war in the 1860s. One American slave, James Johnson from North Carolina, escaped amid the confusion of war and made his way to Liverpool, where he was robbed of his few possessions. He walked 'friendless and hopeless' from town to town, 'where I took to singing, dancing and rattlebones [a game played with bones or dice], which … was easier than begging'. He joined a boxing troupe and performed at fairs around the country before deciding to stay in Oldham, where he found work and married a cotton worker.[20]

The Isles also experienced significant emigration during the nineteenth century, notably from Ireland but also from other places. Some engaged in so-called step migration, from rural areas to towns and then to distant places overseas. Ann Beaton Boggie, from Stromness in Orkney, married a handloom weaver who was forced to go 'on the tramp' for work, moving around various lowland towns before the family left for the US in 1856. There, they were as rootless as they had been in industrial Scotland, passing through Illinois, Nebraska and Iowa before settling in Utah.[21] Most migrants were young, male and single, though many single Irish women also emigrated to the US; the proportion of female migrants increased as overseas settlements became more established. Husbands often went ahead, and wives and children followed later. Prospective emigrants learned about opportunities from letters by family and friends already overseas in a process known as chain migration.

Experiences varied. Peter Hastie, an Edinburgh shopkeeper, emigrated around 1832 to New York state, where he worked as an engineer on canals and aqueducts. In his last surviving letter sent home, he considered himself 'content' and in a good situation. Less contented were John and Martha Kerr from Ayrshire, who emigrated to Madison County, Illinois, in about 1841. John, who had been a joiner in Scotland, mainly worked as a farmer, although he was not very successful. In letters home, he revealed the difficulties endured by many emigrants in the US and advised those thinking of moving there to stay in Scotland. By 1853, he had returned to Dalry in Ayrshire, where he became a baker.[22]

Even for those who made a success of it, emigration could be heartbreakingly difficult. Joseph Johnson, a shepherd, and his wife Louisa emigrated from Grandborough in Warwickshire to New Zealand in 1873–4 on an assisted passage provided by the New Zealand government. There was an outbreak of scarlet fever and measles during the 51-day voyage. Of their five children, only the baby Ellen survived. However, they produced four more daughters and two sons in New Zealand and eventually prospered in the dairy industry. 'If you want to come out of bondage into liberty come out here,' Louisa wrote to a friend.[23]

Emigrants preserved emotional ties with their mother country by creating societies, some purely cultural and others more political. The English-Speaking Union, founded in 1918, promoted exchanges, conferences, scholarships and international use of the English language but also served as a prop to the Anglo-American alliance; its second chairman, 1921–5, was Winston Churchill. Cambrian societies promoted Welsh language, song and literature; the National Welsh-American Foundation, based in Pennsylvania, had counterparts in Canada, Australia, New Zealand and even in Oslo. Irish organisations ranged from the Ancient Order of Hibernians, a society for lay Catholics, to bodies that existed to fund and support the Irish Republican Army (IRA).[24] The Scottish diaspora produced Caledonian societies, Burns clubs and highland gatherings in greater numbers than in the homeland. Emigrants' earnings became crucially important for many families back home, notably in Ireland, where children were 'reared for emigration' in the hope they would not only fund further emigration but provide remittances for their parents that would help to pay rents, rates and shop-debts.

In the twentieth century, emigration was more typical than immigration between the two world wars as economic depression affected large parts of the Isles. Many travelled in Australia on government-assisted passages. Irish migration to Britain rose in the interwar period, partly because of US immigration controls. Many also sought to escape hardship caused by the protectionist policies of Éamon de Valera's Fianna Fáil government, which took office in 1932 and imposed tariffs on imported goods, mainly from Britain, in an effort to make Ireland agriculturally and industrially self-sufficient. Insofar as these had anti-British motives, it was ironic that they provoked more people to seek sanctuary in Britain.

In Scotland, the Irish Catholic community shared in the bloody sacrifices of the Great War. In 1918, Catholic schools were brought into the state system yet allowed to preserve their distinctive ethos, prompting bitter complaints of 'Rome on the Rates' from some Protestants. The Catholic schools have been condemned by some for perpetuating sectarian differences, though others argue that they have assisted assimilation by providing educational opportunity for the Scoto-Irish. The struggle for Irish independence had repercussions in Scotland, where thousands of volunteers joined the IRA and sympathisers supplied powder and gelignite from the quarries and mines where they worked. The interwar period saw a renewed outbreak of anti-Catholicism, but the impact of Irish politics faded, and the Scottish Catholic community became largely loyal to Labour, bringing it into the mainstream of British politics. Later in the century, the erosion of labour market discrimination, wider access to higher education and the effect of the welfare state promoted more rapid assimilation.[25]

Wales saw a huge outflow of people in the wake of the depression, particularly from mining valleys such as the Rhondda and Merthyr. Some went to the US, South Africa, Rhodesia and Australia, but the vast majority went to England – this time mainly to the south-east, which was less hard-hit by the downturn than Merseyside. Scotland suffered less than Wales, Ulster or north-east England, but its exporting industries were badly hit by the slump in international trade; its rate of emigration more than doubled between 1921 and 1931.[26]

The situation changed after the Second World War, when Britain had huge demand for unskilled labour. London Transport set up a recruiting office for bus drivers in Barbados, while Yorkshire woollen mills sent representatives to the Punjab to recruit labour for night-shift work and lower-paid jobs. Immigrants from the West Indies arrived initially on the *Empire Windrush* in 1948, an inflow that accelerated from 1953 when the US imposed entry restrictions. After the 1971 census, it was estimated that more than one-and-a-half million immigrants of 'New Commonwealth' ethnic origins were living in the UK. More than half were from India and Pakistan or were east African Asians, while between a quarter and a third were from the West Indies.[27]

As black and Asian immigration grew, so did ethnic tension. White mobs attacked black people and homes in Nottingham and London's Notting Hill in 1958. The 1962 Commonwealth Immigrants Act applied controls to those whose passports were not issued directly by the UK government. While the 1965 Race Relations Act outlawed discrimination on grounds of race, further immigration acts from 1968 to 1971 removed the remnants of Commonwealth citizens' rights of entry and residence. Riots in 1981 by young blacks who felt marginalised and persecuted by police spread from London's Brixton to Moss Side in Manchester and Toxteth in Liverpool. Disorder in 2001 in Oldham, Burnley, Bradford and Leeds prompted concern that Pakistanis and Bangladeshis were insufficiently integrated into British life.

Immigration into the UK and Ireland has grown in recent decades, raising ethnic minorities' share of the population. According to censuses in 2021 and 2022, non-white groups account for about 18 per cent of England's population, compared with 13 per cent in Scotland, 6 per cent in Wales and 3 per cent in Northern Ireland.[28] In the Irish Republic, almost 13 per cent are non-white or not stated.[29] As in much of the developed world, immigration has become a hot issue in the Isles.

In August 2024, anti-immigrant rioting took place in England and Northern Ireland after a knife attack at a Taylor Swift-themed children's yoga and dance workshop in Southport in which three children were killed and eight others injured. The riots were fuelled by false claims circulated by far-right groups that the perpetrator was a Muslim and asylum seeker. Towns and cities affected included London, Manchester, Hartlepool, Aldershot, Sunderland and Belfast. Protesters clashed with police and counter-protesters, attacked homes and businesses owned by immigrants and attacked hotels housing asylum seekers. More than 1,200 were arrested.

The Labour government, elected in July 2024, and the outgoing Conservative administration have both taken a hard-line approach to try to neutralise a political threat from the populist right. The prime minister, Sir Keir Starmer, vowed to slash inward migration, largely by boosting domestic skills in key sectors that have histori-cally been reliant on overseas labour. In 2023, legal migration to the 38 rich countries in the Organisation for Economic Co-operation and Development (OECD) rose by almost 10 per cent to a record 6.5 million people. The greatest surge was in the

UK, which for the first time became the biggest recipient of migrants after the US, with net immigration of 750,000 driven by recruitment to the care sector.[30]

The most startling change has been in Ireland, where a nation of emigration has turned into one of immigration. A tentative opening to the global economy had begun during the 1960s with reforms by Taoiseach (prime minister) Seán Lemass. These provided a platform for membership of the European Economic Community, which Ireland joined in 1973, and for the subsequent arrival of American technology and pharmaceuticals companies. By the 1990s, the era of the 'Celtic Tiger', Ireland was embracing globalisation enthusiastically and achieved one of the world's highest economic growth rates. The late 1990s saw mass immigration, particularly of people from Asia and eastern Europe. Irish society adopted relatively liberal social policies during this period: divorce was legalised, homosexuality decriminalised and abortion in limited cases allowed by the Supreme Court.

Even in Ireland, however, there has been a backlash. The number of foreign nationals has surged, notably with the arrival of many Ukrainians fleeing the war with Russia at a time when Ireland has been grappling with a severe housing crisis and lack of access to education, healthcare and mental health services. Asylum centres became targets accused of exacerbating the housing crisis, as seen during anti-immigration riots in Dublin in November 2023. Rampaging youths set buses on fire, clashed with police and looted shops after three children and a care worker were stabbed outside a school by a man who far-right groups had claimed was an Algerian immigrant. The government pointed out that the alleged perpetrator was naturalised and had lived in Ireland for 20 years. Since then, other buildings housing asylum seekers have been set on fire across the country. Despite the unrest, however, anti-immigration candidates made little impact on the 2024 general election, which focused mainly on the cost of living and housing. The government has stepped up border checks to try to curb illegal entry.

The irony of a former emigrant country becoming alarmed by immigration has not gone unremarked. As Bryan Fanning, professor of migration and social policy at University College Dublin, put it: 'Freedom of movement, taken for granted by Irish people for centuries, is a prize denied to many millions of desperate people in today's world.'[31]

CHAPTER 11

WOMEN'S FORTUNES

Hastings-born Sophia Jex-Blake was determined to study medicine. She applied to the University of Edinburgh in 1869, attracted by Scotland's supposedly enlightened attitudes towards women's education. The university refused, saying it could not make the necessary arrangements 'in the interest of one lady'. Undeterred, she placed adverts in newspapers to find others to join her. Six replied: Mary Anderson, Emily Bovell, Matilda Chaplin, Helen Evans, Edith Pechey and Isabel Thorne. They became known as the 'Edinburgh Seven', the first women admitted to study medicine in the UK.[1]

Certain male professors whipped up hostility. The women received abusive letters, were spat at and had obscenities shouted at them. When they arrived for an anatomy exam, a jeering crowd tried to block their way. They pressed on, winning support from figures including Charles Darwin, yet the university refused them degrees. When the women sued, the Court of Session ruled in the university's favour and concluded that they should not have been allowed to study at all. Their campaign, though, stoked pressure that led to legislation in 1876 to ensure women could be licensed to practise medicine. Five of the seven went on to gain medical degrees from European universities and worked around the world. Jex-Blake qualified as licentiate of the King and Queen's College of Physicians of Ireland, meaning she could at last be registered with the General Medical Council, becoming the UK's third registered woman doctor.

She returned to Edinburgh in 1878 as the city's first female doctor. In 2019, the university posthumously awarded all seven women the degrees they had fought for.

Throughout the Isles' history, most women were unsung and confined to domesticity. There are some, however, whose stories have survived or been rediscovered. In early times, these were often upper-class women. Boudica, queen of the Iceni tribe in eastern England, led a failed uprising against the Romans in 60 or 61 CE. She became celebrated in Victorian times as a British national heroine. Less well known is Cartimandua, first-century queen of the Brigantes, whose territory centred on Yorkshire and much of Lancashire, Northumberland and Durham. She became forgotten probably because, unlike Boudica, she was not a resistance heroine: she collaborated with the Romans, divorced her husband, married one of his aides and was overthrown by a revolt. Despite her loyalty, she was portrayed by Roman historians as an adulterous betrayer of British men, yet she succeeded in keeping her territory free from annexation for up to 30 years, whereas Boudica's revolt brought down a heavy retribution on her people.[2]

In Anglo-Saxon England, royal women did not always live passive lives as wives and mothers. A number played active, sometimes decisive roles in their kingdoms' fortunes. Monasteries, for example, created opportunities for aristocratic women, notably Saint Hilda (or Hild), great-niece of King Edwin of Northumbria and first abbess of Whitby.[3] Few lives were as eventful as that of Saint Æthelthryth (also known as Etheldreda or Audrey), an East Anglian princess who became queen of Northumbria and also founded an abbey at Ely in Cambridgeshire. She made a vow of perpetual virginity before marrying Tondberct, a Fenland chief, whom she persuaded to respect her vow. After he died, she married Ecgfrith of Northumbria, who was 14 or 15. He initially agreed that Æthelthryth should remain a virgin and allowed her to become a nun but became increasingly insistent on his marital rights. She fled back to the Isle of Ely, where she founded Ely Abbey in 673.[4]

Æthelflæd (c.870–918) governed for seven years as Lady of the Mercians in England's midlands, where she played a big part in the struggle against the Danes, who ruled in England's north and east. She was the daughter of Wessex's Alfred the Great, who had become overlord of the western midlands and married her to Æthelred, the Mercians' lord. After her husband died, Æthelflæd in 917 captured Derby, the first to fall of the five boroughs of Danelaw, the Viking kingdom – seen as her greatest triumph.[5]

Margaret of Scotland (c.1045–93) was a pious woman who became the only Scottish royal to be made a saint. An English princess raised in the Hungarian court (where she was probably born), she came to England in 1057 but fled with her family after the Norman invasion in 1066. Their ship, heading for the continent, was caught in a storm and pushed north to Scotland, where she married King Malcolm Caenn Mór (Malcolm III). She instigated religious reforms to bring Scottish practices closer to those of the continental Roman church. Among charitable works, she established a ferry across the Firth of Forth for pilgrims travelling to St Andrews, which gave the towns of South Queensferry and North Queensferry their names.[6]

Matilda (c.1102–67), Holy Roman Empress, was a claimant to the English throne during the civil war known as the Anarchy. She had gone to Germany as a child to marry Emperor Henry V. After he died, her father, England's Henry I, arranged for her to marry Geoffrey of Anjou in France. Henry I nominated Matilda as his heir, but this was unpopular among England's barons. The throne was seized by her cousin Stephen of Blois, so Matilda crossed to England to try to take the kingdom by force, backed by her uncle David I of Scotland. The war descended into stalemate after her attempt to be crowned at Westminster Abbey collapsed amid opposition from London's crowds. Eventually, her and Geoffrey's son succeeded Stephen as Henry II.[7]

Eleanor, Countess of Leicester (1215–75), youngest child of King John and sister of Henry III, was anything but meek and submissive.

During a war among barons, her second husband Simon de Montfort captured the king and became England's de facto ruler. A year later, de Montfort and their eldest son were killed in battle. Eleanor, at Dover Castle, tried to hold out against Henry's forces. Betrayed from within the castle and attacked from outside, she negotiated a settlement that pardoned her supporters, although she was exiled to France.[8]

In Wales, Gwenllian ferch Gruffudd (c.1097–1136) was a rebel against the Normans and the only woman known to have led a Welsh army into battle in medieval times. She was the daughter of Gruffudd ap Cynan, king of Gwynedd, and married Gruffydd ap Rhys of the kingdom of Deheubarth in south-west Wales. An opportunity arose during England's Anarchy for the Welsh to recover lands lost to marcher lords (nobles appointed by the English king to guard the border). In the Great Revolt of 1136, while her husband was away seeking an alliance with her father, Gwenllian raised an army to defend Deheubarth, but she was captured and executed. The spot is still known as Maes Gwenllian. Even after her death, her revolt inspired other rebels.[9]

In Scotland, Isabella MacDuff, Countess of Buchan (died c.1314), was the daughter of the Earl of Fife and a member of the MacDuff clan. During the Scottish Wars of Independence, her husband John Comyn pledged allegiance to the English after being defeated in battle, but Isabella defied him and rode to Scone, where she crowned Robert Bruce king of Scotland. As the highest-ranking family, the earls of Fife claimed the right to crown the king. However, after Bruce's defeat she fell captive to England's Edward I and was imprisoned in an open-air cage at Berwick Castle for four years. She may have perished in captivity.[10]

Agnes, Countess of Dunbar (c.1312–69), defended her home, Dunbar Castle, against a six-month siege by English forces led by the Earl of Salisbury. The earl eventually gave up, describing her as 'a brawling, boisterous Scottish wench'.[11] Joan Beaufort (c.1404–45), English-born daughter of the Earl of Somerset, married James I and became queen of Scots. She is said to have inspired James's romantic poem *The Kingis Quair*, written while a prisoner in England, after he saw her from his window. The poem described her as 'beautee eneuch to mak a world to dote'. The marriage was at least partly political, as it was part of the agreement for his release, intended by the English to ally Scotland with England rather than France.[12]

Julian of Norwich (1342–c.1416) – an anchoress who lived in seclusion in a cell attached to St Julian's Church, Norwich – wrote *Revelations of Divine Love*, the first book written by a woman in English that has survived. She is best known for the phrase 'alle shalle be wele, and alle maner of thynge shalle be wele', quoted by T.S. Eliot in the *Four Quartets*.[13] Margery Kempe (c.1373–after 1438), another Norfolk mystic, who met Julian, wrote by dictation *The Book of Margery Kempe*, considered by some the first surviving autobiography in English. She was mother of at least 14 children and had religious visions and illusions during an illness (possibly postpartum psychosis) after the first birth. The book chronicles her domestic troubles, extensive pilgrimages to sites in Europe and the Holy Land and conversations with God.[14]

Women played a significant role in England's Wars of the Roses, including Margaret of Anjou (1430–82), who twice became England's queen as the wife of Henry VI. She at times led the Lancastrians owing to her husband's frequent bouts of insanity. Margaret Beaufort (1443–1509), another Lancastrian, great-granddaughter of John of Gaunt, was a skilled politician and mother of Henry VII, the first Tudor monarch, who defeated Yorkist Richard III at Bosworth. Henry's eldest daughter Margaret Tudor married James IV of Scotland, leading to the Union of the Crowns a century later.[15]

In Tudor times, Lady Jane Grey, 'nine days' queen' of England and Ireland, was nominated as heir by Edward VI to try to prevent his Catholic half-sister Mary from succeeding. After Edward died, Jane was proclaimed queen on 10 July 1553 and awaited coronation, but the Privy Council changed sides and deposed Jane in favour of Mary on 19 July. Mary I or 'Bloody Mary' was queen of England and Ireland from 1553 and queen of Spain as wife of Philip II from 1556 until her death in 1558. She sought to reverse the English Reformation begun under her father, Henry VIII, and had more than 280 Protestants burned at the stake. Elizabeth I, the last Tudor monarch from 1558 until her death in 1603, reinstated Protestantism as the state religion but tried to avoid alienating Catholics. Mary, Queen of Scots, after ruling her nation personally for just six years, fled south to seek her cousin Elizabeth's protection after being accused of involvement in her husband's murder. She was held captive for almost 19 years, feared as a rallying point for Catholic rebels, and executed for allegedly endorsing a plot to murder Elizabeth.[16]

Among the era's colourful figures, Elizabeth Cavendish (c.1527–1608), known as Bess of Hardwick (Hardwick Hall, Derbyshire), rose through Elizabethan society, making herself one of England's wealthiest women through four advantageous marriages and increasing her assets by investing in coal mines and glass works. A Scottish noblewoman, Lady Agnes Campbell (1526–1601), spoke several languages and displayed military and political skills. After her Scottish husband died in captivity in Ulster, she married his captor's successor, Turlough Luineach O'Neill, Lord of Tír Eoghain or Tyrone, bringing with her a dowry of 1,200 highland troops that she led against English occupying forces.[17]

The early modern era was tough for many women as hysteria about witchcraft peaked, influenced by religious convulsions, although both Protestants and Catholics hunted witches. Estimates put the number strangled, hanged or burned across Europe at 30,000–60,000, mostly women, from around 1400 to 1775. Scotland, where James VI was witch-obsessed, was the worst-affected part of the Isles, with perhaps 1,500 executed. In England, the figure may have been nearer 500. Among the best known are the Pendle witch trials of 1612 in Lancashire, in which nine women and two men were hanged. Most of those accused came from two families competing to scrape a living from healing, begging and extortion. It began when a young woman called Alizon Device was accused of bewitching a pedlar who had stumbled and fallen down lame, possibly from a stroke.[18]

Wales and Ireland, by contrast, had only a handful of executions. Reasons advanced for this include the suggestion that wise women who made potions and charms were an accepted part of small, rural communities, as well as differences in legal systems. In 1594, Gwen ferch Ellis of Llandyrnog, Denbighshire, was the first to be executed as a witch in Wales. Accusations were that, although she provided healing to animals and sick people in return for gifts of food or goods, she had used her charms to cause a child's madness and murder a sick man. The first such execution in Ireland is believed to have been that of Petronilla de Meath, maidservant to a wealthy woman in Kilkenny in 1324. Her boss, Alice Kyteler, was accused of using witchcraft to poison her four husbands for their money; they died one after the other, and de Meath was accused of being a co-conspirator. She is thought to have been tortured before confessing. Kyteler fled, leaving only de Meath to be flogged and burned.[19]

In 1727, 'Janet Horne' – probably a generic name – was Britain's last person to be tried and executed for witchcraft when she and her daughter were arrested in Dornoch, north-east Scotland. Janet's daughter suffered from a deformity in her hands and feet; neighbours gossiped that she looked as though she had hooves. Janet was accused of turning her daughter into a pony so she could ride to meet the devil. The sheriff-depute ordered both to be burned. Her daughter escaped, but Janet, perhaps showing signs of dementia, was tarred and feathered and paraded through Dornoch in a barrel. She was said to have smiled and warmed herself at the fire that was about to consume her.[20]

More cheerily, the first woman in England to be granted a patent was Amye Everard Ball, a widow, whose patent for her medicinal 'Mrs Ball's Tincture of Saffron and Essence of Rose' was registered in 1637. Margaret Cavendish (1623–73), Duchess of

Newcastle upon Tyne, who lived at Bolsover Castle, was a prolific philosopher, poet, scientist, fiction writer and playwright. Labelled 'Mad Madge' by later writers for eccentricities such as swearing and a colourful dress sense, she also published works such as *Observations upon Experimental Philosophy*, a critique of a movement that sought to promote experimentation and careful observation over speculative theorising. She argued that artificial instruments 'delude' us and that people could gain a better understanding of the natural world by using their senses combined with reason.[21]

Margaret Hughes is credited by many as the first professional actress to play a female role on the English stage when she played Desdemona in Shakespeare's *Othello* on 8 December 1660 in a production by the King's Company. Previously, male actors had played female roles. Aphra Behn (c.1640–89), Canterbury-born playwright, poet and prose writer, was one of the first English women to earn her living by writing. She also spied in Antwerp for Charles II under the name Astrea, which became her literary pseudonym. Her best-known works are *Oroonoko: or, the Royal Slave*, sometimes described as an early novel, and the play *The Rover*. A periodical published in London by the Athenian Society in 1693, *The Ladies' Mercury*, was probably the world's first women's magazine, although its publisher was a man, John Dunton. It promised to answer readers' queries about love and relationships with 'the zeal and softness becoming to the sex' but lasted just four issues.[22]

The poet Elizabeth Melville, Lady Culross (c.1578–c.1640), became the earliest-known Scottish female writer to see her work in print, when Edinburgh publisher Robert Charteris issued *Ane Godlie Dreame*, a Calvinist dream-vision poem, in 1603. Other prominent women included Mary Erskine (1629–1707), a successful businesswoman in Edinburgh. Born in Clackmannanshire, she married twice and, after her first husband died, became a shopkeeper. She later became a private banker, lending money to businessmen and other widows to encourage them into business. In 1694, she established an institution for educating orphaned and impoverished Edinburgh girls, which later became Mary Erskine School.[23]

Outside the elite, women played a big role in Scotland's fishing industry. Fishwives gutted and cured catches, worked in open-air markets and carried creels to hawk around the countryside. In communities such as the Outer Hebrides, most weavers were women. The gender imbalance in textiles continued through the Industrial Revolution: in nineteenth-century Dundee, women outnumbered men by more than two to one, leading to the city being nicknamed 'she town'. It was similar in other textile-dominated parts of the Isles. Cotton's explosive growth meant that more than one-third of Lancashire's population was employed in the industry by 1811, though women earned much less than men.[24]

In England, Mary Wollstonecraft (1759–97), writer and philosopher, was a passionate advocate of women's rights. In *A Vindication of the Rights of Woman*, she argued that women were not naturally inferior to men but needed better education. The novels of Jane Austen (1775–1817) offer an enduring critique of women's place in the English landed gentry. Social reformer Elizabeth Fry (1780–1845) was a driving force behind legislation to improve treatment of prisoners, especially female inmates. Anne Lister (1791–1840) from Halifax left diaries that led to her being dubbed 'the first modern lesbian'. Palaeontologist Mary Anning (1799–1847) became known internationally for her discovery of Jurassic fossils at Lyme Regis in Dorset.

North of the border, Màiri NicLeòid, or Mary MacLeod (c.1615–c.1707), was a seventeenth-century Gaelic poet and composer. She was exiled from Dunvegan in Skye to the Isle of Scarba, allegedly because she wrote a song that praised one of the MacLeod chiefs' relatives too highly. Jedburgh-born scientist Mary Somerville (1780–1872) studied subjects such as mathematics, astronomy, botany and geology; her works brought together many scientific disciplines. Isobel Gunn (1781–1861) from Orkney joined the Hudson's Bay Company in Canada. As only men could work for the company, she disguised her identity, assumed her father's name 'John Fubbister' and became a labourer; she was the first European woman to reach western Canada.[25]

Colourful characters in Ireland included Margaret Leeson (1727–97), also known as Peg Plunkett, a witty and beautiful brothel keeper amid the hedonism of Georgian Dublin. When her house was vandalised by a gang of wealthy ne'er-do-wells known as the Pinking Dindies, she won damages in court from the gang leader. Dr James Barry (1789–1865), born in Cork as Margaret Ann Bulkley, lived as a man in order to be accepted as a university student and eventually held the second-highest medical office in the British Army.[26]

Welsh-born Hester Lynch Piozzi (1741–1821), from the Salusbury family of Anglo-Welsh landowners, published eight books including *Retrospection*, the first history of the world by a British woman. She became Hester Thrale by marrying a London brewer and became friends with Dr Samuel Johnson. However, they fell out when she married her second husband, Gabriele Mario Piozzi, an Italian music teacher Dr Johnson felt was below Hester's social status.[27]

The Victorian era saw several remarkable women, not least the queen. Florence Nightingale (1820–1910) was the founder of modern nursing, organising care for injured soldiers in the Crimean War. Others in Crimea included Kingston-born Mary Seacole (1805–81), daughter of a Scottish soldier and Jamaican mother. Her offers to serve as an army nurse in Crimea were refused, which she attributed to racial prejudice, so she set up the British Hotel to sell food, supplies and medicines to troops. She also visited the battlefield to nurse the wounded. Welsh nurse Betsi Cadwaladr (1789–1860) went to Crimea aged 65 but clashed frequently with Nightingale. She moved closer to the frontline, where her fight with bureaucracy to ensure supplies got through finally won Nightingale's approval. Mary Clare Moore (1814–74), an Irish Sister of Mercy, also nursed in Crimea. She and Nightingale became lifelong friends.[28]

English reformers included Northumberland-born Josephine Butler (1828–1906), who did much to end coverture (whereby woman's legal rights were subsumed by her husband's) and criminalise child prostitution and human trafficking. Elizabeth Garrett Anderson (1836–1917) was the first woman to qualify in Britain as a physician and surgeon. Mathematician Ada Lovelace (1815–52) has been described as the first computer programmer, having created a program for Charles Babbage's prototype digital computer. Among writers, Charlotte Brontë (1816–55) and her sisters Emily (1818–48) and Anne (1820–49) shaped the world's view of northern England. Mary Ann Evans, writing as George Eliot (1819–80), wrote novels celebrated for realism and psychological insight. Bermuda-born Mary Prince (1788–after 1833), sold as a slave multiple times, dictated her life story while living in London, published as *The History of Mary Prince* in 1831, the first autobiography of a black enslaved woman published in the UK. Millicent Garrett Fawcett (1847–1929), born in Suffolk, co-founded Newnham College, Cambridge and led Britain's largest women's rights association, the National Union of Women's Suffrage Societies. Social campaigner Annie Besant (1847–1933) embraced causes such as the London matchgirls' strike for better conditions in 1888. She supported both Irish and Indian self-rule and became the first female president of the Indian National Congress in 1917.[29]

In Scotland, Eliza Wigham (1820–99), a Quaker, campaigned against slavery, helped to establish the Edinburgh chapter of the National Society of Women's Suffrage and campaigned against laws permitting forced medical examinations on women suspected of prostitution. Skye-born Gaelic poet and songwriter Màiri Mhòr nan Òran (Mary MacPherson, 1821–98), known as Great Mary of the Songs, fought for land reform and the rights of crofters who were being evicted. Dublin-born Phoebe Anna Traquair (1852–1936) was one of the first women artists in Scotland to achieve professional recognition. She contributed to the Arts and Crafts movement in disciplines including embroidery, manuscript illumination, enamelwork, furniture decorations, murals, watercolours and easel paintings. Dundee-born astronomer Williamina Fleming (1857–1911) pioneered a designation system for stars and catalogued thousands of them. After she and her husband emigrated to Boston when she was 21, he abandoned her and their young son, and she worked as a maid in the home of Professor Edward Charles Pickering, director of Harvard College Observatory. On his wife's recommendation, Pickering gave Williamina a role at the observatory.[30]

Opera singer Catherine Hayes (c.1818–61) was an Irish soprano who performed across the world. Her voice was said to be more than two octaves in range. She married her manager, but he died the following year from consumption, while she herself died of a stroke at 42. Wexford-born Lady Jane Wilde (1821–96), less famous than her middle son Oscar later became, was a linguist, poet, women's rights activist and nationalist. She faced poverty after her husband died; when she herself was dying from bronchitis, she was refused permission to visit Oscar in Reading Gaol, where he had been imprisoned for gross indecency. Astronomer Agnes Clerke (1842–1907), born in Skibbereen, developed an early interest in stars by looking through her father's telescope. Her book *A Popular History of Astronomy during the Nineteenth Century* remains a classic. In 1981, NASA named a crater on the moon, close to where *Apollo 12* landed, in her honour. Nellie Cashman from County Cork (1845–1925), who migrated to America as a child during the Great Famine, became a fearless prospector in Canada's Yukon during the Klondike gold rush. She once rescued dozens of miners in a snowstorm. Lady Augusta Gregory (1852–1932), Anglo-Irish dramatist and folklorist, was a catalyst for Ireland's 'Celtic Revival' at the end of the century and co-founded Dublin's Abbey Theatre.[31]

Lady Charlotte Guest (1812–95), an English aristocratic linguist from Lincolnshire, married Welsh ironmaster John Guest, owner of Dowlais ironworks in south Wales. Apart from having 10 children and running the business after her husband died, she is best known for translating the 11 medieval tales of the *Mabinogion*, a cornerstone of Welsh culture, from Middle Welsh into English. Oxfordshire-born Rose Crawshay (1828–1907), another Englishwoman who married a Welsh ironmaster – Robert Thompson Crawshay of Cyfarthfa works at Merthyr – was less keen on Welsh culture but became a suffragist, philanthropist and one of Britain's first women to sit on a school board. Emmeline Lewis Lloyd (1827–1913) from Powys was one of the first women to climb in the Alps. Sarah Jane Rees (1839–1916) was a teacher, poet, editor, master mariner and temperance campaigner in Cardiganshire. She taught navigation, became the first female editor of a woman's magazine in Wales and had two same-sex relationships. Frances Hoggan (1843–1927) from Brecon was the first British woman to qualify as a medical doctor and a leading figure in the campaign to improve girls' education. Bristol-born Millicent Mackenzie (1863–1942) became professor of women's education at the University College of South Wales, making her Wales's first female professor. In 1918, she stood for Labour as the only female parliamentary candidate in Wales; she also became a leading promoter of Steiner-Waldorf educational methods.[32]

In 1903, Manchester's Emmeline Pankhurst (1858–1928), frustrated by the failure of suffrage bills, formed the Women's Social and Political Union, dedicated to 'deeds, not words'. A *Daily Mail* journalist first used the diminutive term 'suffragette', which the movement seized as its own. At first, it indulged in peaceful activities such as rallies, but before long members started smashing windows and assaulting police officers. Pankhurst, her daughters and other activists received repeated prison sentences and staged hunger strikes to secure better conditions, which led to them being force-fed. The first hunger strike was by Marion Wallace Dunlop (1864–1942), a talented artist born at Leys Castle near Inverness, as a protest when refused political prisoner status. She had been arrested for damaging a wall in the Houses of Parliament.[33]

Flora Drummond (1878–1949), born in Manchester but raised on Arran, became known as 'The General' to fellow suffragettes for marshalling demonstrations in London and Edinburgh while wearing a military-style uniform. In her youth, she was angered when, after qualifying as a postmistress, she was unable to follow that career because of new regulations that raised the height standard to 5 feet 2 inches, an inch above her height. She became known for daring protests, bursting into 10 Downing Street, finding subterranean entrances to parliament and dancing a highland fling outside Holloway prison. She once hired a motor launch on the Thames opposite the terrace of the House of Commons to harangue members taking afternoon tea.[34]

Margaret Haig Thomas, Viscountess Rhondda (1883–1958), was a businesswoman from a wealthy industrial family and also Wales's most famous suffragette. She attended London demonstrations and even jumped on to the running board of Prime Minister Herbert Asquith's car in St Andrews. She was briefly imprisoned and went on hunger strike after setting a post box alight in Newport. When the First World War broke out, Emmeline Pankhurst halted militant action and supported the war effort. Lady Rhondda ensured women played a vital role, rising to become chief controller of women's recruitment at the Ministry of National Service in London. She even survived the sinking of the *Lusitania* when it was torpedoed. When her father died, she inherited coal-mining, shipping, newspapers and other businesses. She sat on the boards of 33 companies, chairing seven of them, and was elected the first female president of the Institute of Directors.[35]

In Ireland, many nationalist women participated in the 1916 Easter Rising and the War of Independence. Voting rights activist Hanna Sheehy Skeffington (1877–1946) described the Rising as 'the only instance I know of in history when men fighting for freedom voluntarily included women'. Constance Markievicz (1868–1927) became the first-ever female MP elected to Britain's House of Commons in 1918 but refused to take her seat because of Sinn Féin's abstentionist policy. She became a senior minister in the Dáil or parliament after Ireland became independent in 1922.

Other nationalists included businesswoman Jennie Wyse Power (1858–1941), Dr Kathleen Lynn (1874–1955), aristocrat Mary Spring Rice (1880–1924), teacher Margaret Skinnider (1893–1971), trade unionist Rosie Hackett (1892–1976) and actor and editor Helena Molony (1883–1967). But while the first Irish Free State government supported women's rights, a 1937 constitution under Taoiseach Éamon de Valera enshrined the Catholic Church's conservative social teachings. Contraception and divorce were banned, and women were told to stay at home.[36]

In the early twentieth century, Elsie Inglis (1864–1917), Scottish doctor and suffragist, created a maternity hospital for the poor in Edinburgh. After suggesting female doctors and nurses should be sent to the front during the First World War, Inglis was told by the War Office: 'My good lady, go home and sit still.' Undeterred, she formed the Scottish Women's Hospitals – all-female units that provided support for Britain's allies. Edinburgh-born Marie Stopes (1880–1958) was a birth control pioneer. In 1921, she and her husband founded Britain's first birth-control clinic in London, free and open to all married women to learn about birth-control methods and reproductive health, and later created a regional network. Perthshire-born Victoria Drummond (1894–1978), god-daughter to Queen Victoria, became the UK's first female marine engineer. She was awarded an MBE for bravery at sea during the Second World War when she kept the engines of the SS *Bonita* running under German bombardment.[37]

Virginia Woolf (1882–1941), from South Kensington, London, was an important modernist author who pioneered use of the stream of consciousness. Her best-known works include novels *Mrs Dalloway*, *To the Lighthouse* and *Orlando*. Agatha Christie (1890–1976) was dubbed 'queen of crime' during the golden age of detective fiction. She started writing as a nurse during the First World War, inspired by refugees she saw in Torquay. Her first novel, *The Mysterious Affair at Styles*, introduced Hercule Poirot, a retired Belgian police officer, clever, meticulous and self-important. She remains the best-selling novelist ever, known for 66 detective novels and 14 short story collections as well as the world's longest-running play, *The Mousetrap*. Her books have sold more than a billion copies in English and a billion in translation.[38]

American-born Nancy Astor (1879–1964) was the first woman to take up a seat in the Commons, serving from 1919 to 1945. She was elected as a Unionist candidate in a by-election at Plymouth Sutton in 1919, caused by her husband becoming a peer. She was an advocate for temperance, welfare, education reform and women's rights but has been criticised as antisemitic, anti-Catholic and a Nazi sympathiser. Megan Lloyd George (1902–66), daughter of Prime Minister David Lloyd George, became Wales's first female MP as Liberal member for Anglesey in 1929. She campaigned for a Welsh parliament and a secretary of state. She also served as the Liberals' deputy leader before later becoming a Labour MP. Katharine (Kitty) Stewart-Murray (1874–1960), Duchess of Atholl and Unionist Party politician, became Scotland's first female MP in 1923 as member for Kinross and West Perthshire. In the 1930s, she helped to rescue thousands of child refugees fleeing General Franco's forces in Spain. She resigned her seat in 1938 in opposition to Neville Chamberlain's policy of appeasing Adolf Hitler.[39]

Hull-born Amy Johnson (1903–41) was the first woman to fly solo from England to Australia and went on to break many long-distance records. On 5 May 1930, setting off from Croydon in a second-hand de Havilland Gipsy Moth, Johnson was virtually unknown. Arriving at Port Darwin 19 days later, she was hailed as an international celebrity. At least 10 songs were written about her – the most famous, 'Amy, Wonderful Amy', was performed by Jack Hylton. She flew in the Second World War for the Air Transport Auxiliary but disappeared during a flight; she is believed to have died in the Thames Estuary, though her body has never been found.

Women in the Second World War include Violette Szabo (1921–45), a British-French woman who was working in the perfume department of Bon Marché in Brixton when the war began. She joined the Special Operations Executive after her husband died in action and was sent twice into occupied France. She was captured by the Germans and executed at Ravensbrück concentration camp. She was posthumously awarded the George Cross, the highest civilian decoration for gallantry. Noor Inayat Khan (1914–44), a British woman of Indian descent, was sent as a wireless operator to aid the French resistance. She was betrayed, captured and then executed at Dachau concentration camp. She also received a posthumous George Cross.[40]

After the war, chemist Rosalind Franklin (1920–58) in London conducted ground-breaking work on the X-ray diffraction images of deoxyribonucleic acid (DNA), a constituent of chromosomes that serves to encode genetic information. One of her students' photographs led to the discovery of the DNA double helix, a discovery that enabled three others – Francis Crick, James Watson and Maurice Wilkins – to share a Nobel prize in 1962. Franklin died of ovarian cancer at 37, and her contribution for a long time went unrecognised. Another English chemist, Dorothy Hodgkin (1910–94), won the 1964 Nobel Prize for Chemistry for work determining the structure of penicillin and vitamin B12 – the only British woman to be awarded a Nobel Prize for science.[41]

Queen Elizabeth II (1926–2022) came to the throne in 1952 when her father George VI died. Her reign was the longest of any British monarch, and she was noted for a strong sense of duty. While her family faced challenges, particularly after the breakdown of her children's marriages and the death in 1997 of former daughter-in-law Diana, support for the monarchy and her personal popularity remained high. Manchester-born Ellen Wilkinson (1891–1947), minister of education in the post-war Labour government, was nicknamed 'Red Ellen' or the 'Fiery Particle', partly because of her red hair. As Labour MP for Jarrow, she played a big part in the 1936 Jarrow march of the unemployed to London. As education minister, she raised the school-leaving age from 14 to 15 and oversaw the creation of grammar schools and secondary moderns. Labour's Barbara Castle (1910–2002), Blackburn MP, became transport minister, employment secretary and health and social services secretary – and introduced the Equal Pay Act 1970.[42]

Margaret Thatcher (1925–2013), from Grantham, Lincolnshire, was Conservative prime minister from 1979 to 1990, the UK's first female premier and the longest continuously serving PM since Lord Liverpool in 1827. She shifted the centre of British politics to the right, disrupting the post-war consensus. To her delight, Russian media nicknamed her the 'Iron Lady'. Her economic policies became known as 'Thatcherism', a broad term embracing her views and instincts more than a consistent philosophy. She tamed the trade unions and reversed the trend towards nationalisation but failed to curb public spending significantly. When her long-serving foreign secretary, Sir Geoffrey Howe, resigned in 1990 in protest at her attitude to Europe, his resignation speech brought about events that led to her exit.[43]

Mary Robinson (b.1944) was Ireland's first female president, serving as an independent from 1990 to 1997. Afterwards, she became United Nations High Commissioner for Human Rights 1997–2002. Her time as president is seen as a transformative period for Ireland during which homosexuality was decriminalised and contraception and divorce legalised. Veronica Guerin (1959–96) was a journalist for *The Sunday Independent* who became famous for hard-hitting exposés of Dublin's drug culture. She ignored death threats from the city's crime lords, and in 1996 she was shot dead in her car on the outskirts of Dublin by a passenger on a motorcycle.[44]

Scottish novelist Muriel Spark (1918–2006) was born in Edinburgh to a Jewish father and Episcopalian mother. Success came suddenly at age 39 after obscurity and near-poverty as a single mother following the failure of her marriage. Her second novel, *The Prime of Miss Jean Brodie*, published in 1961, was adapted for stage, film and television and assured her financial security. Based around her schooldays, it tells the story of an Edinburgh spinster schoolteacher who devotes her middle years to her 'gerrils', to Mussolini and to having illicit sex. Spark wrote more than 20 novels.[45]

Winnie Ewing (1929–2023), lawyer and politician, won a 1967 by-election at Hamilton that heralded a breakthrough for the Scottish National Party (SNP). She was later member of the European parliament for the Highlands and Islands. She became a founding member of the devolved Scottish parliament in 1999 and, as the oldest MSP, chaired its first session. Nicola Sturgeon, another lawyer, served as Scotland's first minister and SNP leader 2014–23, the first woman to hold either position, taking over from Alex Salmond after Scots rejected independence by 55.3 per cent to 44.7 per cent in a 2014 referendum. A talented communicator, Sturgeon nonetheless struggled to find a path to independence. She and ex-SNP chief executive Peter Murrell announced in January 2025 that they planned to end their marriage. Murrell had been charged the previous year with embezzling SNP funds; Sturgeon was arrested but released without charge in 2023.[46]

In Wales, Esmé Kirby (1910–99) was a conservationist and sheep farmer who formed the Snowdonia National Park Society in 1958 to ensure the mountains would be protected from development. Mary Quant (1930–2023), born in London to parents from Welsh mining families, was the 1960s fashion designer behind hotpants and miniskirts. Betty Campbell (1934–2017), born into a poor household in Cardiff's Butetown, commonly known as Tiger Bay, became Wales's first black head teacher as head of Mount Stuart Primary School. Shirley Bassey, born in Tiger Bay in 1937 to a Nigerian father and English mother, became a singer famed for her powerful voice. In a career spanning more than 70 years, she has sold more than 140 million records. Julia Gillard, born in 1961 in Barry and raised in Adelaide, became Australia's first female prime minister. Tanni Grey-Thompson, born in Cardiff in 1969, is a former wheelchair racer who won 16 Paralympic medals and 13 World Championship medals before becoming a television presenter and life peer.[47]

While many women from around the Isles have reached meta-phorically for the stars, one has done so literally. Helen Sharman, born in Sheffield in 1963, was a research chemist at a confectionery company when she was chosen as the first British citizen to go into space, on a mission to the Soviet space station Mir in 1991. She has said: 'We should push forward not only our own individual boundaries, but also the boundaries of what humans believe is possible.'[48]

CHAPTER 12

SMALL ISLANDS

The Isles' story is one of small as well as large. The archipelago contains not only Ireland and Britain but also islands or groups such as the Isle of Man, the Inner and Outer Hebrides, the Northern Isles of Orkney and Shetland and more than 6,000 smaller islands. The bailiwicks of Jersey and Guernsey, off France's north coast, are usually considered part of the Isles, even though geographically they are outside the archipelago. The Isle of Man, Jersey and Guernsey are classed by the UK government as Crown Dependencies (a term criticised by some on the islands), meaning that they are self-governing, while the UK government is responsible for their defence and represents them abroad. These three have sought modern-day salvation as offshore finance centres because island economies can be precarious.

Hunter-gatherers in the Middle Stone Age (8000–4000 BCE) were the first to leave traces on the Isle of Man, which became an island when melting glaciers caused sea levels to rise. Large-scale immigration from Ireland began in the fifth century CE when missionaries established Celtic Christianity and the Manx language emerged. Saint Maughold, a legendary saint, was said to have been converted to Christianity by St Patrick after being a bloodthirsty robber. He was sent to Man in a rudderless, oarless coracle and there led an austere life and was chosen as bishop for his holiness. After a period of Northumbrian control from the seventh century, Vikings arrived at the end of the eighth, first to plunder and then to settle.

The island became a staging post connecting Viking outposts of Dublin, north-west England and the Hebrides. The Isle of Man was nominally under Norwegian kings' sovereignty until ceded to Alexander III of Scotland in the 1266 Treaty of Perth, in which Scotland acknowledged Norwegian sovereignty over Shetland and Orkney, while Norway recognised Scottish sovereignty over Man and the Hebrides.[1]

England's Edward I seized the Isle of Man in 1290. After that came a few decades of alternating Scottish and English rule before the struggle was decided in England's favour. A more settled period began in 1405 when Henry IV granted the title Lord of Man to Sir John Stanley of Lancashire, with fees and homage promised to the English crown. Successive generations of the Stanley family governed, aside from a brief interregnum in the Wars of the Three Kingdoms, until the title was revested in the British crown in 1765; today it is used by Charles III. The island became a centre for smuggling, which Britain tried to control through the Smuggling Act 1765, giving customs and excise officials the authority to search vessels. For a while, it was also a haven for debtors, who could not be reached by off-island creditors.[2]

The island's first general election took place in April 1867. Previously, the House of Keys, the lower house of Tynwald, the ancient parliament, had been self-elected; when a vacancy arose, the Keys nominated two persons to the lieutenant governor, who decided whom to appoint. After a campaign, the UK authorities agreed to give the vote to men who owned property worth at least 8 pounds, or tenants paying annual rent of at least 12 pounds, and also to allow Tynwald some say over finance. In 1881, the franchise was extended to property-owning widows and spinsters – making it the first place in the world where women could vote in a national election – and in 1919 to all adults. Tourism grew in the Victorian era, initially attracting wealthier British families through Isle of Man Steam Packet Company sailings between Douglas and Liverpool. The Edwardian era brought mass tourism by Lancashire cotton workers enjoying Wakes Week holidays. The annual Isle of Man Tourist Trophy motorcycle races, often called one of the world's most dangerous racing events, began in 1907.[3]

During the world wars, camps were created for internees from enemy countries living in Britain. When Éamon de Valera, the Republic of Ireland's taoiseach, visited the island in 1947 he was so dissatisfied with lack of support for the Manx language that he had two recording vans sent over to capture it before native speakers died. A greater appreciation of indigenous Manx culture has grown from the 1990s, including the opening of the first Manx-language primary school. Tourism declined in the late twentieth century as the British and Irish started flying to Spain for package holidays. The Manx government responded by promoting the island, with its low tax rates, as an offshore financial centre. Leading sectors include insurance, online gambling, information and communications technology and offshore banking. Critics point to potential tax evasion, but the island has avoided being placed on tax haven blacklists by the OECD and the European Union and insists it complies with international standards on tax transparency and co-operation.[4]

Notable Manx-born people include William Christian or Illiam Dhone ('Brown William'), who led a 1651 rebellion against inheritance and tenancy laws during England's civil wars. Naturalist Edward Forbes (1815–54) proposed a mechanism to explain distributions of species on now-isolated islands and mountain tops, for which he was credited by Charles Darwin. Barry, Maurice and Robin Gibb of the Bee Gees pop group were born on the island, as was cyclist Mark Cavendish, one of the greatest road sprinters, along with photographer Chris Killip, known for black-and-white images especially of north-east England, and American attorney and psychologist Elizabeth Holloway Marston, credited as an inspiration for her husband's comic book creation Wonder Woman. Science fiction screenwriter Nigel Kneale (1922–2006), best known for creating the character Professor Bernard Quatermass, was raised on the island. Those who moved to the Isle of Man include Florrie

Forde (1875–1940), an Australian vaudeville performer known as 'The Queen of Music Hall'; comedian Norman Wisdom (1915–2010); and actress Mollie Sugden (1922–2019). Arrivals in recent times include keyboard player Rick Wakeman and north-west property mogul John Whittaker.

The Channel Islands comprise the Bailiwick of Jersey, the largest island, and the Bailiwick of Guernsey, consisting of Guernsey, Alderney, Sark, Herm and some smaller islands. Historically, these are remnants of the Duchy of Normandy. As with the Isle of Man, the UK is responsible for their defence and represents them internationally. They have been administered separately since the late thirteenth century and each has its own laws, elections and representative bodies, although the islands' leaders keep in regular contact. There is friendly banter between the islands. Jersey folk are nicknamed *crapauds* (toads, of which the island has a unique species), while Guernsey people are *ânes* (donkeys, denoting either strength of character or stubbornness), those from Sark are *corbins* (crows) and those from Alderney *lapins* (rabbits).

The earliest evidence of human occupation of the Channel Islands – at La Cotte (cave), St Brelade, Jersey – has been dated at up to 250,000 years ago. As well as animal bones found there, 13 Neanderthal teeth were discovered in 1910. Rising sea levels after the last Ice Age detached the islands from continental Europe's landmass around 6000–7000 BCE. Roman officials and traders are likely to have visited the islands, which they called *Insulae Lenuri*, though evidence of settlement is sparse. Christian missionaries visited in the sixth century, including saints such as Helier, from today's Belgium, after whom Jersey's capital St Helier is named; and Welsh-born Samson, Guernsey's patron saint. Vikings began raiding in the ninth century and then settled; many place names are of Norse origin, including, it is believed, the islands' modern names.[5]

William I 'Longsword', ruler of Normandy, seized the islands and made them part of the duchy in 933. Normandy's dukes also became kings of England, starting with William the Conqueror in 1066.

King John in the thirteenth century lost Normandy but held on to the Channel Islands; the bailiwicks were governed separately and never absorbed into England, with no attempt made to introduce English laws or customs. French forces invaded the islands several times during the Hundred Years' War, but the English retook them. The French again occupied Jersey in 1461 during the Wars of the Roses and held it for seven years before being expelled. After the loss of Calais in 1558, the Channel Islands were the English crown's last remaining holdings in France.[6]

During the Wars of the Three Kingdoms, Jersey was royalist, reflecting the loyalties of the influential de Carteret family, and provided refuge for Charles, Prince of Wales – though it was eventually captured by parliamentarian forces. Guernsey mostly favoured parliament. When Charles became King Charles II at the Restoration, he gave Sir George Carteret, Jersey's bailiff and governor, a large grant of land in the American colonies, which he named New Jersey, now a US state. In 1781, there was another failed French invasion during the American War of Independence.[7]

The nineteenth century saw a growth in tourism as transport links improved, leading to the immigration of thousands of English residents and a cultural shift towards a more anglicised culture, with the English language gaining ground at the expense of traditional Jèrriais and Guernésiais, varieties of the Norman language. Victor Hugo, French Romantic novelist, fled to exile in Jersey after Louis-Napoléon Bonaparte seized dictatorial powers in 1851 but was expelled for supporting *L'Homme*, a newspaper run by French refugees in Jersey that had published an open letter to Queen Victoria by republicans, which was deemed treasonous. He finally settled with his family in St Peter Port, Guernsey's capital, where he lived from 1855 to 1870. Jersey's agriculture, meanwhile, received a boost when a farmer, Hugh de la Haye, cut up two huge potatoes and planted the pieces, which produced an early crop of kidney-shaped potatoes, unlike the round parent potato. At first, these were named Royal Jersey Flukes, later shortened to Jersey Royals. In

1891, 70,000 tons were exported, bringing the growers nearly half a million pounds.[8]

When the Second World War began, the British government decided not to defend the Channel Islands, ironic in view of past efforts to hold on to the British monarchy's oldest offshore possession. Tens of thousands chose to evacuate, including those who signed up with British forces. German occupation began at the start of July 1940. Telephone connections with Britain were severed, wireless sets confiscated, checkpoints created, meetings of societies banned and a range of restrictions introduced. It was to be a traumatic experience, with residents' reactions ranging from sullen defiance to varying degrees of collaboration.[9]

Hitler ordered the islands to be fortified with artillery and anti-aircraft batteries, land mines and underground ammunition stores. Concrete towers encircled the islands and are still in evidence. He called for non-native islanders to be deported and interned: more than 2,000 were shipped to France and Germany. Anti-Jewish orders were issued, though most Jews had left the island before the invasion. Three Jewish women who remained on Guernsey – Therese Steiner, an Austrian nanny; Auguste Spitz, an Austrian cook; and Marianne Grünfeld, a Polish farm worker – had fled central Europe in the 1930s. In 1942, they were deported to France and later sent to Auschwitz, where they were killed or died. Thousands of forced workers, male and female, were brought in from eastern Europe. They were horribly mistreated, and many died in the work camps. Any islanders who helped them faced punishment. Louisa Gould, a grocer from St Ouen, Jersey, sheltered an escaped Russian worker for nearly a year in 1943. When a neighbour betrayed her, she was arrested by the Gestapo and interned in France. She was later transferred to Ravensbrück concentration camp near Berlin and died in a gas chamber there in 1945.[10]

As the war ground on, tensions increased. Young women thought too friendly with German soldiers were derided as 'Jerry bags'. Some people were tempted to co-operate with the Germans by betraying those who infringed regulations. When allied forces landed in Normandy on D-Day in June 1944, islanders became excited, relishing the thought of liberation, but it did not arrive. The Channel Islands were left for almost a year as troops fought their way to Berlin. The population came close to starvation as German supply lines were disrupted by the allied presence in France. Eventually, the Red Cross managed to send a vessel with canned food and other supplies.

The occupation finally ended after Victory in Europe Day on 8 May 1945, with Jersey and Guernsey liberated on 9 May and Alderney on 16 May. Emotions were mixed. Farewells were waved to those Germans whose considerate acts were remembered. There were reprisals, however, against women who had fraternised with German soldiers. One such was Alexandrine Baudains, nicknamed 'Ginger Lou', who had flaunted her favoured status as the girlfriend of a high-ranking German officer; she was attacked by a crowd of angry women and saved by British soldiers from being lynched. Islanders have generally been unwilling to dredge up the past for outsiders to criticise. Along with evacuees, traumatised soldiers and prisoners-of-war returned, yet in many cases they felt alienated from those who had not fought. One perverse outcome of the occupation was that it increased anglicisation because evacuated island children had had an English education in Britain.

Since the war, the islands' ancient legislatures have been reformed to be more democratic. Jersey adopted free, universal secondary education and a social security system. Tourism increased. A subsequent decline in the profitability of agriculture and tourism has been more than offset by the development of Jersey and Guernsey as offshore finance centres, accounting for almost 40 per cent of economic output. Low, stable income tax rates, coupled with a lack of capital gains, estate or inheritance duties attracted wealthy British tax exiles, while a tax-free interest policy on funds deposited in island banks brought in money from non-residents too. After Thatcher's government lifted exchange controls in 1979, the banks were joined on the islands by accountancy businesses, insurance and reinsurance companies, investment funds and fiduciaries handling trusts and company management. As with the Isle of Man, the islands have been accused of encouraging tax evasion and money-laundering, though they have largely avoided inclusion on international black-lists by pledging to share information with other countries' tax authorities. A particular bugbear was what media dubbed the 'Sark lark', in which light regulation encouraged a boom in offshore company registrations, with local residents paid to be nominee stockholders and directors. Regulations were tightened, though critics said some problems persisted.[11]

Jersey-born people include socialite and actress Lily Langtry (1853–1929), 'Jersey Lily', who had affairs with men including the future king Edward VII and Prince Louis of Battenberg. Also born there were artist Edmund Blampied (1886–1966), journalist and feminist Rosie, Baroness Boycott (b.1951) and England footballer Graeme Le Saux (b.1968). Painter Sir John Everett Millais (1829–96) was born in Southampton to a Jersey-based family. Comedian Will Smith (b.1971) grew up on the island. Among incomers, Sir Walter Raleigh, Elizabethan statesman and explorer, was governor of Jersey 1600–3; Billy Butlin, founder of the holiday camp empire, moved to Jersey in 1972; Gerald Durrell, naturalist and author, founded Jersey Zoological Park. Others included television presenter Alan Whicker; industrialist and Blackburn Rovers owner Jack Walker; racing driver Nigel Mansell; Irish singer-songwriter Gilbert O'Sullivan; Simon Nixon, founder of Moneysupermarket.com; and retailer Sir Philip Green.

Guernsey-born people include printer Thomas de la Rue (1793–1866), known as the father of the English playing card; actor Roy Dotrice (1923–2017); radio presenter Sarah Montague (b.1966); former footballer Matt Le Tissier (b.1968); and tennis player Heather Watson (b.1992). In addition to Victor Hugo, who wrote *Les Misérables* while living on Guernsey, painter Pierre-Auguste Renoir created 15 paintings of the island in 1883. Writer Mervyn

Peake (1911–68) wrote the first two of his Gormenghast novels while living on Sark. Nicholas Monsarrat (1910–79), author of *The Cruel Sea*, lived on Guernsey for a time; 'hell-raising' actor Oliver Reed (1938–99) spent more than 20 years there. Actress Julie Andrews (b.1935) had a house on Alderney; Elisabeth Beresford (1926–2010), creator of fictional furry creatures the Wombles, also lived on the island. David and Frederick Barclay, media and property tycoons, built a mock-Gothic castle on Brecqhou, off Sark, and fought several legal disputes with the Sark government. Mary and Doug Perkins established Specsavers, the retail optometry chain, in Guernsey in 1984.

Other populated islands located in the English Channel and close to the coast of Britain, such as the Isle of Wight, are not regarded as 'Channel Islands'. The Isle of Wight was home to poets Algernon Charles Swinburne and Alfred, Lord Tennyson; the latter wrote 'The Charge of the Light Brigade' there. Queen Victoria loved the island so much that she built her summer residence and final home, Osborne House, at East Cowes. In modern times, indie rock band Wet Leg were formed on the island (the phrase is said to be Isle of Wight slang for non-locals, though there are differing versions of why the band chose the name). Just off the tip of Cornwall lie the Isles of Scilly, whose unforgiving rocks have sent countless vessels to a watery grave. During England's civil wars, parliamentarians captured the Scilly isles, only to see their garrison mutiny and return them to the royalists; parliament later recaptured them. The Scilly isles were briefly famous in the 1960s and 1970s when Labour prime minister Harold Wilson and his wife Mary had a holiday home there. In 1973, he was rescued from drowning by passers-by after falling into the sea.

The Northern Isles of Orkney and Shetland lie more than 650 miles north of the Channel Islands. Shetland is so far north that on most maps it is dragged ignominiously southwards and placed in a box off Scotland. Their climates are cool and temperate, and they have the UK's highest average wind speeds.[12] Orkney has 20 inhabited islands and Shetland 16, the largest in each case being known as the Mainland. Orkney is agriculturally fertile, while rugged Shetland is more dependent on fishing and extracting oil. Both have a developing renewable energy industry. They share a Pictish and Norse history and were part of the kingdom of Norway before being absorbed into Scotland in the fifteenth century.

Orkney is particularly rich in prehistoric remains from the Neolithic period, four of which make up a UNESCO world heritage site designated in 1999: Skara Brae, Europe's most complete Neolithic village; Maeshowe chambered cairn and passage grave; the Standing Stones of Stenness; and the Ring of Brodgar. Skara Brae comprises 10 dwellings with stone furniture such as dressers, bed frames, seats, fireplaces and a primitive sewer system with water closets. By the late Iron Age, the Northern Isles were part of the mysterious kingdom of the Picts, about whom there is abundant debate but limited evidence. Archaeological relics include stones carved with symbols, notably one on the Brough of Birsay, off the north-west coast of Orkney's Mainland, which depicts three warriors in stately robes as well as characteristic Pictish symbols. Orkney's formal conversion to Christianity may have come as late as the early eighth century, less than 100 years before the onset of Viking raids.[13]

The Vikings soon settled and created the earldom of Orkney, ruled by earls (or *jarls*) from the ninth century until 1472; it covered Orkney, Shetland plus Caithness and Sutherland on the Mainland and owed allegiance to Norwegian kings. Medieval documents named Orkney and Shetland as *Nordr-eyjar* or 'Nordreys' (Northern Isles) to distinguish them from the Hebrides and Isle of Man, called *Sudr-eyjar* or 'Sudreys' (Southern Isles). The Vikings brought a different culture, initially pagan and later Christian, and a new language, Norn. Theories for what happened to the Pictish population range from peaceful integration to enslavement and genocide. Orkney's story is told in the *Orkneyinga Saga*, a unique account of British Norse culture by an unknown thirteenth-century Icelandic scribe, though its version of some early events is disputed. Work on

St Magnus Cathedral in Kirkwall, the UK's most northerly cathedral and Scotland's oldest, began in 1137. It was named after Magnus Erlendsson, Earl of Orkney, who had a reputation for piety and gentleness.[14]

Scottish influence grew steadily, and in 1472 Scotland's parliament absorbed the earldom of Orkney into the kingdom of Scotland, after failure to pay a dowry promised to James III by the family of his bride, Margaret of Denmark. During the Wars of the Three Kingdoms, the Marquess of Montrose raised hundreds of Orcadians and Shetlanders to fight for the royalist cause after Charles I's execution in 1649, but the force was routed by Scottish covenanters at Carbisdale, north-east Scotland, in 1650. During the eighteenth-century risings, Orkney was largely Jacobite in sympathy, but not all islanders agreed. After the Jacobites were defeated at Culloden in 1746, an Orkney naval captain, Benjamin Moodie, went after Orcadian Jacobites and burned several of their homes; apparently, Jacobites had killed his father 20 years earlier.[15]

Ships of Canada's Hudson's Bay Company were in the habit of calling at Stromness in Orkney to recruit a large part of the company's workforce. The company found them 'more sober and tractable than the Irish ... a close, prudent, quiet people, strictly faithful to their employers', although 'sordidly avaricious'.[16] By 1779, more than three-quarters of the company's servants were Orcadians. The nineteenth century brought transport improvements, including regular steamship services, which made it easier to export cattle and sheep. Land enclosure helped cereal output. The 1886 Crofters Act gave some protection from arbitrary eviction, but the landless became paupers or emigrated. Orkney's population fell by a third between 1850 and 1950.[17]

After the end of the First World War in 1918, the German high seas fleet was transferred to Scapa Flow in Orkney to await a decision on its future, but German sailors opened the seacocks and scuttled the ships. Just over a month into the Second World War, a German U-boat sank the Royal Navy battleship *Royal Oak* there.

Population declined significantly in the post-war years, but there has been some economic recovery in recent decades.[18]

Notable Orcadians include author Mary Brunton (1778–1818), whose two novels combined fast-paced plots with moral instruction; John Rae (1813–93), a surgeon who explored parts of northern Canada; William Balfour Baikie (1825–64), explorer and naturalist, remembered for opening navigation of Africa's River Niger; Margaret Manson Graham (1860–1933), nurse and missionary in Nigeria; folklorist Florence Marian McNeill (1885–1973), a founder member of the SNP; artist Stanley Cursiter (1887–1976); Edwin Muir (1887–1959), poet and novelist; George Mackay Brown (1921–96), poet, author and dramatist with a strongly Orcadian flavour; and Anne Brundle (1958–2011), who was curator of archaeology at Tankerness House Museum, later the Orkney Museum, and did much to develop public appreciation of Orkney's archaeology. Others associated with Orkney include Eliza Anne Fraser (c.1798–1858), an Englishwoman who lived with her mariner husband in Orkney, travelled with him to Australia and became famous after being shipwrecked on the Great Barrier Reef; American writer Washington Irving (1783–1859), whose father was Orcadian; Welsh-born Eric Linklater (1899–1974), poet and novelist who spent years in Orkney, where his father was born; Salford-born composer Sir Peter Maxwell Davies (1934–2016), who lived in Orkney for 50 years and founded the St Magnus arts festival; and Fife-born Jo Grimond (1913–93), who was MP for Orkney and Shetland 1950–83 and led the Liberal Party for 11 years.

Shetland is particularly notable for brochs, or distinctive round towers, from the Iron Age, which sheltered animals and humans. Like Orkney, Shetland was part of the obscure Pictish kingdom and then colonised by Vikings before being absorbed into Scotland. The Norse period left a particularly strong legacy. Almost all place names have Norse origin, and the Shetland dialect is infused with Norse influence. The Up Helly Aa (Up Holy Day All) fire festival, held annually from January to March in various Shetland communities, dates back to the nineteenth century and draws inspiration from Viking history.

Shetlanders' maritime skills were sought by Britain's Royal Navy, and press gangs were rife during the Napoleonic wars. During the First World War, thousands of ships sailed from Lerwick, Shetland's capital, as part of an escorted convoy system. During the Second World War, when Norway was occupied by the Nazis, the Special Operations Executive established an operation nicknamed the 'Shetland bus' in which Shetland fishing boats sailed there to land supplies, weapons and saboteurs and to liberate refugees.[19]

In the later twentieth century, the discovery of oil in the North Sea around Shetland gave a huge boost to the islands' economy. Sullom Voe, built in 1978, became Europe's largest oil and gas terminal, and the UK became the European Economic Community's biggest oil producer in the 1970s. For 25 years, it brought Shetland unprecedented prosperity, with reduced unemployment and leaps in public services. Its population rose sharply after decades of decline. The boom has since faded, though oil and gas remain important, while Shetland also has the controversial Viking onshore wind farm. Fishing, agriculture, creative industries and tourism are important sectors.[20]

Among notable Shetlanders, Lerwick-born Arthur Anderson (1792–1868) was co-founder of the Peninsular and Oriental Steam Navigation Company (P&O), having started as a shipping clerk in London after serving in the Napoleonic wars. He used his wealth and global experience to promote liberalisation of the islands' economy, notably through his short-lived newspaper *The Shetland Journal*, and became the first Shetlander to sit as an MP (Liberal), elected for Orkney and Shetland. Betty Mouat (1825–1918), spinner and hand knitter, became famous for surviving nine days alone on a boat that drifted to Norway; May Moar (1825–94), a crofter, was awarded a Royal National Lifeboat Institution silver medal for rescuing fishermen off the island of Yell; Thomas Edmondston (1825–46) became professor of botany at Anderson's University in Glasgow;

Jessie Saxby (1842–1940) was a writer and folklorist; Sir Watson Cheyne (1852–1932), born at sea but raised in Shetland, was a surgeon and bacteriologist who pioneered the use of antiseptic methods; Lerwick nurse Nellie Gilbertson was a sister in the Territorial Force Nursing Service during the First World War; Tom Anderson (1910–91) was a fiddler, composer and collector of traditional tunes; physician Douglas Black (1913–2002) wrote the Black report on health inequalities, published in 1980. Norman Lamont (b.1942), Conservative chancellor of the exchequer 1990–93, was born in Lerwick, where his father was the islands' surgeon; as a child, he was known locally as 'peerie Norrie' (little Norman).

Occupation of the Hebrides or Western Isles, usually divided into Inner and Outer, also dates from the Mesolithic era. They are a large collection of islands, of which about 50 are inhabited; Lewis and Harris, a single island in the Outer Hebrides, is the biggest in area and population. The islands have names of varying etymology reflecting the successive influence of Celtic-, Norse- and English-speaking peoples. Neolithic remains include the standing stones at Calanais on Lewis. The kingdom of Dál Riata was founded in the sixth century CE, broadly including what is now Argyll and Bute and Lochaber in Scotland and County Antrim in Ireland, while the northern Hebrides were a loose Pictish confederation. The foundation of a monastery at Iona by Columba or Colmcille, an aristocrat from what is now Donegal, was important to the spread of Christianity.[21]

Viking raids began in the late eighth century, and the Hebrides came under Norse control. King Edgar of Scotland signed the islands over to Magnus 'Barefoot' Olafsson, king of Norway, in 1098, creating the Kingdom of the Isles after the latter conquered Orkney, the Hebrides and Isle of Man, which had all been held by local Norse chiefs. The Hebrides and Isle of Man were later handed back to Scotland under the 1266 Treaty of Perth. As the Norse era ended, there was strife among Gaelic-speaking clan chiefs, though by the early fourteenth century the MacDonald Lords of the Isles, based on Islay, exerted some control.[22]

After the 1707 Treaty of Union, the Hebrides became part of Great Britain, but loyalties to a distant monarch were not strong. Several clan chiefs backed Jacobite risings, after which the clan system was severely weakened. In the mid-nineteenth century, communities were hit by the clearances, under which people were replaced by sheep farms, exacerbated by the failure of the kelp industry. There was large-scale emigration to places such as Australia and Canada. The 1886 Crofters Act gave crofters security and heritability of tenure. Depopulation continued, however, especially in the Outer Hebrides during the twentieth century, because of poor economic opportunities. After the First World War, Lewis suffered a terrible blow in 1919 with the sinking of the vessel *Iolaire* on New Year's Day within sight of Stornoway's harbour, killing more than 200 naval reservists returning home. Commercial activity is now based on tourism, crofting, fishing and weaving. The northern parts of the Outer Hebrides (Lewis, Harris, North Uist) have historically embraced a distinctively austere form of Presbyterianism, while those of the southern islands (Benbecula, South Uist, Barra) were predominantly Catholic.[23]

Figures from the Outer Hebrides include South Uist-born Flora Macdonald (1722–90), rescuer of Bonnie Prince Charlie. From Lewis, there was Sir Alexander Mackenzie (c.1764–1820), explorer and fur trader who made the first crossing of North America by a European; art collector Louisa Baring, Lady Ashburton (1827–1903); Mary Anne MacLeod Trump (1912–2000), mother of US president Donald Trump; and Donald Stewart (1920–92), SNP MP for the Western Isles 1970–87. Poet and novelist Iain Crichton Smith (1928–98), who wrote in both English and Gaelic, was born in Glasgow but moved to Lewis aged two. From Harris came Gaelic poet Màiri nighean Alasdair Ruaidh (c.1615–c.1707), also known as Mary Macleod, and Angus Matheson (1912–62), inaugural professor of Celtic languages and literature at the University of Glasgow. County Durham-born author Sir Compton Mackenzie (1883–1972) had a house on Barra and wrote *Whisky Galore*, based on an incident in 1941 when the SS *Politician* ran aground on Eriskay with a cargo including 28,000 cases of malt whisky.

In the Inner Hebrides, figures from Skye include explorer Angus McMillan (1810–65), once revered as a pioneer but now known as the 'butcher of Gippsland' in Australia for his massacre of a large group of Gunaikurnai men, women and children; Romantic poet William Ross (1762–c.1790); Gaelic poet and songwriter Màiri Mhòr nan Òran (Mary MacPherson, 1821–98); Alexandrina Matilda MacPhail (1860–1946), a missionary doctor in India; and Anne MacKinnon (1879–1953), a nurse who joined the French Flag Nursing Corps in the First World War and was awarded the Croix de Guerre for bravery. Ulva-born Major General Lachlan Macquarie (1762–1824) became governor of New South Wales and led its transition from penal colony to free settlement. Novelist George Orwell (1903–50) wrote *Nineteen Eighty-Four* while living on Jura in 1947–8 to escape London literary life. Gourock-born illustrator and author Mairi Hedderwick (b.1939) is known for the Katie Morag series of children's books set on the Isle of Struay, a fictional counterpart of Coll, where she has lived at various times.

All these islands, which have seen numerous ups and downs, have played an important part in the archipelago's story.

CHAPTER 13

LEISURE BLOOMS

If there is one place that generations of English comedians grew to fear, it was the Glasgow Empire, notorious during the twentieth century as the 'graveyard of comics', especially English ones. Those who had a hard time included Bob Monkhouse and Tommy Cooper. Des O'Connor was so badly received that he faked fainting and was dragged offstage. Max Miller refused to make a return visit, saying: 'I'm a comic, not a missionary.' Mike and Bernie Winters' act started routinely with Mike onstage playing a lively tune on the clarinet. After a couple of minutes, Bernie's face peeked through the curtains wearing a silly grin. Legend has it that an audience member then shouted: 'Christ, there's two of them!'

It was possible to win audiences over, as Morecambe and Wise gradually did, but it was tough. Locals had usually been drinking in the pub after a hard week's manual labour and had little patience with acts they thought thin or slow. Scottish comedian Janey Godley explained:

I have seen comedians struggle because they let the audience smell the fear. If they get a sniff of that, they will attack like a bunch of straggly, one-legged dogs from Easterhouse. Glasgow audiences are unforgiving but, if you hit them on the funny bone, they will go with you down a hundred routes of madness. They have to trust you first to make them laugh.[1]

164

Comedy was a release from tough conditions. Life for many in the Industrial Revolution was grim, but real incomes rose in the later nineteenth century (by an estimated 80 per cent for Britain as a whole between 1850 and 1900[2]), and people started to get some leisure time. That led to a growth in popular entertainment in the form of music halls, variety theatres, shopping and excursions. There were new parks, libraries and museums. A Saturday half-holiday was introduced, crucial to the rise of football as a professional spectator sport, and a week-long unpaid summer holiday appeared in several towns.

The seaside had become popular among wealthier people in the eighteenth century, with visitors attracted to resorts such as Brighton and Scarborough for the health benefits of sea air and bathing. Visitor numbers grew rapidly in the nineteenth century as the advent of the railway made it easier for working-class people to travel to the coast, while new piers and pleasure gardens made the resorts more attractive. Blackpool became hugely popular not just for northern English families but for many from the midlands and the west of Scotland. Steamboats allowed Glaswegians go 'doon the watter' to Clyde seaside resorts, or they could take the train to explore the southern highlands by day excursion. Resorts developed in Wales including Rhyl, Prestatyn, Colwyn Bay, Tenby, Porthcawl and Mumbles. By 1861, Llandudno was known as 'the Queen of the Welsh Watering Places'.[3] Bray in County Wicklow, south of Dublin, found itself hailed as the 'Brighton of Ireland' because of its popularity with day-trippers. Bundoran in County Donegal became one of Ulster's main resorts.

Entrepreneurs were keen to exploit the new market for leisure. Music halls began as pub music rooms or saloon bars where singers, dancers, comedians and speciality acts performed. One such was the Grecian Saloon, established in 1825 at the Eagle (a former tea-garden) in east London, the subject of a curious English nursery rhyme: 'Up and down the City Road / In and out The Eagle / That's the way the money goes/ Pop goes the weasel.' Music hall theatres soon developed, where people could eat, drink and smoke in the auditorium during a performance (unlike conventional theatres, in which the audience sat in stalls with a separate bar-room).

Music hall was flourishing in most towns and cities by mid-century. Among the most prominent was London's Canterbury Music Hall, based in Lambeth, which opened in 1852. Glasgow had its first pub halls from the early 1850s, such as Shearer's Whitebait Concert Rooms and Davie Brown's Royal Music Hall. Within a decade, larger Glasgow halls were opening, a surviving example being the Britannia (1859) in Trongate. Victoria Hall in Settle, north Yorkshire, is reckoned to be England's oldest surviving music hall, having opened as Settle Music Hall in 1853. Cardiff's first music hall is thought to have been the Coliseum in Bute Street. Swansea's Albert Hall opened in 1864 with a 'Grand Concert' featuring operatic tenor Sims Reeves singing 'Come into the Garden Maud' and 'My Pretty Jane'. In Dublin, Connell's Monster Saloon opened in 1855. Belfast's Alhambra opened in 1872.[4]

Popular stars of the late nineteenth century included singer and comedian Marie Lloyd (Matilda Alice Victoria Wood) from London, famed for performing songs such as 'Don't Dilly Dally on the Way' and 'Oh! Mr Porter'. Dan Leno (George Wild Galvin), billed as 'the funniest man on earth', created a host of mostly working-class characters as he told stories mixed with comic songs. Gateshead-born George Leybourne (Joseph Saunders), who co-wrote and performed songs including 'Champagne Charlie' and 'The Daring Young Man on the Flying Trapeze', played a 'lion comique', a parody of an upper-class toff. Edinburgh-born Arthur Lloyd was a prolific singer-songwriter. Singer and pantomime actress Marie Loftus, born in Glasgow to Irish parents, became a pin-up beauty among young men. Welsh strongwoman Vulcana (Miriam Kate Williams) toured Britain, Europe and Australia. Dublin-born comedian Joe O'Gorman formed a popular duo with Manchester-born Joe Tennyson. The stress of maintaining careers told on many performers. Mark Sheridan, born in Sunderland, became famous for singing 'I Do Like to Be Beside the Seaside'. Thinking that his career was in decline, he shot himself in the head in Glasgow's Kelvingrove Park in 1918.[5]

In Scotland, the sentimental caricature of the 'Bonnie Hieland Laddie' emerged, developed by W.F. Frame, who demonstrated its potential among north American immigrants from Scotland when he took Carnegie Hall in New York by storm in 1898. Sir Harry Lauder took it further, deploying his kilt and cromach (walking stick) as he sang hits such as 'Roamin' in the Gloamin'' and 'I Love a Lassie'. His performances and recordings became hugely popular with audiences across north America, Australasia and South Africa, reputedly making him the world's highest-paid performer and the first Briton to sell a million records. Sir Winston Churchill described him as 'Scotland's greatest ever ambassador'.[6]

Music hall was not without controversy. Religious and moral campaigners objected to lewd performances and accused the halls of encouraging prostitution. In 1894, London's Empire, Leicester Square, was required by London County Council to place a screen to separate the auditorium from the bar – a notorious pick-up place. But the screen was torn down by a group of young bloods, among them Churchill. The temperance lobby exerted considerable influence in northern England, where Manchester's Palace Theatre of Varieties and Sheffield's Empire Palace were denied an alcohol licence. From the 1890s, proprietors themselves began to seek a new, lower-middle-class audience – the sober, industrious clerk or shop assistant and their families. 'Variety theatre' or 'theatre of varieties' was becoming the fashionable term. Content was similar, but tables and chairs were replaced by rows of theatre seats. Entrepreneurs began to build national chains. Edward Moss, born in Droylsden near Manchester but educated in Edinburgh and Glasgow, made his initial fortune in Scotland before joining forces with Richard Thornton from South Shields and later Australian-born Oswald Stoll to create Moss Empires, Britain's largest group. Glasgow's Palace Empire, opened in 1897, was among many designed by prolific theatre architect Frank Matcham for Moss Empires.[7]

Alongside activities such as music hall and variety, retailing expanded in city centres as shopping became popular among the growing middle class. By 1851, more than half of Britain's population lived in towns or cities. Local councils in northern England commissioned covered markets such as Grainger Market in Newcastle, Europe's biggest, and County Arcade in Leeds. Department stores became common on high streets, with Harding, Howell & Co, opened in 1796 on London's Pall Mall, among contenders to have been the first. Bookseller and stationer W.H. Smith, founded in London in 1792 by Henry Walton Smith and his wife Anna, is reckoned to be the world's oldest national retail chain.[8]

Working-class communities meanwhile sometimes managed to create their own entertainment. By the mid-nineteenth century, activities pursued by local people in the Lanarkshire mining town of Wishaw included throwing quoits (which sparked fierce rivalry among teams from different pits, works and communities), pigeon racing and fancying, whippet racing, music-making (which led to the creation of brass, silver and pipe bands) and betting and gambling.[9] Brass bands grew strongly in Britain, notably in small industrial towns and villages in northern England, which also produced amateur orchestras, operatic societies, concertina bands and handbell teams. Wales's choral tradition, especially male voice choirs, arose through industrialisation and the Methodist revival, with hymns popularised by writers such as William Williams. The Temperance Choral Union organised singing festivals, while the Cymanfa Ganu movement of hymn festivals in villages and towns began in 1859 in Aberdare. The Irish took their traditional music around the world as vast numbers emigrated after the Great Famine.

Industrialisation, coupled with rising real wages and increased leisure time, created conditions for the growth of professional spectator sports, notably football. Sheffield FC, founded in 1857, is recognised by FIFA as the world's oldest football club. Professional football developed rapidly from the 1870s, when it became clear that spectators were willing to pay, especially in Lancashire textile towns where family incomes were above average and a Saturday half-holiday was available. The Football Association initially tried to outlaw professionalism but accepted it in 1885. England's Football League was created in 1888. All 12 founder members came from the north and midlands, including six from Lancashire. Preston North End won the first season, going through the 22 league games unbeaten. They also won the FA Cup and became known as the Invincibles.[10]

The origin of golf is often traced to fifteenth-century Scotland, where the first documented mention was a 1457 edict by James II prohibiting the playing of golf and football as these were a distraction from military archery practice. Cricket, rugby, rowing and bowling all gained popularity among Scotland's skilled working class in the 1860s, but none could compete with football's appeal. Teams often began as works sides and then extended to neighbourhoods and communities. Playing football offered a way out of the industrial system; by some estimates, at the peak one in four of all males aged 15 to 29 in central Scotland belonged to a football club. Football also developed a mass spectator following. The first club was Queen's Park in Glasgow, founded in 1867. The Scottish Cup was founded in 1873 and the Scottish Football League in 1890. Rangers, seen as the main Protestant club in Glasgow, was founded in 1872. Celtic was founded by Irish Marist Brother Walfrid in 1887 with the aim of raising money for charity in Glasgow's East End. At first, these two clubs enjoyed a good relationship, but they later became deadly rivals. The first official international football match was played between Scotland and England at Hamilton Crescent, Partick, in 1872; it was a nil–nil draw. That match was watched by 3,500 people, but by 1937 the fixture attracted more than 149,000 at Hampden Stadium.[11]

In Ireland on 1 November 1884, a group of men gathered in the billiards room of the Hayes Hotel in Thurles, County Tipperary, to found the GAA in order to revive and preserve native Irish sports such as hurling and Gaelic football. These remain the most popular sports in the Republic in terms of attendance. In Northern Ireland, association football grew strongly in popularity, though most sports remain organised on an all-Ireland basis, such as rugby union and the Gaelic games of football, hurling, handball and rounders, along with basketball, rugby league, hockey and cricket. In Wales, rugby union is widely seen as central to national identity. Rugby-like games such as *cnapan*, a form of Celtic medieval football, had been played for centuries, but this was eclipsed after 1850, when Reverend Professor Rowland Williams brought rugby union from Cambridge to St David's College, Lampeter, and fielded the first Welsh rugby team. The first club was Neath, formed in 1871, after which came the big four south Wales clubs: Newport, Cardiff, Llanelli and Swansea. The first international match was against England in 1881, in which Wales suffered a crushing defeat, though this did not stop rugby union being adopted as the national sport. Association football also became popular, with Cardiff City and Swansea City among the most successful teams.[12]

The end of the nineteenth century saw a growth in activities by socialist organisations, including swimming clubs, competitive galas, picnics and choirs, from which emerged, for example, Glasgow Orpheus Choir in 1906. The weekly *Clarion*, a popular newspaper launched in Manchester in 1891 by journalist Robert Blatchford, inspired the Clarion movement of social, recreational and political groups such as glee clubs, choirs and rambling and cycling clubs. Stella Davies, a switchboard telephonist, described life in Manchester's Clarion Cycle Club:

> The Clarionets, as we called ourselves, met at appointed places on the outskirts of Manchester … furnished with stacks of leaflets, pamphlets and the Clarion … Arriving at some village in Derbyshire or Cheshire we held an open air meeting trying to catch the people as they came out of church or chapel. We were young and given to buffoonery … we scrawled slogans in chalk on

barns and farmhouse walls ... We sang 'England arise, the long, long night is over' outside pubs and on village greens.[13]

Music hall and variety began to decline in the 1920s with the arrival of cinema, though many twentieth-century stars began their careers on the boards. Gracie Fields made her professional debut at Rochdale Hippodrome in 1910. Stan Laurel, born in Ulverston, Lancashire, gave his first professional performance aged 16 at Glasgow's Panopticon.[14] Charlie Chaplin, born in poverty in London, became one of Hollywood's greatest stars of the silent film era. Dundee-born Will Fyffe, who wrote 'I Belong to Glasgow', was one of Britain's highest-paid music hall stars in the 1930s and appeared in many films, both American and British.

The world's first moving picture was shot in Leeds by Frenchman Louis Le Prince in 1888, and the first moving pictures developed on celluloid film were made in Hyde Park, London, in 1889 by English inventor William Friese Greene. The number of films made in the UK peaked in 1936, though by the mid-1920s Britain was losing out to heavy US competition. London-born filmmaker Alfred Hitchcock is among those who started in the UK but made careers in Hollywood. The earliest-known film footage shot in Ireland, of Dublin's O'Connell Street in 1897, was recorded by a cameraman for French inventors the Lumière brothers. Many Hollywood directors have made films in Ireland, notably Irish-American John Ford, whose best-known Irish movie is *The Quiet Man*, a 1952 Oscar-winning film shot in County Mayo about a retired Irish-American boxer, played by John Wayne, who returns to the town he was born in. The first feature films made in Northern Ireland were in the 1930s, but production was erratic in the following decades and overshadowed by the Troubles from 1969; in later years, there has been a boom in TV and film production, including global hits such as the series Game of Thrones. The first film known to have been made in Wales was by American Birt Acres featuring a royal visit to Cardiff by the Prince of Wales, later Edward VII. The first Wales-based filmmaker of enduring stature was fairground showman William Haggar, who made more than 30 fiction films in 1901–8 and achieved a worldwide audience. Filmmaking in the Isles has often been held back by lack of infrastructure and finance: Ford's 1941 film of Richard Llewellyn's novel *How Green Was My Valley* was notable for starring just one Welsh actor in a significant role, Rhys Williams, and for being shot in the US.[15]

Despite the difficulties, the 1940s are seen as a golden age of British cinema, with critically acclaimed works by filmmakers such as Surrey-born David Lean, Kent-born Michael Powell and London-born Carol Reed. One of British cinema's greatest stars was Edinburgh-born actor Alastair Sim, who made more than 50 films including *Scrooge*, a celebrated adaptation of Charles Dickens's *A Christmas Carol* in 1951. Hollywood stars during the twentieth century included Wales's Richard Burton, Stanley Baker, Anthony Hopkins and Catherine Zeta-Jones; Ireland's Maureen O'Hara, Richard Harris and Maureen O'Sullivan; Northern Ireland's Liam Neeson, Kenneth Branagh and Michelle Fairley; and Scotland's Sean Connery, Ewan McGregor and Kelly Macdonald.

Ballroom dancing rivalled cinema as the most popular pastime from the 1920s and 1930s, with public ballrooms built across the Isles. The waltz had been introduced in the early nineteenth century, followed by dances such as the polka, mazurka and schottische. In the early twentieth century, American ragtime and the Parisian tango fuelled the dancing craze, as did the 1930s films of Fred Astaire and Ginger Rogers. There was a moral panic, particularly about female drunkenness. The *Daily Herald* in 1925 described a move in Glasgow to ban girls under 18 from dance halls as they 'might be subjected to drink and moral temptation'. Dance halls reached their peak in the 1950s with an estimated 200 million visitors per year, when it was thought that up to 70 per cent of couples met there. The craze also invited criminal behaviour. In 1950, two young men from Malahide, near Dublin, were fined for 'disorderly behaviour and for using obscene language outside a dance hall'. In 1953, a young miner in

Wallsend, Tyneside, forced his way into a dance at the Memorial Hall, to which he had been denied access, then brandished an automatic pistol and said: 'If anybody touches my mates, I'll blow their brains out.' By the 1970s, ballroom dancing had largely fallen out of favour, but there has been a resurgence in recent years with popular TV shows *Strictly Come Dancing* and *Dancing with the Stars*.[16]

Britain's first national radio broadcasting service was launched on 14 November 1922 from Marconi House in the Strand, London, by Arthur Burrows, director of programmes at the British Broadcasting Company (BBC), created by manufacturers of wireless sets. He read each bulletin twice, once quickly and once slowly, and asked listeners to say which they preferred. The company was replaced by the publicly owned British Broadcasting Corporation in 1927, funded by a tax on receiving sets. Its first director-general was John Reith, a moralistic Scottish Presbyterian born in Stonehaven who had been the private company's managing director. He established the BBC's aim to 'inform, educate and entertain', to which it still adheres. An imposing figure at 6 feet 6 inches, he had been severely wounded by a sniper's bullet through his left cheek in France in 1915. In his diaries during the 1930s, Reith expressed admiration for Hitler and Benito Mussolini.[17]

Scottish radio broadcasting had begun in 1923, when, after a skirl of bagpipes, Reith announced that '5SC, the Glasgow station of the BBC, is calling.' BBC broadcasting also began from Cardiff that year and from Belfast in 1924. Ireland's first radio bulletins came during the 1916 Easter Rising in Dublin, when rebels issued a declaration of independence from the disused Irish School of Wireless Telegraphy above a jeweller's shop. The British identified the building by its tall aerial, and by the next evening the station was in flames and broadcasts ended. Regular broadcasting began with test transmissions in 1925 by 2RN, the Irish Free State's first radio station, run by the Post Office. Commercial radio was outlawed in Ireland until 1989, leading to a proliferation of pirate stations.[18]

Experimental television broadcasts by the BBC started in 1929 using an electromechanical system developed by John Logie Baird, a

Scottish inventor from Helensburgh. Limited regular broadcasts began in 1932 and an expanded service started from London's Alexandra Palace in 1936, alternating between an improved Baird mechanical system and an all-electronic Marconi–EMI system; Baird's system was dropped early the following year. Television broadcasting was suspended during the Second World War, and the BBC moved most radio operations out of London, initially to Bristol and then to Bedford. Prime Minister Winston Churchill delivered 33 major wartime speeches by radio, all carried by the BBC. The BBC faced competition from 1955 with the creation of the commercial Independent Television network, but the BBC monopoly on radio persisted until 1973, when the first independent local radio station, LBC, came on-air in the London area. BBC Radio Scotland began shortly after, as did Radio Clyde, the first independent station outside London.[19]

Popular BBC radio comedies included: *It's That Man Again* (*ITMA*) (1939–49), starring Liverpudlian Tommy Handley, a fast-talking figure around whom other characters orbited; *The Goon Show* (1951–60), surreal humour with Spike Milligan, Welshman Harry Secombe, Peter Sellers and initially Michael Bentine; *Hancock's Half Hour* (1954–61, radio then television), in which Tony Hancock played a down-at-heel comedian living at 23 Railway Cuttings in East Cheam; and *The Hitchhiker's Guide to the Galaxy*, a comedy science fiction franchise created by Douglas Adams, which began as a radio sitcom 1978–80, then became a TV series in 1981 and a feature film in 2005. *Welsh Rarebit* was a popular radio variety show broadcast from Cardiff by the BBC 1940–52, whose regulars included actress, comedian and singer Maudie Edwards (who also spoke the first lines in TV soap opera *Coronation Street*) and comedians Gladys Morgan and Stan Stennett. Cardiff-born entertainer Tessie O'Shea, who adopted 'Two Ton Tessie from Tennessee' as her theme song, was known for her BBC radio broadcasts.

Popular television programmes included Scottish variety show *The White Heather Club*, with dance musician Jimmy Shand and singer Andy Stewart, which ran on and off from 1958 to 1968. Glasgow-born comedian Stanley Baxter had a successful television series from the 1960s to the 1980s. Gregor Fisher starred as *Rab C. Nesbitt*, an alcoholic Glaswegian, 1988–2014. Also celebrated was drama series *Tutti Frutti* about a Scottish rock-and-roll band, transmitted in 1987 and written by John Byrne. Irish television stars included Dublin-born Dave Allen (David Tynan O'Mahony), best known for observational comedy. Sitcom *Father Ted*, about a group of exiled priests living on an island off Ireland's west coast, ran on Britain's Channel 4 1995–8. *Mrs Brown's Boys*, a sitcom created by and starring Brendan O'Carroll and produced by the BBC and Irish broadcaster Raidió Teilifís Éireann, has been a ratings success despite poor reviews by critics. *Derry Girls*, a teen sitcom set in Northern Ireland and written by Lisa McGhee, was a hit for Channel 4 in 2018–22. In Wales, comedian and singer Max Boyce made several television series. Paul Whitehouse, born in Stanleytown, Glamorgan, was co-creator and star of BBC comedy sketch show *The Fast Show*, which ran 1994–7 with specials in 2000 and 2014. Ruth Jones, born in Bridgend, Glamorgan, co-wrote and co-starred in the BBC sitcom *Gavin & Stacey*.

Commercial pop music arose in the sixteenth and seventeenth centuries with broadside ballads, or songsheets sold cheaply and widely, and developed in the nineteenth century with parlour music, brass bands and the music hall. Dance bands emerged in the 1930s, influenced by American jazz and swing music, with leaders such as London-born Billy Cotton and Jack Hylton from Great Lever in Lancashire. The mid-1950s brought skiffle, influenced by American folk and country blues. Its leading exponent was Lonnie Donegan, born in Glasgow to an Irish mother and Scottish father but raised in East Ham, Essex.

The 1960s saw a surge in beat bands including Liverpool's The Beatles, Gerry and the Pacemakers and The Searchers. The Rolling Stones, rooted in blues and rock and roll, formed in London, where other bands included The Dave Clark Five, The Kinks and The

Who. Popular female singers included London's Dusty Springfield, Liverpool's Cilla Black and Sandie Shaw from Essex. Singers Tom Jones and Shirley Bassey dominated Welsh pop music. Performers from Belfast included rock band Them, who launched the career of singer-songwriter Van Morrison. Irish folk music was revitalised in the 1960s by groups such as The Chieftains, The Dubliners and The Clancy Brothers and Tommy Makem, followed in the 1970s by the likes of Planxty and Clannad. In 1970, Dana (Dana Rosemary Scallon), while still a schoolgirl, won the Eurovision Song Contest with 'All Kinds of Everything'. She later served as a member of the European parliament. Sandie Shaw had won it in 1967 with 'Puppet on a String' and Scottish singer Lulu (Lulu Kennedy-Cairns) in 1969 with 'Boom Bang-a-Bang'.

The progressive rock and glam rock era of the early 1970s was followed by punk and new wave trends and then ska and the New Romantics. Dublin's U2 and The Boomtown Rats were formed in the 1970s, as were The Undertones from Derry. Singer-songwriter Annie Lennox from Aberdeen had international success with the Eurythmics in the 1980s, which saw the rise of indie pop bands such as East Kilbride's Aztec Camera, Glasgow's Orange Juice and later Belle and Sebastian. Other Scottish bands included Simple Minds, Deacon Blue, Hue and Cry, The Proclaimers and Fairground Attraction. Ireland's The Cranberries, including singer and guitarist Dolores O'Riordan, formed in Limerick in 1989. Enya (Eithne Pádraigín Ní Bhraonáin), from Donegal, who has been recording since the 1980s, is the best-selling Irish solo artist.[20] Singer-songwriter Sinéad O'Connor from Dublin achieved international chart success. Welsh rock band Manic Street Preachers formed in Blackwood, Caerphilly, in 1986. Cocteau Twins were a Scottish rock band formed in Grangemouth.

The indie dance or 'Madchester' scene of the late 1980s included Manchester bands such as Happy Mondays and The Stone Roses. The 1990s brought boy bands such as Manchester's Take That and Ireland's Boyzone and Westlife, along with girl groups such as

England's Spice Girls. The Britpop era included bands such as London's Blur, Manchester's Oasis and Sheffield's Pulp. 'Post-pop' bands in the 1990s and 2000s included Stereophonics, a rock band from the Cynon Valley in south Wales, and Glasgow bands Travis and Franz Ferdinand. Female soul singers included (Aimée Anne) Duffy from Bangor in north Wales.

Many of these artists would undoubtedly have been popular in the pub music rooms or saloon bars of the nineteenth century.

CHAPTER 14

SHARED YET SEPARATE CULTURES

The Kardomah Boys, a group of bohemian would-be artists, musicians and writers in 1930s Swansea, exemplified a quandary that has often perplexed ambitious young people in towns and cities across the Isles. While artistic types drew nourishment from their local roots, many felt an urge to escape provincial confines that kept them trapped. This particular group – notably including a young newspaper reporter called Dylan Thomas, later Wales's most famous poet – frequented the Kardomah Café in Castle Street to talk and dream of what their talents might achieve.[1]

Leading lights of the group, a male clique typical of the culture of the time, also included Marxist scholar Bert Trick, composer and linguist Daniel Jones, painter Alfred Janes, poet and translator Vernon Watkins, artist and art dealer Mervyn Levy and novelist and poet John Prichard. These were individualists with no shared manifesto or grand theory of art. Thomas, a precocious talent who wrote in English, was born in 1914 in Swansea, his 'ugly, lovely town'. In the Kardomah years, he was soon also visiting London but spent much of his life alternating between the UK capital's literary scene and rural, Welsh-speaking Carmarthenshire and Cardiganshire, where his family roots lay. Famed for poems such as 'Do Not Go Gentle Into That Good Night' and his radio play *Under Milk Wood*, he acquired a reputation as a hard-drinking womaniser and died aged just 39 in New York.[2]

Artistic people around the Isles have grappled not only with truth, beauty and the perplexities of existence but also with their feelings about their native lands and their neighbours. Much of Thomas's work centres on the cycle of birth, love, procreation and death. Although he had a deep connection with Wales, he disliked Welsh nationalism. 'Land of my fathers, and my fathers can keep it' is a line he wrote for a character in a film screenplay. Others such as R.S. Thomas, another poet, took a different view. In Ireland, poet William Butler Yeats, though raised as a member of the Protestant Ascendancy, became a nationalist. In Scotland, Hugh MacDiarmid (Christopher Murray Grieve), poet, journalist and essayist, was a founding member of the National Party of Scotland in 1928 but left and joined the Communist Party of Great Britain, only to be expelled for his nationalist sympathies.[3]

History's legacy can be complex and disturbing. 'Other people have a nationality. The Irish and the Jews have a psychosis,' wrote the staunch republican Brendan Behan for a character in the play *Richard's Cork Leg* (1972). Novelist Edna O'Brien put it more positively: 'When anyone asks me about the Irish character, I say look at the trees. Maimed, stark and misshapen, but ferociously tenacious.'[4] Each nation's experiences bubble through into art. R.S. Thomas wrote in 'Welsh Landscape' (1952): 'To live in Wales is to be conscious / At dusk of the spilled blood / That went into the making of the wild sky.' Underlying it all is sensitivity about domination by England, whose glittering history of Elizabethan drama, Romantic poetry and landscape art could appear as daunting as its imperial ambitions. 'Let not England forget her precedence of teaching nations how to live,' wrote John Milton in 1643.[5] Or alternatively, as Dublin-born Oscar Wilde is said to have put it: 'The English came and took our lands and turned them into barren wastes. We took their language and made it beautiful.'[6]

The arts embody a tension in the relationship between the nations: there have been elements of shared Britishness, particularly at the height of Empire, but there have also been efforts to preserve different identities. These include a long struggle to protect Celtic language and culture, the origins of which lie deep in pagan prehistory. Four epic cycles form a central part of early Irish literature: the Mythological Cycle about the Tuatha Dé Danann, a supernatural race who dwell in the Otherworld but interact with humans; the Ulster Cycle, whose characters include warrior hero Cú Chulainn; the Fenian Cycle, focusing on the exploits of Fionn mac Cumhaill (Finn McCool) and his warrior band, the Fianna; and the Historical Cycle, covering various high kings. These cycles are, however, a modern categorisation; not all tales fit easily into them.

The eighteenth century saw a flowering of Irish writing in English, notably Dublin-born satirist Jonathan Swift (1667–1745), best remembered for *Gulliver's Travels*, published in 1726. Swift held positions of authority in England and Ireland and became dean of St Patrick's Cathedral, Dublin. He gained a reputation as an Irish patriot through works such as *Proposal for Universal Use of Irish Manufacture* (1720), *Drapier's Letters* (1724) and *A Modest Proposal* (1729), which suggested that Ireland's poor might escape their poverty by selling their children as food to the rich. Irish writers who made careers in England included Clonmel-born Laurence Sterne, an Anglican cleric who wrote *The Life and Opinions of Tristram Shandy, Gentleman*; Oliver Goldsmith, author of *The Vicar of Wakefield*; Dublin-born playwright Richard Brinsley Sheridan; and Dublin-born poet Mary Tighe, whose allegorical poem 'Psyche' was admired by John Keats and others. In Ireland, poet Mary Barber was a member of Swift's circle. Sydney, Lady Morgan was best known for *The Wild Irish Girl* (1806), a 'proto-feminist' romantic novel that extolled the beauty of Irish scenery and the noble traditions of its early history.

In the nineteenth century, Maria Edgeworth (1768–1849), a pioneer of the realist novel, was born in Oxfordshire but moved to

Ireland when young. Abraham 'Bram' Stoker, born in Clontarf, wrote the 1897 Gothic horror novel *Dracula*. Oscar Wilde became one of late Victorian London's most popular playwrights as well as notorious for his criminal conviction for gross indecency for homosexual acts. A 'Gaelic revival' of interest in the Irish language and culture was spurred by Douglas Hyde's Gaelic League. Important writers included Peadar Ua Laoghaire from County Cork, author of the story *Séadna*; modernist poet Patrick Pearse (Pádraig Anraí Mac Piarais), later a leader of the 1916 Easter Rising; and prolific writer Pádraic Ó Conaire from Galway.

In the twentieth century, Ireland had four winners of the Nobel Prize for Literature: Yeats, playwrights George Bernard Shaw and Samuel Beckett and Northern Irish poet Seamus Heaney. Yeats was a driving force behind an Irish literary revival, linked to the Gaelic revival. With Augusta, Lady Gregory, he founded Dublin's Abbey Theatre and later served two terms as a senator of the Irish Free State. He spent much of his life in fruitless pursuit of his muse, republican activist Maud Gonne. Of the Easter Rising, he wrote: 'All changed, changed utterly / A terrible beauty is born', recognising that he had underestimated the leaders because of their apparent ordinariness.[7]

Shaw (1856–1950) moved to London as a young man and struggled at first to establish himself. He became a leading pamphleteer of the newly formed Fabian Society, which advocated socialism by gradual means, and a theatre and music critic. Eventually he became a dramatist, writing more than 60 plays, of which the best known include *Man and Superman*, *Pygmalion* and *Saint Joan*. Influenced by the realist theatre of Norway's Henrik Ibsen, Shaw was irreverent, witty and used plays to air his political, social and religious ideas. He remained popular despite his often contentious opinions, such as promoting eugenics and making positive statements about Hitler, Stalin and Mussolini.[8] Dublin-born novelist James Joyce (1882–1941) is another who left Ireland and in his case lived in Trieste, Zurich and Paris. He was a celebrated modernist whose landmark *Ulysses* chronicles the experiences of three Dubliners in a single day – 16 June 1904, now celebrated by fans as Bloomsday – drawing on Homer's *Odyssey* and using innovations such as interior monologue and wordplay. It was published in Paris in 1922 but prohibited in the UK and the US until the mid-1930s because of its perceived obscenity. Other notable works include the short-story collection *Dubliners* and novels *A Portrait of the Artist as a Young Man* and *Finnegans Wake*.[9]

Beckett (1906–89), born in Dublin from an Anglo-Irish Protestant background, lived most of his adult life in Paris. A key figure in the 'theatre of the absurd', he is best known for his 1953 play *Waiting for Godot*, in which two characters, Vladimir and Estragon, hold a variety of discussions while awaiting the titular Godot, who never arrives. Beckett was a member of the French resistance during the Second World War.[10]

Among other writers, Belfast-born Clive Staples 'C.S.' Lewis (1898–1963) was sent to boarding schools in England and held academic posts in English literature at Oxford and Cambridge. He was an Anglican whose faith profoundly affected his work, best known for The Chronicles of Narnia, a series of fantasy novels set in a world of magic, mythical beasts and talking animals. Elizabeth Bowen (1899–1973), born in Dublin to an Anglo-Irish gentry family, wrote novels and stories about awkward relationships among the upper-middle class. Limerick-born Kate O'Ryan (1897–1974) wrote novels largely featuring young women yearning for independence and equality. Prominent among Irish-language writers was modernist Máirtín Ó Cadhain (1906–70), best known for his novel *Cré na Cille* (Earth of the Church), a conversation between dead characters in a Connemara graveyard.

Heaney (1939–2013), born near Castledawson in County Derry, was the most prominent among a number of post-Second World War poets from Northern Ireland that also included Derek Mahon, Paul Muldoon, James Fenton and Michael Longley. Heaney, a Catholic, lived in the Irish Republic for much of his later life. His poems often depicted Ireland's grey and damp landscape and were connected with daily experiences, while reaching into history. When he was awarded the Nobel Prize in 1995, the committee described his oeuvre as 'works of lyrical beauty and ethical depth, which exalt everyday miracles and the living past'.[11]

Irish art began with Neolithic stone carvings. In the sixth to eighth centuries, newly Christianised Irish art mixed with Mediterranean and Germanic traditions through missionary contacts, creating Insular art including masterpieces such as the Book of Kells, Ardagh Chalice and Tara Brooch. Modern artists include Dublin-born Francis Bacon (1909–92), who lived much of his life in London. Noted for raw, grotesque imagery, his subjects included crucifixions, portraits of popes, self-portraits and portraits of close friends, often with contorted limbs and howling mouths – an exploration of nihilism after two world wars.[12]

Ireland's musical history, aside from its vibrant culture of traditional music, encompasses medieval Gregorian chants, Renaissance choral and harp music, court music of the Baroque and early Classical period and Romantic and twentieth-century modernist works. Among the best-known harpists was Turlough Carolan (Toirdhealbhach Ó Cearbhalláin, 1670–1738), a blind man from County Meath, who for almost 50 years journeyed from one end of Ireland to the other, composing and performing his tunes.[13] Among modern figures was Sir Herbert Hamilton Harty (1879–1941) composer and conductor, born in Hillsborough, County Down, who conducted the Hallé orchestra in Manchester and the London Symphony Orchestra. Performers include soprano Catherine Hayes (1818–61), the first Irish woman to perform at La Scala in Milan; tenor Josef Locke, popular in the 1940s and 1950s; and flautist Sir James Galway (b.1939) from Belfast, nicknamed 'the man with the golden flute'.

With so many artistic people from around the Isles attracted to London – and in view of England's dominance – it can sometimes be difficult to separate England's culture from that of the UK as a whole. Old English literature such as the epic poem *Beowulf* was followed by Middle English, notably including Geoffrey Chaucer, author of *The Canterbury Tales*. The English Renaissance ushered in authors such as William Shakespeare, widely regarded as the world's greatest playwright. He was attuned to the politics of the Isles. When James VI of Scotland also became James I of England, Shakespeare welcomed him with *Macbeth*, set in James's native Scotland, which portrays the king's ancestor, Banquo, as a good man destined to have monarchs among his descendants. The witch scenes were probably inspired by James's *Daemonologie*, a book that explained witchcraft as a pact between humans and the devil. In two later plays, *King Lear* and *Cymbeline*, Shakespeare appears to support James's desire to unite England and Scotland.[14] The Romantic era produced poets such as William Wordsworth, Samuel Taylor Coleridge, John Keats, William Blake and Percy Bysshe Shelley. Nineteenth-century novelists included Jane Austen, Charles Dickens, the Brontë sisters, George Eliot and Thomas Hardy. Twentieth-century novelists included George Orwell, D.H. Lawrence and Virginia Woolf.

English art in the eighteenth and nineteenth centuries produced the satirical tradition of William Hogarth, James Gillray and George Cruikshank. England was a leader in the trend for landscape painting, notably in the work of John Constable and J.M.W. Turner; the latter painted watercolours around Scotland, Wales, England and western Europe. Notable twentieth-century figures included sculptors Henry Moore and Barbara Hepworth, along with L.S. Lowry, painter of the industrial north, and Bradford-born David Hockney. In music, the Renaissance period produced Thomas Tallis, John Taverner and William Byrd, followed by the Baroque work of Henry Purcell and George Frideric Handel. In the late nineteenth century, figures such as Sir Edward Elgar and Sir Arthur Sullivan showed a new vitality. In the twentieth century, Benjamin Britten and Michael Tippett were internationally recognised opera composers, while Ralph Vaughan Williams adapted English folk tunes for the concert hall.

The oldest surviving poetry in Scotland is reckoned to be *Y Gododdin*, attributed to the bard Aneirin in the kingdom of Gododdin, south-east Scotland, in the sixth century. It memorialises a battle and was composed in the Brythonic language, a precursor of today's Welsh. Over the following centuries, writers employed Latin, Old English, Gaelic and French. In the early modern era, Sir David Lyndsay, a courtier under James V, wrote *Ane Pleasant Satyre of the Thrie Estaitis* (1552), an attack on the clergy, lords and burgh representatives in parliament. In the Romantic era, poet James Macpherson became known throughout Europe in 1761 when he began publishing the poems of Oisín or Ossian, supposedly third-century Gaelic originals that he had discovered and translated. Although based in part on genuine Gaelic ballads, the works were largely Macpherson's invention. They infuriated Irish scholars because they mixed up legends from the Fenian and Ulster cycles and because Macpherson claimed the Irish heroes were Caledonians and therefore a glory to Scotland's past rather than Ireland's.[15]

Romanticism also produced Ayrshire-born Robert Burns (1759–96), regarded as Scotland's national poet, who wrote lyrics and songs in Scots and English. He was famous for his love affairs, radicalism and Scottish patriotism. His poem (and song) 'Auld Lang Syne' is sung at Hogmanay, or New Year's Eve, while 'Scots Wha Hae' is regarded by some as an unofficial national anthem. Other well-known poems and songs include 'A Red, Red Rose', 'A Man's a Man for A' That' and 'Ae Fond Kiss'. In later life, he worked as an exciseman, though he almost lost his job for indiscreet outbursts of support for the French and American revolutions. He has particularly inspired the Scottish diaspora, with Burns clubs created around the world. Burns Night is widely celebrated with suppers on his birthday, 25 January.[16]

In the nineteenth century, Edinburgh-born Sir Walter Scott (1771–1832), novelist, poet and historian, did much to define and popularise Scottish cultural identity. He was prominent in Edinburgh's Tory establishment and combined writing and editing with his daily work as a law court official in Selkirkshire. He has been acclaimed as the main inventor of the historical novel, with works including *Waverley, Rob Roy, The Heart of Midlothian* and *Ivanhoe*.[17] Authors later in the Victorian era included novelist Robert Louis Stevenson, best known for *Treasure Island, Kidnapped* and *Strange Case of Dr Jekyll and Mr Hyde*; Arthur Conan Doyle, whose Sherlock Holmes stories helped found the genre of detective fiction; J.M. Barrie, most famous for creating *Peter Pan*; and George MacDonald, remembered chiefly for allegorical fairy stories.

The twentieth century brought a surge of interest in literature and the arts known as the Scottish Renaissance. Its leading figure, Hugh MacDiarmid, was a postman's son from Langholm, Dumfriesshire, who sought to revive the Scots language as a medium for serious literature. In his long poem *A Drunk Man Looks at the Thistle* (1926), a blend of philosophical musings and personal reflections, he tries to grapple with 'this root-hewn Scottis soul' and analyse the Scottish nation. Novelist Lewis Grassic Gibbon (James Leslie Mitchell, 1901–35) is best known for *A Scots Quair*, a trilogy set in north-east Scotland, which combines stream-of-consciousness, lyrical use of dialect and social realism. Later poets included Glasgow's Edwin Morgan, who became the first Makar (official national poet), appointed by the Scottish government in 2004. Dame Carol Ann Duffy, also from Glasgow, was appointed Britain's Poet Laureate in 2009 – the first woman, first Scottish-born person and first openly lesbian poet to hold the position.

In art, several nineteenth-century painters were influenced by neoclassicism, including Allan Ramsay, a portraitist, and Gavin Hamilton, painter of historical scenes whose best-known works were inspired by Homer's *Iliad*. Romanticism encouraged landscape painting that focused on the Highlands, including artists such as Alexander Nasmyth. In the 1880s and 1890s, a group known as the Glasgow Boys emerged; keen on realism and naturalism, they painted rural, prosaic scenes. Architect Charles Rennie Mackintosh, born in Glasgow, was a leading figure in the art nouveau style. In the early twentieth century, the Scottish Colourists – Francis Cadell, John Duncan Fergusson, Leslie Hunter and Samuel Peploe – combined the influence of French Impressionism with Scottish traditions. Later in the century, John Bellany, born in the fishing village of Port Seton, created large compositions dealing with original sin, guilt, sex and death, often featuring personal symbolism derived from the sea.

Scotland is known internationally for its folk music, with a variety of styles such as ballads, reels, jigs and airs, and is closely associated with the bagpipes. James V in the sixteenth century was a talented lute player who introduced French chansons and consorts of viols to his court. Scotland's Calvinist Reformation was generally opposed to church music, leading to the removal of organs and an emphasis on metrical psalms. That slowed the development of an art music tradition, but several composers in classical style emerged in the eighteenth century, including Thomas Erskine, Sixth Earl of Kellie, who wrote several symphonies. The Edinburgh Festival's creation in 1947 led to an expansion of classical music. Leading modern composers include Dame Judith Weir and James MacMillan.

Wales is seen as the 'land of song', famed for folk music, choirs, religious music and brass bands. Since at least the twelfth century, bards and musicians have taken part in musical and poetic contests called *eisteddfodau*. Male choirs emerged in the nineteenth century, originally as the tenor and bass sections of chapel choirs. In the twentieth century, Welsh classical and operatic soloists included tenor Robert Tear and bass-baritones Sir Geraint Llewellyn Evans and Sir Bryn Terfel Jones. From the 1980s, a number of crossover artists emerged including mezzo-soprano Katherine Jenkins, who performs operatic arias and popular songs, Charlotte Church, a classical singer who tried less successfully to move into pop music, and Aled Jones, a teenage chorister who became famous for singing a cover version of 'Walking in the Air', originally from the 1982 television film *The Snowman*.

Literature in the Welsh language dates back to Aneirin, the *Gododdin* poet, in the sixth century, and his contemporary Taliesin, whose authentic work is believed to have survived in 12 praise poems in the medieval *Book of Taliesin*. Poetry was followed by prose in medieval stories such as those in the collection known in modern times as the *Mabinogion*, which are tales from the oral tradition that depict royal lives and themes of fall and redemption, loyalty, marriage, love, fidelity, a wronged wife and incest. In the seventeenth century, Puritan author Morgan Llwyd wrote in both English and Welsh, recounting his spiritual experiences, while Captain Gwilym Puw (William Pugh), a royalist, wrote Welsh-language poetry defending the Catholic faith. Ann Griffiths (1776–1805), a Calvinistic Methodist from Montgomeryshire, wrote Welsh-language hymns reflecting her intense faith and was the only female poet included in 1962's *Oxford Book of Welsh Verse*. Nineteenth-century *eisteddfodau* encouraged poets including Talhaiarn (John Jones) from Denbighshire, a colourful character known for his willingness to argue with adjudicators. The first Welsh-language novelist to achieve lasting popularity was Daniel Owen (1836–95) from Mold in Flintshire. His novel *Rhys Lewis* deals with issues of evangelical Christianity in a rapidly changing society affected by increasing exposure to outside influences and industrialisation.[18]

Several writers embraced nationalism in the twentieth century, notably Saunders Lewis (1893–1985), a dramatist, poet, novelist and critic born in Wallasey, Cheshire, to a Welsh-speaking family. He was co-founder of the Welsh Nationalist Party (later Plaid Cymru) in 1925, served as its president 1926–39 and was jailed for his part in burning an RAF bombing school at Penyberth, Gwynedd, in a 1936 protest, which led to him being dismissed from his post as lecturer in Welsh at Swansea University. Despite his Calvinistic Methodist upbringing, he converted to Catholicism, criticised Wales's Nonconformist and socialist traditions and embraced European nationalist culture, especially French. He supported the nationalists during Spain's civil war and believed Welsh-speaking communities were at their most vital in the Middle Ages. His varied literary output included 21 plays, which explored themes such as honour and the responsibilities of leadership. His 1962 radio lecture on the fate of the Welsh language triggered the creation of the Welsh Language Society (Cymdeithas yr Iaith Gymraeg).[19] Another prominent nationalist was Kate Roberts (1891–1985), short-story writer and novelist from Rhosgadfan near Caernarfon. Her work ranged from the harsh life of slate-quarrying society to the loneliness she felt after her husband's death.[20]

Welsh-born writers who wrote in English include metaphysical poets George Herbert (1593–1633), a priest in the Church of England who was born in Montgomery to a wealthy family and largely raised in England, and Henry Vaughan (1622–95) from Brecknockshire, who also wrote religious verse. John Dyer (1699–1757), a painter and poet from Carmarthenshire, was another Anglican priest. Royalist-leaning English poet Katherine Philips (1631/2–64), best known for poems on female friendship, lived at Cardigan Priory for much of her life after marrying a Welsh parliamentarian.[21]

David Caradoc Evans (1878–1945), a story writer, novelist and poet from Cardiganshire, is widely seen as the first modern Welsh writer in English. He cultivated a reputation as 'the most unpopular man in Wales' with stories that pilloried aspects of rural life such as Nonconformism, the *eisteddfod* and the Welsh language. Newport-born writer William Henry ('W.H.') Davies (1871–1940) became famous principally for his *The Autobiography of a Super-Tramp*, which described his life wandering across north America, finding sporadic work on farms and wintering in jails. He wrote poems on subjects including humans' relationship to nature. Among his famous poems is 'Leisure', which begins: 'What is this life if, full of care / We have no time to stand and stare?' David Jones (1895–1974), born in Kent to a Welsh father and English mother, is famed for *In Parenthesis*, a modernist epic poem drawing on his experience as an infantryman in the First World War.[22]

Rhys Davies (1901–78) from the Rhondda Valley probably wrote more fiction about the industrial south Wales valleys than anyone, but he did so from London, where he was living by the time he was 20. Gwyn Thomas, a miner's son also from the Rhondda, wrote novels, short stories, plays and radio and television scripts, most of which focused on unemployment in the Rhondda Valley in the 1930s. Richard Llewellyn Lloyd (1906–83), author of the most famous novel about Wales, *How Green Was My Valley* (1939), appears to have been born in London to parents of Welsh descent, though he claimed to have been born in St David's, Pembrokeshire. His famous novel portrays an idealised mining community whose hard work and solidarity are spoiled by greed on the part of both owners and workers. Poet Idris Davies (1905–53), born in Rhymney near Merthyr Tydfil, worked as a coal miner before qualifying as a teacher.[23]

Much of Welsh art has been variants of forms and styles seen elsewhere in the Isles. The earliest-known artwork is a decorated horse jaw from the end of the last Ice Age found at Kendrick's cave in Llandudno. The eighteenth-century vogue for landscape painting sparked interest in Wales. Richard Wilson (1713–82), a clergyman's son from Penegoes in Montgomeryshire, was a central figure in the development of British landscape painting and a precursor to Constable and Turner. Wilson painted Welsh scenes as well as English and Italian ones. In the twentieth century, Augustus John (1878–1961) and his sister Gwen John (1876–1939) were the most famous Welsh-born painters, though they lived mostly in London and Paris. Sir John Kyffin Williams (1918–2006) who was born and lived on the island of Anglesey, is widely seen as the defining Welsh artist of the past century. His landscapes and portraits were painted in a boldly expressionist style. He also described himself as 'the first painter that people in Wales have been able to relate to'.[24]

Kyffin Williams was a prime example of the talent for art, music and literature that has existed in all parts of the Isles, not just in London. In conjunction with politics and the economy, the arts will continue to play an important part in shaping the Isles' culture.

CHAPTER 15

WAR, NATIONALISM AND IMPERIAL DECLINE

The apparent self-confidence of imperial Britain was reaching its apogee in the early twentieth century. As *The Times of India* put it in 1911 on the eve of the coronation of Queen Victoria's grandson as George V:

> We are impressed, almost awed, by the antiquity of this rite. For the ceremony at Westminster carries us back to the year 785 when Ecgfrith, Prince of Mercia, was 'hallowed to be king' by Offa, his father. The Coronation then, symbolises the growth of the British Nation and the British Empire through twelve centuries.[1]

The coronation was celebrated with a Festival of Empire in London. The new king and queen went on to visit Ireland, where they received a warm welcome, and India, where they were presented to dignitaries and princes as Emperor and Empress at the Delhi Durbar.

The political background, though, was turbulent: a Liberal government was seeking to curb the powers of the House of Lords; a merchant seamen's strike was paralysing the ports; troops had been used against striking coal miners in Tonypandy, south Wales; and

Ulster unionists were desperately campaigning to obstruct the progress of another Irish home rule bill. That was just a taste of what was to become a brutal century involving fascism, communism and two world wars. Most of the Isles – except for the Channel Islands – avoided occupation and totalitarianism, but many died, the Empire disintegrated and Ireland left the union after an armed struggle. Industrial Britain, which had fallen behind Germany and the US, suffered deep recessions in the 1920s and 1930s. In the second half of the century, living standards rose to unprecedented levels along with those of other developed countries, though there was also a widening economic divide as south-east England pulled ahead of other regions.

Victoria's son Bertie had succeeded her in 1901 as Edward VII, giving his title to the Edwardian era, a time of peace and relative prosperity but also rapid and sometimes disconcerting changes in society and politics. Arthur Balfour, born at Whittingehame House, East Lothian, succeeded his uncle Lord Salisbury as Conservative prime minister in 1902 but ran into trouble when he cautiously embraced 'imperial preference', or trade tariffs on goods from non-Empire counties, championed by Joseph Chamberlain, former secretary of state for the colonies. The issue divided his party. Balfour resigned in December 1905, and the next month the Conservatives suffered a landslide defeat by the Liberals at the 1906 election, in which he lost his Manchester East seat.

The new prime minister was Glasgow-born Sir Henry Campbell-Bannerman, a supporter of free trade and Irish home rule. The Liberals were helped by a secret pact with the LRC not to compete against each other. After the election, the LRC's MPs adopted the name 'The Labour Party', and Lanarkshire-born Keir Hardie, MP for Merthyr Tydfil and Aberdare in Wales, became their parliamentary leader. The Campbell-Bannerman government passed reforms such as allowing local councils to provide free school meals and giving some workers a right to compensation for accidents at work. After some prevarication, the government met a demand by trade unions to legislate to overturn fully the 1901 Taff Vale ruling, resulting from a dispute between strikers and a railway company in which the union was ordered to pay £23,000 damages. The judgment had in effect made strikes illegal by opening union funds to sequestration.

Campbell-Bannerman, the last Liberal leader to win an absolute parliamentary majority, resigned in 1908 after heart attacks and was succeeded by his chancellor, Herbert Henry Asquith. The new chancellor was David Lloyd George, MP for Carnarvon Boroughs, born in Chorlton-on-Medlock, Manchester, to Welsh parents. His People's Budget of 1909 proposed taxes on lands and incomes of the wealthy to fund old-age pensions, national insurance and unemployment assistance. It was blocked for a year by the Conservative-dominated House of Lords, leading to two general elections in 1910 and the Parliament Act 1911, limiting the Lords' power of veto.

There was a dramatic increase in industrial conflict from 1908, with strikes in sectors including cotton, shipbuilding and coal mining, driven in part by workers demanding their share of rewards created by expansion in recent decades. A dispute in the Rhondda began in 1910 when coal-mine owners resisted a demand for special pay for 'abnormal work', resulting in a riot, which led Winston Churchill, home secretary, to send troops to Tonypandy. In the baking summer of 1911, there were racist attacks by striking seamen on Chinese shopkeepers in Cardiff, while in Tredegar Jewish shops were attacked. In Llanelli, troops fired on striking railwaymen, killing two and triggering another riot that caused an explosion and four more deaths. There was extensive unrest in Liverpool, Hull, Glasgow and London's East End. The first national railway workers' strike began with an unofficial stoppage in Liverpool, coinciding with a strike there by dock and transport workers. Churchill sent 2,000 soldiers and a cruiser to Merseyside. In Ireland, James Larkin, a docker born in Liverpool to Irish parents, created the Irish Transport and General Workers' Union and led a 1913 strike over the right to unionise that led to the 'Dublin lock-out', the most severe industrial dispute in Irish history.[2]

The Liberals depended on Irish nationalists led by John Redmond for a majority, forcing Asquith to introduce a third home rule bill in 1912. That provoked fierce opposition from Ulster unionists led by barrister Sir Edward Carson, who created the Ulster Volunteer Force to resist it; they received a shipment of arms and ammunition from Germany. In response, nationalists created the Irish Volunteers, part of which later became the forerunner of the IRA. James Larkin and James Connolly, an Edinburgh-born Marxist of Irish parentage, formed the Irish Labour Party to represent workers in the home rule debate. Unionists had strong support from the Conservatives, now led by Andrew Bonar Law, born in Canada of Scottish and Ulster Scots descent. The bill was finally passed, with Ulster set to be temporarily excluded, but implementation was suspended when the First World War broke out.

The UK was on the winning side in the First World War but at high cost to the home nations and the dominions, colonies and protectorates. Almost 900,000 troops from Britain and the Empire died in the fighting, while civilian deaths exceeded the pre-war level by almost 300,000.[3] Both nationalists and unionists served in respective Irish divisions. Scotland bore a particularly heavy burden, with some sources putting total losses at more than 134,000.[4] Scotland's industries were harnessed to the war effort. Singer's Clydebank sewing machine factory, for example, made artillery shells, aeroplane parts, grenades and horseshoes; its workforce was about 70 per cent female at war's end. In Glasgow and the west of Scotland, poor working and living conditions led to industrial and political unrest. Welsh troops fought on all the main battlefields. Lord Kitchener, war secretary, had intended to scatter the Welsh among various regiments and efforts were made to prevent them speaking Welsh on parade or in billets; but Lloyd George had publicly promised a Welsh division, so after a cabinet row the 38th (Welsh) Division was created.[5]

Pressure for more effective leadership grew as the war became bogged down, forcing Asquith to form a coalition with the Conservatives and

Labour early in 1915. Conscription was introduced in January 1916; Asquith had tried to cling to the principle of voluntary recruitment but was forced to yield amid pressure from Lloyd George and Tory allies. Lloyd George became minister for munitions and later war secretary after Kitchener was killed when his ship struck a German mine near Orkney. Asquith, weakened by indecision, was replaced in December 1916 by Lloyd George, the first and only Welshman to become Britain's prime minister.

The Irish issue had erupted earlier in 1916 when 1,600 republicans staged a rebellion known as the Easter Rising, led by Connolly and Padraig Pearse. The rebellion lacked popular support and was put down within a week, but the execution of its leaders and heavy-handed arrests of other activists upset the nationalist public. Support swung towards Sinn Féin, a pro-independence party, which won a large majority of seats at the 1918 election, boosted by a backlash against proposals to extend conscription to Ireland. Its MPs refused to take seats at Westminster and, in January 1919, 27 assembled in Dublin's Mansion House, where they established Dáil Éireann (an Irish parliament) and proclaimed a republic.[6]

In 1919–21, the IRA waged guerrilla war against the British Army and paramilitary police units known as the Black and Tans in what became known as the War of Independence, during which both sides engaged in brutal acts. Britain passed an act granting home rule separately both to the north-easternmost six counties of Ulster and Ireland's remaining twenty-six counties, thus partitioning Ireland. Northern Ireland's parliament came into being in 1921, with Sir James Craig as prime minister, but the southern institutions were boycotted by nationalists and never became functional. In July 1921, a ceasefire led to an Anglo-Irish Treaty in which southern and western Ireland was to be given dominion status, modelled on Canada. The Dáil narrowly passed the treaty, and a provisional government was established under Michael Collins, the IRA intelligence chief who had led negotiations, and William Thomas Cosgrave.[7]

The Irish Free State came into being in December 1922. However, the treaty was bitterly opposed by Éamon de Valera, Sinn Féin's president, and many of the IRA on the grounds that it accepted partition, failed to create a fully independent republic and imposed an oath of fidelity to the UK monarch on Irish parliamentarians. The result was a civil war lasting several months in which many anti-treaty fighters were interned or executed, while Collins was killed in an ambush in Cork. Fighting petered out in victory for the pro-treaty side in May 1923 but left Irish society embittered for generations. Today, Ireland's three largest political parties are descended from the civil war: Fine Gael from the pro-treaty side; Fianna Fáil, formed by de Valera from anti-treaty republicans; and Sinn Féin, comprising republicans who refused to join any partitionist party.[8]

After the First World War ended in victory, Lloyd George's prestige was at its height, and his coalition government, comprising mainly Conservatives and Liberals, was re-elected by a landslide in December 1918. Lloyd George promised to make the UK 'a fit country for heroes to live in'.[9] There was a brief post-war economic boom and a vigorous programme to extend health and educational services, subsidise house-building by local authorities, raise pensions and spread universal unemployment insurance. The boom ended abruptly, however, when interest rates and unemployment rose and social spending was slashed in 1921–2 to curb a ballooning budget deficit.

Aside from the Irish crisis, there was trouble in India, where the 1919 Amritsar Massacre, in which British troops fired on peaceful protestors, led Mahatma Gandhi to campaign for Indians to cease co-operation with the UK government. In the UK, there was a wave of strikes in 1919–21 in the police, railways, cotton, iron and coal as workers sought to protect living standards. In Glasgow, where 'Red Clydeside' had produced anti-war activists such as John Maclean and James Maxton, troops and tanks were sent – though not deployed – in response to a 1919 demonstration for a 40-hour working week. A 'cash for patronage' scandal erupted in 1922 when it became known that Lloyd George had sold peerages, knighthoods and other honours to raise funds for his party via a fixer called Maundy Gregory, which was not illegal at the time. The coalition collapsed in October, and an election was won by the Conservatives under Bonar Law, with Labour more than doubling its seats and overtaking the divided Liberals. Bonar Law, who became seriously ill with throat cancer, resigned in May 1923 and died soon after, to be replaced by his chancellor Stanley Baldwin, the son of a prosperous Worcestershire family involved in iron and steelmaking.

Baldwin called an election in 1923 to seek a mandate for protectionist policies, but the result was a hung parliament. Lossiemouth-born Ramsay MacDonald, MP for the Welsh seat of Aberavon, formed the first Labour government. It lasted only nine months; its biggest achievement was an act pushed through by Scottish socialist John Wheatley, health minister, which expanded municipal housing for low-paid workers.[10] Baldwin's Conservatives won the 1924 election by a landslide. In 1926, the new government faced Britain's only general strike when mine owners, demanding wage cuts, began to lock miners out. Rhondda miner Arthur James Cook was general secretary of the Miners' Federation of Great Britain; his slogan 'Not a penny off the pay, not a second on the day' became the miners' cry. The Trades Union Congress (TUC) ordered a strike by rail and transport workers, printers, dockers, ironworkers and steelworkers in support of the miners. The government proclaimed a state of emergency and enlisted middle-class volunteers to maintain essential services. After nine days, the TUC called off the strike, fearing a drift back to work. The miners stayed out for several months but were eventually forced to accept longer hours and lower wages. Strikes declined afterwards, though memories of what many miners saw as the TUC's betrayal were still raw as late as the 1984–5 coal strike.

The economy worsened again as the 1929 Wall Street crash led to the great depression. Countries raised tariffs and world trade shrank by a third. The impact in the UK, which had not experienced a

1920s boom, was less severe than in countries such as the US, but again it was concentrated in older industrial areas, with mass unemployment in northern England, south Wales, Clydeside and Belfast. Wales, heavily dependent on mining, was particularly hard-hit by the slump in world markets combined with a lack of investment capital. Unemployment there among insured males reached a peak of 42.8 per cent in August 1932.[11] Its steel and iron, transport and shipping sectors also went into decline. Glamorgan and Monmouthshire had the UK's highest proportion of people on poor relief, apart from County Durham.[12] New and expanding industries such as car manufacture, electrical engineering, paper and publishing and rayon production tended to be concentrated in England's midlands, which deepened Britain's economic divide. With the help of these newer industries, the living standards of people who remained in employment actually improved by about 16 per cent between the wars.[13]

MacDonald formed a second minority government in 1929, which became engulfed by economic crisis. The cabinet split over unemployment benefit cuts, and MacDonald formed a national government with Conservatives and Liberals, leading to his expulsion from Labour, which was routed at the 1931 election. The Treasury was forced to abandon the gold standard, after which the pound fell by 25 per cent, making exports more competitive. In 1932, 10 per cent tariffs were introduced on all imports except those from the Empire. Baldwin took over again from MacDonald in 1935.

The economy began to recover from 1932. Average unemployment during the 1930s was half that of the US. Britain saw a rise in fascism, though less so than in other European countries. The government passed the Special Areas Act 1934, designating west Cumberland, Tyneside and most of county Durham, Scotland's central belt, west Monmouthshire and most of Glamorgan for development. Financial incentives were too weak to have much effect, though things improved a bit when Neville Chamberlain, the chancellor, introduced rent and tax rebates and Treasury loans in 1937, resulting in the construction of trading estates at Team Valley near Gateshead, Treforest in south Wales and North Hillington outside Glasgow.

In Ireland, Fianna Fáil, created in 1926, came into office in 1932, with de Valera as president of the executive council (prime minister). He ditched free trade and used tariffs and subsidies to encourage domestic industries. He also withheld land annuities owed to the UK for loans to Irish farmers, launching an Anglo-Irish trade war in which the UK imposed sanctions against Irish exports; de Valera responded with levies on British imports, which lasted until 1938. The government pursued conservative social and cultural policies, with divorce and contraception prohibited and a stringent system of literary censorship. In 1937, a new constitution renamed the Irish Free State as Éire (Ireland) and the prime minister became the taoiseach, with greater powers. In Scotland, new nationalist and independent political groupings began to emerge, including the National Party of Scotland in 1928 and Scottish Party in 1930. They joined to form the SNP in 1934, with the aim of eventual independence.

As the threat of war with Nazi Germany grew, Neville Chamberlain, the UK's Conservative prime minister from 1937, pursued an unsuccessful strategy of trying to appease Hitler, notably in the 1938 Munich agreement ceding Czechoslovakia's Sudetenland to Germany. When Germany invaded Poland in September 1939, Chamberlain was forced to declare war. He led the UK through the first eight months of the Second World War before being replaced by Churchill, who had opposed appeasement and championed rearmament. Churchill formed a coalition government. Ireland insisted on remaining neutral, though it shared intelligence with the allies and would probably have accepted military assistance if the Germans invaded Ireland.

CHAPTER 16

UNEVEN PROSPERITY AND DEVOLUTION

Churchill's powerful speeches and radio broadcasts did much to boost morale, particularly during the Battle of Britain. Years later, Labour's Clement Attlee wrote that, if someone asked him, 'What, exactly, Winston did to win the war, I would say, "talk about it".'[1] The war was to claim the lives of almost 400,000 UK troops (less than half the number killed in the First World War) and 70,000 civilians, while millions were made homeless by the Blitz or V1/V2 rockets.[2] Despite this, the UK, which had been such a divided society between the wars, pulled together to a remarkable degree. The heaviest bombing was in London, but a wide range of cities including Liverpool, Hull, Bristol, Cardiff, Swansea, Belfast, Glasgow, Sunderland, Manchester, Coventry and Sheffield were also hit. There were many difficult times: 1942 was a terrible year until victory at El Alamein enabled the British Eighth Army to seal victory in north Africa.

Shipyards and heavy engineering factories in Glasgow and Clydeside played a key part in the war effort. Contributions by Scots include the development of radar by Brechin-born Robert Watson-Watt, which was invaluable in the Battle of Britain, as was the leadership of Moffat-born Air Chief Marshal Hugh Dowding, head of RAF Fighter Command. In Wales, there were fears that the war might damage Welsh culture and language, notably because of the inflow of evacuated English children, and there was concern about the War Office's takeover of 10 per cent of Welsh land. However, the war also revived the Welsh economy, rural and industrial, curbed unemployment and revived coal miners' bargaining power. After a strike by 100,000 in March 1944, miners won a minimum wage that put them high up in the table of working-class wages.[3]

After the war, Churchill ran an over-confident election campaign in 1945, but Labour won unexpectedly by a landslide, and Attlee became prime minister. Labour created the National Health Service (NHS) – overseen by health minister Aneurin Bevan, MP for Ebbw Vale – and legislated to nationalise and universalise sickness, unemployment and retirement benefits that had previously existed unevenly. It nationalised coal, rail, steel, some road transport, electricity and gas, which impressed the public less. A 1951 Gallup poll found approval only for nationalisation of health and coal, with other industries seen as having suffered under public ownership.[4] India gained independence in 1947 and was partitioned into two nations, India and Pakistan, kicking off waves of post-war decolonisation. Financial help from the US obliged Britain to fight in the Korean war of 1950–53, combat communist insurgents in Malaya and remain engaged in the Middle East to protect oil supplies.

In Scotland, full employment during the war had pushed up real incomes by about 25 per cent. Labour's Tom Johnston, wartime secretary of state for Scotland, managed to attract 700 enterprises and 90,000 new jobs north by creating a Scottish Council of Industry.[5] He also created a prototype NHS on Clydeside and brought hydro-electricity to the highlands. After the war, the government mounted an export drive, boosting Scotland's shipbuilding and heavy engineering sectors, helped also by the fact that competitors Germany and Japan were temporarily crippled. Scotland began a 20-year drive to build new homes, mostly council houses. In Wales, full employment was maintained, and the nation benefited from government policies to spread industrial development around the

UK: in 1945–9, 179 factories were established in south Wales, 112 of them with direct government assistance. There was huge investment in steel, leading to the opening of Britain's largest steelworks at Margam, Port Talbot, in 1951.[6]

Labour won the 1950 election by just five seats and called a snap election for October 1951 to try to increase its majority, but the Conservatives won by 17 seats despite Labour having the most votes – a unique event caused by the collapsing Liberal vote. The Tories had promised not to dismantle the welfare state or the NHS but denationalised steel. Churchill returned for a second term before retiring in 1955, to be succeeded by Anthony Eden, from a landed gentry family in County Durham. Eden's term was wrecked by the 1956 Suez crisis, a British–French–Israeli invasion to regain control of the Suez canal, through which most of Europe's oil arrived from the Middle East, after Egypt's president Gamal Abdel Nasser had nationalised it. It was a bungled attack, criticised by the US and the United Nations, which led to humiliating withdrawal. Eden resigned and was replaced by Harold Macmillan, a one-nation Tory who continued the post-war consensus. Benefiting from favourable international conditions, he presided over low unemployment and high, if uneven, growth and was re-elected with an increased majority in 1959. Macmillan told the nation in a 1957 speech that 'most of our people have never had it so good', though he also warned of the dangers of inflation.[7]

In Scotland, unemployment remained low, health improved and incomes rose. Among new independent TV stations was Scottish Television in 1957, headed by Scots-Canadian tycoon Roy Thompson, who memorably described his franchise as 'a licence to print money'.[8] Scottish Opera began in 1962; a folk music revival in the 1950s was led by figures such as Hamish Henderson. Robert McIntyre, SNP leader, won his party's first parliamentary seat in 1945 at a Motherwell by-election, though he lost it at the general election a few weeks later. Post-war politics were dominated first by Labour and then by the Unionists (known as Conservatives from 1965). Nationalism surfaced sometimes, however: on Christmas

Day 1950, four students seized Scotland's Stone of Destiny from Westminster Abbey, the coronation stone that had been moved to London by Edward I during the Wars of Independence. It turned up in Arbroath Cathedral, wrapped in the Saltire. Scottish pride was also hurt by Churchill's decision to call the new monarch Elizabeth II, though she was the first of that title in Scotland. A few postboxes with the QEII symbol were blown up. The Unionists won a record 50.1 per cent of the vote in the 1955 election, but by the late 1950s unemployment was starting to rise. Scotland's growth rate lagged behind the British average, while emigration, both overseas and to England, remained high. Scotland had seen little economic diversification, leaving its industries vulnerable. Coal faced a particularly bleak future, and shipbuilding had slumped. One result was that at the 1959 election Scotland voted against the UK trend and Labour won the most seats.[9]

Cardiff was recognised as Wales's capital in 1955 in a written reply by Gwilym Lloyd George, 'National Liberal' home secretary in the Conservative government and son of David Lloyd George. Caernarvon had also vied for the title. Welsh unemployment fell to a record low of 1.4 per cent of the insured workforce in July 1955. The situation deteriorated, however, and by the start of 1959 the jobless rate was back up to 4.7 per cent. With cheap oil coming in from the near east, the National Coal Board closed 50 pits in Wales's southern coalfield in 1957–64, and the number of miners there fell from 104,600 to 76,500. The biggest fall was in the slate quarries of Caernarfonshire, where the number employed fell from 3,607 in 1951 to 1,650 in 1961. The government stepped up regional policy, investing £260 million in Wales. Manufacturers attracted to Wales included Prestcold in Swansea, Rover in Cardiff, Fisher/Ludlow in Llanelli, Hoover in Merthyr, Revlon in Maesteg, Hotpoint in Llandudno and Ferodo in Caernarfon. Esso built an oil refinery near Milford Haven in 1960, followed by other companies.[10]

Ireland declared itself a republic in 1949 and left the Commonwealth. It missed out on the post-war boom, with its economy growing by only 1 per cent a year during the 1950s, leading to higher emigration and a decline in population to a low of 2.81 million. Protectionist policies and low public spending since the 1930s were seen as failing. Seán Lemass, who succeeded de Valera as leader of Fianna Fáil and taoiseach in 1958, dropped many tariffs and offered tax incentives to foreign manufacturing companies to set up in Ireland, creating economic growth of 4 per cent a year between 1959 and 1973.[11]

In the UK, Macmillan's government was rocked by a scandal in which John Profumo, war secretary, was revealed to have had an extramarital affair with 19-year-old model Christine Keeler, reported as simultaneously involved with a Soviet naval attaché. Macmillan resigned and was replaced by Alec Douglas-Home, a Scottish aristocrat who renounced his peerage to take a seat in the Commons. Labour's Huddersfield-born Harold Wilson ended 13 years of Tory rule by winning the 1964 election by just four seats. He called another election in 1966 and won a 98-seat majority, though economic pressures soon piled up, and in 1967 he was forced to devalue the pound by 14 per cent (and criticised for saying the 'pound in your pocket' had not lost value). The 1960s were an era of liberalising reforms including abolition of the death penalty and legalisation of homosexual acts. With student numbers expanding, a youth counterculture grew across much of the western world. Wales suffered a catastrophe in 1966 when heavy rain caused a colliery spoil tip above the village of Aberfan, near Merthyr, to slide downhill, killing 116 children and 28 adults as it engulfed a primary school and a row of houses. An inquiry blamed the National Coal Board for the disaster.

In Scotland, the SNP's Winifred Ewing, a young Glasgow solicitor, sensationally won a by-election in Hamilton, Lanarkshire, one of Labour's safest seats, in November 1967. The SNP also performed well in local elections. Labour depended on support from Scotland and Wales to counter Conservative strength in England, so it felt threatened by a nationalist surge in both nations. In Wales, Labour created a secretaryship of state and a Welsh Office. Gwynfor Evans, president of nationalist Plaid Cymru, won a by-election at Carmarthen in 1966, the first parliamentary seat for the party, which had been founded in 1925. Militant separatists emerged such as the Free Wales Army and Mudiad Amddiffyn Cymru (Movement for the Defence of Wales); the latter carried out bomb attacks on infrastructure, notably before Prince Charles's investiture as Prince of Wales at Caernarfon Castle in 1969. Wilson prevaricated towards nationalism and set up a Royal Committee on the Constitution in 1969, headed initially by Lord Crowther and later by Lord Kilbrandon, which did not report until 1973. To the horror of many Scots Tories, the Conservative leader, Edward Heath, committed the party to a devolved Scottish assembly in his 'Declaration of Perth' at its Scottish conference in 1968, reversing a century of Tory opposition to home rule; he would later shelve the idea.[12]

In Northern Ireland, frustration among nationalists about discrimination against the Catholic minority boiled over into what became known as the Troubles, lasting 30 years. A Northern Ireland Civil Rights Association was created in 1967, fuelled by half-fulfilled promises of reform by Terence O'Neill, Northern Ireland's moderate Unionist prime minister. Clashes between marchers and the Royal Ulster Constabulary began the following year, and violence erupted in August 1969 when a Protestant Apprentice Boys' march was forced through the nationalist Bogside area of Derry, leading to disorder known as the Battle of the Bogside. Even more severe rioting broke out in Belfast and elsewhere in response to it. The British Army was deployed by Home Secretary James Callaghan at the Northern Ireland government's request. At first, the soldiers received a warm welcome from nationalists, who hoped they would protect them from loyalist attack, but tensions rose in subsequent years.[13]

Heath's Conservatives won a surprise victory in the 1970 election, after which Heath took the UK into the European Economic Community in 1973. In Northern Ireland, internment without trial was introduced for suspected terrorists in 1971. In 1972, the most violent year of the conflict, 14 unarmed civilians were killed in Derry by the First Battalion, Parachute Regiment, in what was dubbed Bloody Sunday. The Provisional IRA, a breakaway in 1970 from what became known as the Official IRA, carried out indiscriminate bombing campaigns, while there were also sectarian attacks by loyalist paramilitary groups such as the Ulster Defence Association. The Northern Ireland parliament was prorogued and direct rule from London introduced. The Sunningdale Agreement was reached with various parties in 1973, bringing in a cross-community government, but a strike by the Ulster Workers' Council brought Northern Ireland to a standstill by shutting down electricity stations, leading to the collapse of the power-sharing executive in 1974.[14]

The Heath government broke with interventionist economic policies and asserted that 'lame duck' industries would not be propped up with taxpayers' money. That policy hit the buffers when partly state-owned Upper Clyde Shipbuilders announced in 1971 that it was going into receivership with the loss of 8,500 jobs at a time of rising unemployment. A campaign involving a 'work-in' led by two young shop stewards, Jimmy Reid and Jimmy Airlie, resulted in a reprieve in which the government restructured the yards. A Middle East oil crisis coupled with a miners' strike led to a three-day working week in early 1974. Heath called an election in February on the issue of 'who governs Britain?', but the result was a hung parliament in which Wilson again became prime minister. He called another election in October that gave Labour a small majority. The SNP won 11 seats, nine from the Tories, on the back of a campaign for an independent Scotland to take control of the enormous oil reserves discovered in 1970, when British Petroleum struck oil 110 miles off Aberdeen in the Forties field.[15]

Wilson resigned in 1976 and was replaced by Callaghan. By this time, Labour had lost its slim majority, and after early by-election defeats and defections he was forced to reach a pact with the Liberals, which lasted from March 1977 until August the following year. The government also had to concede referendums on its plans for Scottish and Welsh devolution, which were held in March 1979. In Wales, there was a large majority of 79.7 per cent against, while the Scottish referendum returned a narrow majority of 51.6 per cent in favour but failed to meet a threshold of 40 per cent of the electorate in support that parliament had set – an amendment proposed by George Cunningham, Dunfermline-born MP for Islington South and Finsbury. When the government refused to go ahead with setting up a Scottish assembly, it lost a no-confidence motion tabled by the SNP, necessitating a general election that the Conservatives, now led by Margaret Thatcher, won. The SNP lost nine of its 11 seats, confirming Callaghan's gibe that this was 'the first time in recorded history that turkeys have been known to vote for an early Christmas'.[16]

Thatcher, prime minister from 1979 to 1990, left the post-war consensus far behind and became the UK's longest-serving prime minister in the twentieth century, as well as the first woman in the office. 'Thatcherism' comprised elements such as monetary control, liberalisation of markets, privatisation, the virtue of self-help and curbing trade union power. She survived an assassination attempt by the Provisional IRA in the 1984 Brighton hotel bombing and won eventual victory over the National Union of Mineworkers in the 1984–5 miners' strike. A deep recession in the early 1980s, coupled with North Sea oil pushing up the pound's value and damaging exports, was severely felt, particularly by traditional industries in Scotland, northern England and Wales. Scotland's 30.8 per cent drop in manufacturing capacity in 1976–87 was the UK's steepest. The number of active coal mines in Scotland dropped from 15 to two in the 1980s. Shipbuilding and textiles were also hard-hit. Closures included Talbot's Linwood car plant, Singer in Clydebank, the Invergordon aluminium smelter, Caterpillar in Uddingston, Monsanto in Ayrshire and Plessey in Bathgate.[17]

Wales lost jobs in coal mining and steel, including the end of steel-making at Shotton, Ebbw Vale and Cardiff. Scotland's Ravenscraig steel plant was starved of investment and finally closed in 1993. Against that, the Isles' economies were becoming more diverse as service sector employment grew in areas such as tourism and business services. Finance was particularly strong in Scotland: by 1993–4, 10 of the largest 15 Scottish companies by turnover were in finance, and by some measures Scotland had the fourth largest financial sector in Europe after London, Frankfurt and Paris. North Sea oil recovered after a mid-1980s oil price slump, enabling Aberdeen to become Europe's oil capital. Electronic manufacture became a Scottish strength, with 'Silicon Glen' stretching from Ayrshire to Dundee.[18]

Thatcher was re-elected in 1983 and 1987, though in Scotland the Tories lost 11 of their 21 MPs in 1987, their worst result since 1910, while in Wales they lost six out of 14. Thatcher sought to reform local government taxes by replacing domestic rates, based on a home's nominal rental value, with a community charge or 'poll tax' in which the same amount was charged to each adult resident. The new tax was introduced in Scotland in 1989 and in England and Wales the following year and proved deeply unpopular. There was a massive campaign of non-payment in Scotland, though it was riotous protests in England that ensured its eventual demise. As the Tories fell behind in opinion polls, Port Talbot-born Sir Geoffrey Howe resigned as deputy prime minister and used his resignation speech to criticise her hostility to moves towards European monetary union. Former minister Michael Heseltine, born in Swansea, challenged her for the party leadership. She won the first ballot, slightly short of the required majority, but resigned in November 1990 before a second ballot, leaving Downing Street in tears after consultation with cabinet members persuaded her to withdraw.[19]

Thatcher was replaced by her chancellor, John Major, a mild-mannered man with a more moderate political stance. He replaced the poll tax with a council tax, assigning properties to various bands, and steered the UK through the early 1990s recession. Two thousand Welsh businesses collapsed in 1991. In 1992, Major led the Conservatives to a fourth consecutive election victory, winning more than fourteen million votes, a British record. However, his government's economic credibility was severely dented by 'Black Wednesday', 16 September 1992, when the chancellor, Shetland-born Norman Lamont, was forced to withdraw sterling from the European Exchange Rate Mechanism (ERM) after a failed attempt to keep its exchange rate above the lower limit required for ERM participation.[20]

In Scotland, pressure was mounting for devolution. A Scottish Constitutional Convention was created in 1989 to press for change. The SNP withdrew because the convention was unwilling to discuss independence, but the party was now recovering from recent internal turmoil. In 1988, it unveiled a new flagship policy, 'Independence in Europe', and in 1990 Banff and Buchan MP Alex Salmond became leader following Gordon Wilson. Michael Forsyth, Scotland's Tory secretary of state from 1995, played the patriotic card and pulled off an eye-catching coup in 1996 by securing the return of the Stone of Destiny from Westminster Abbey. Labour leader John Smith, a popular Scottish politician, died suddenly in 1994 and was replaced by Tony Blair – born in Edinburgh, raised mainly in Durham but educated at Edinburgh boarding school Fettes College from age 13. Blair's shadow cabinet decided that a referendum would be needed to create a Scottish parliament, in which two questions would be asked, one on the principle of a parliament and the other on a proposed power to vary the basic income tax rate by up to 3 pence in the pound, which Forsyth labelled a 'tartan tax'. It was inevitable that there would have to be a referendum in Wales too.[21]

Ireland, meanwhile, was becoming less socially conservative, with liberalisation championed particularly by Mary Robinson, president from 1990 to 1997. The constitutional ban on abortion was softened in 1992, homosexual sex decriminalised in 1993 and divorce legalised in 1995 after a referendum. After a disappointing economic performance for much of the state's existence, Ireland became one of the world's fastest-growing economies by the 1990s, known as the 'Celtic Tiger'. Factors that helped included offering ultra-low taxes on profits to attract foreign investors, investment to create a better-educated workforce and a 'social partnership' with trade unions to control pay rises and get public spending under control.

Blair, a centrist whose project was dubbed 'New Labour', won a landslide victory at the 1997 Westminster election, ending 18 years of Conservative government; the Tories were wiped out in Scotland and Wales. Aged 43, he was the youngest person to become prime minister since Lord Liverpool, who was aged 42, in 1812. Blair's government introduced a minimum wage, student tuition fees and raised public spending on health, coupled with market-based reforms. His first cabinet contained a record seven Scottish MPs: Gordon Brown, Robin Cook, Derry Irvine, Alistair Darling, George Robertson, Donald Dewar and Gavin Strang. The Welsh secretary was Ron Davies, MP for Caerphilly. In September 1997, the referendum in Scotland resulted in 74.3 per cent voting for a Scottish parliament and 63.5 per cent for tax-raising powers. In Wales, voters backed a National Assembly by a narrow majority of 50.3 per cent, which was nonetheless substantially higher than the 20.3 per cent that had backed devolution in 1979.[22]

Blair's government also made a major breakthrough in Northern Ireland after three decades of conflict. Major's government had already advanced the peace process by holding secret talks with the Provisional IRA and agreeing the 1993 Downing Street Declaration with Albert Reynolds, Ireland's taoiseach, stating among other things that Britain would uphold the right of Northern Ireland's people to decide between the union with Great Britain or a united Ireland. The IRA declared a ceasefire in 1994, as stalemate in the war convinced a republican majority that progress might be achieved better through negotiation. With the help of US president Bill Clinton, the 1998 Good Friday Agreement was reached between the British and Irish governments and most Northern Irish political parties. It included a devolved, inclusive government, prisoner release, troop reductions, targets for paramilitary decommissioning, provisions for polls on Irish reunification, civil rights measures and 'parity of esteem' for Northern Ireland's two communities. Referendums north and south of the border approved the agreement. Voters elected a Northern Ireland Assembly, and then a power-sharing executive was formed in which Ulster Unionist leader David Trimble was first minister and Seamus Mallon of the Social Democratic and Labour Party was his deputy. Among republicans, Gerry Adams, Sinn Féin president 1983–2018, was an important figure in the peace process. The assembly and executive had a stop-start existence over following decades. Dissident republicans who refused to accept the Good Friday Agreement formed the Real IRA, which carried out a bombing in Omagh in August 1998, killing 29 people.

In October 1998, Welsh Secretary Ron Davies was assaulted while apparently seeking homosexual experiences on Clapham Common and resigned the next day over what he called 'a moment of madness'. He was replaced by Alun Michael. Elections to the Scottish parliament and National Assembly of Wales were held in May 1999 under a mixture of first-past-the-post and proportional representation. In Scotland, Labour formed a coalition with the Liberal Democrats, with Donald Dewar as first minister. In Wales, Labour won less than half the seats, with Plaid Cymru performing strongly even in south Wales. Alun Michael became first secretary and formed a minority government rather than a coalition.[23]

When the Scottish parliament convened in May 1999 at its temporary home, the Church of Scotland's General Assembly Hall in Edinburgh, SNP member Winnie Ewing became the presiding officer as its oldest qualified member. She opened the session by saying: 'The Scottish Parliament, adjourned on the twenty-fifth day of March in the year 1707, is hereby reconvened.'[24]

CHAPTER 17

THE BREAK-UP THAT DIDN'T HAPPEN

Any expectations that Labour's devolution strategy for Scotland, Wales and Northern Ireland might settle the UK's constitutional future proved short-lived. The picture has remained in flux, as it has in one way or another for much of the Isles' history.

Almost a century after most of Ireland left the union, Scotland held an independence referendum in 2014 in which voters rejected independence by 55.3 per cent to 44.7 per cent. Pressure for a second referendum has since eased, though the issue may no doubt at some point move back up the agenda. Northern Ireland's assembly and power-sharing executive have been suspended six times because of various disputes. In England, 14 directly elected 'metro' or regional mayors have been created in places such as Greater London, Greater Manchester, Liverpool City Region and the West Midlands. However, plans by Tony Blair's government for English regional assemblies died after north-east voters rejected such an assembly by four-to-one in 2004. The National Assembly of Wales meanwhile won the power to make primary legislation in 2011 and in 2020 was renamed Senedd Cymru, or Welsh parliament.

The Northern Ireland institutions, created in 1999, were first suspended for three months in 2000 as unionist parties refused to participate alongside Sinn Féin until it was clear that the IRA had discontinued its activities, decommissioned its weapons and disbanded. In Wales, Alun Michael – widely seen as having been imposed on Welsh Labour by Blair – resigned as first minister after less than nine months in office, to avoid a no-confidence vote called by Plaid Cymru over what it claimed was his failure to secure Treasury funding to match European Union development grants. He was replaced by Rhodri Morgan, who had stood twice but had been seen by Blair as too traditionalist. Morgan became Wales's longest-serving first minister, in office for almost 10 years. Blair also suffered a rebuff when the mayoralty of London and assembly were created in 2000, the first of England's metro mayors. Ken Livingstone, a vocal left-wing critic of Blair's New Labour project, after failing to become Labour's candidate, ran as an independent and won. He was in office for eight years.[1]

The Scottish parliament also got off to a difficult start. Donald Dewar, long prone to black moods and self-doubt, looked weary by the time he took office in 1999. There were mishaps, and Dewar and his team seemed to be in a constant state of crisis. Dewar commissioned a new building for the parliament opposite Edinburgh's Royal Palace of Holyroodhouse designed by Spanish architect Enric Miralles, but criticism grew when it became clear that costs had been drastically underestimated. It eventually opened in 2004, more than three years late, with an estimated final cost of £414 million compared with initial estimates of £10–40 million. Also in 2000, the parliament abolished Section 28 of the Local Government Act 1988, which prevented local authorities from 'promoting' homosexuality, in the face of intense opposition from the Catholic Church, led by Cardinal Tom Winning, and millionaire bus tycoon Brian Souter, an evangelical Christian; it was subsequently also repealed in England and Wales in 2003. Dewar, who had acute heart problems, died of a brain haemorrhage following a fall in October 2000 after less than 18 months in office. He was widely hailed as the 'father of the nation' for his work in creating the parliament, even by popular newspapers that had portrayed him as bumbling and incompetent.

Other achievements included plans for radical reform of land ownership in the highlands and a bold scheme to transfer Glasgow's huge
council housing stock to tenant-managed housing associations.[2]

Blair was re-elected by a second landslide in June 2001. The elec-
tion campaign was enlivened when John Prescott, Prestatyn-born
deputy prime minister, punched a protester after being hit by an egg
on his way to a rally in Rhyl, north Wales. In Northern Ireland, the
Ulster Unionist Party (UUP) lost four seats to the more hard-line
Democratic Unionist Party (DUP), while the moderate nationalist
Social Democratic and Labour Party lost votes to Sinn Féin. In
Scotland, the Conservatives went from zero seats to one by winning
Galloway and Upper Nithsdale from the SNP but otherwise failed
to regain their former strongholds. Dewar was succeeded by Henry
McLeish, enterprise minister and former professional footballer, who
lasted only a year before resigning over a controversy about having
sub-let part of his office in Glenrothes while an MP without declaring it in the register of interests. After him came Jack McConnell,
first minister from 2001 to 2007. He implemented a ban on smoking in public places and successfully bid for the 2014 Commonwealth
Games to be hosted in Glasgow. In March 2002, more than 800
years of underground coal mining in Scotland ended when the last
deep mine of any significance, Longannet in Fife, closed after flooding. Tower Colliery near Aberdare, the last deep mine in south
Wales, closed in 2008.[3]

Blair's second term was dominated by the 'war on terror' after the
11 September 2001 al-Qaeda Islamist attacks on the US. Blair
supported President George W. Bush and committed British troops
to war in Afghanistan to overthrow the Taliban government and
destroy al-Qaeda. More controversially, Britain joined the US in
invading Iraq in 2003 in the inaccurate belief that Saddam Hussein's
regime possessed weapons of mass destruction. The policy faced
large-scale opposition, including among Blair's own MPs. Robin
Cook, MP for Livingston, resigned as leader of the Commons in
protest. As casualties mounted, Blair's popularity declined sharply.

In March 2002, Queen Elizabeth the Queen Mother, mother of Elizabeth II, died at age 101. She was the daughter of Claude Bowes-Lyon, Lord Glamis (later the 14th Earl of Strathmore and Kinghorne) and his wife Cecilia Cavendish-Bentinck, and spent her childhood partly at Glamis Castle in Angus, the earl's ancestral home. As George VI's queen consort in the Second World War, she cheered the public by refusing to leave London during the Blitz. In later years, she was the royal family's matriarch and remained popular even when other royals suffered low public approval.[4]

In Ireland, the Fianna Fáil–Progressive Democrat administration led by Bertie Ahern was re-elected with a larger majority in May 2002. Ahern had played an important part with Blair in negotiating the Good Friday Agreement. The Northern Ireland Assembly and executive were suspended again from October 2002 until May 2007 as a result of 'Stormontgate': unionist parties withdrew from the executive after Sinn Féin's offices at the assembly were raided by police, investigating allegations of intelligence-gathering on behalf of the IRA by members of the party's support staff. Charges were later dropped against three men including Denis Donaldson, the Sinn Féin group's head of administration, who subsequently confessed to having been a British MI5 spy for 20 years. He was later shot dead, for which the dissident republican Real IRA claimed responsibility.[5]

Blair's government was re-elected in 2005, helped by the UK's strong economic performance, but with a substantially reduced majority, down from 167 seats to 66, as a result of the Iraq War controversy. This victory made him the only Labour leader to have achieved an overall majority at three consecutive general elections. In Northern Ireland, the UUP was reduced from six MPs to one, with leader David Trimble unseated; the DUP became the largest party with nine MPs. Charles Kennedy, Liberal Democrat leader and MP for Ross, Skye and Lochaber, resigned in January 2006 after admitting he had received treatment for alcoholism. He was succeeded by Menzies Campbell, MP for North East Fife.[6]

The government faced problems such as failures by the Home Office to deport illegal immigrants. Blair, Labour's longest-serving prime minister, resigned in June 2007 after 10 years in office and was succeeded by Gordon Brown, his chancellor. Brown had been raised in Kirkcaldy, Fife, as a 'son of the manse' – his father was a Church of Scotland minister – and studied history at the University of Edinburgh. When Labour leader John Smith died in 1994, Brown had left the way clear for Blair so as to avoid splitting the modernising, centrist vote in the leadership election, allegedly after a deal was struck between them at Granita restaurant in Islington. If there was such a deal, each appeared to have a different idea of what it entailed. There were tensions during Blair's prime ministership, with Brown apparently impatient to take over quickly, though they remained united in public. As chancellor, Brown presided over a long period of economic growth, transferred interest rate-setting to the Bank of England, extended the Treasury's powers over domestic policy and transferred banking supervision to the Financial Services Authority. He also set five economic tests that resulted in Britain staying out of the euro, the currency of most European Union member states, introduced in 1999.[7]

In Northern Ireland, a new election to the suspended assembly was held in March 2007 in which the DUP and Sinn Féin remained the largest parties and agreed to enter government together. An administration was formed in May with the DUP's Ian Paisley as first minister and Sinn Féin's Martin McGuinness as deputy. Paisley was co-founder and leader of the Free Presbyterian Church of Ulster, famed for his fiery sermons and denunciations of Catholicism, ecumenism and homosexuality. After an election in the Irish Republic, Ahern remained taoiseach and the Fianna Fáil–Progressive Democrat administration was joined by the Green Party. A Welsh Assembly election resulted in a Labour–Plaid coalition, with Morgan remaining first minister until he retired in 2009, succeeded by Swansea-born Carwyn Jones.[8]

There was a major change at the Scottish parliament election in May 2007 when the SNP came first, one seat ahead of the governing

Labour Party, and a minority SNP government was formed with Alex Salmond as first minister.[9] Salmond, a former Royal Bank of Scotland economist, had led the SNP from 1990 to 2000 before standing down to lead the SNP group at Westminster, but he returned to the party leadership in 2004 and became the Scottish parliament's member for Gordon in 2007. His government passed significant legislation including abolition of university tuition fees, scrapping of prescription charges and commitment to renewable energy.

Brown's premiership was dominated by the 2008 global financial crisis, which triggered the deepest UK recession since the Second World War, lasting five quarters. The government took majority shareholdings in Northern Rock and Royal Bank of Scotland, which had experienced severe financial trouble, and injected public money into other banks. Economic output shrank by 4.8 per cent in Scotland, slightly less severe than the UK's 6 per cent overall decline. Wales experienced a sharp rise in unemployment, a downturn in the housing market and a squeeze on wages. Steelmaker Corus announced the loss of up to 1,100 jobs at its plants in Wales and the mothballing of the Llanwern hot strip mill. Hoover at Merthyr and Indesit at Kinmel Park, Bodelwyddan, in Denbighshire, both ceased washing machine production. UK unemployment rose to 8.3 per cent or 2.68 million by August 2011, the highest number since 1994.[10]

In Ireland, Brian Cowen, finance minister, became taoiseach in May 2008 after Ahern resigned amid an investigation into possible past financial misconduct. Cowen's government mounted a bailout of Ireland's banking system, thrown into crisis by the housing market's collapse, but the rescue came at the cost of a soaring budget deficit. As economic difficulties mounted, Cowen increased income taxes and cut services. In November 2010, as concern for Ireland's financial stability grew among its eurozone partners, Cowen was forced to agree a bailout of €85 billion (£72 billion) from the European Union and International Monetary Fund. That was regarded as a national humiliation, and Cowen was heavily criticised for failing to stem the crisis. The *Irish Times* editorialised: 'There is the shame of it all. Having obtained our political independence from Britain to be the masters of our own affairs, we have now surrendered our sovereignty to the European Commission, the European Central Bank, and the International Monetary Fund.'[11]

In England, Conservative politician and former journalist Boris Johnson became mayor of London, defeating Livingstone in the 2008 mayoral election. The DUP's Peter Robinson, finance minister, succeeded Paisley as first minister in Northern Ireland. Away from politics, Scotland's Roman-era Antonine Wall was designated a UNESCO World Heritage Site, joining St Kilda, Edinburgh Old and New Towns, the Heart of Neolithic Orkney and New Lanark. In February 2009, Northern Irish golfer Rory McIlroy achieved his first professional win at the Dubai Desert Classic at age 19.[12]

Brown lost popularity during the recession, and Labour lost 91 seats at the UK's 2010 general election. The result was a hung parliament in which the Conservatives won the most seats. Their leader David Cameron became prime minister by forming a coalition with the Liberal Democrats.[13] Cameron's government sought to cope with the recession's effects by adopting austerity policies, mainly public spending cuts, to reduce the budget deficit and the role of the welfare state. It also made big changes to healthcare and education, tried to enforce stricter immigration policies, privatised Royal Mail and legalised same-sex marriage in England and Wales.

Ireland's Cowen, under pressure from his Fianna Fáil party, announced his departure and called an election in February 2011 after the Green Party left the coalition. Micheál Martin, foreign affairs minister, took over as leader of Fianna Fáil, which suffered a crushing defeat by Fine Gael. Enda Kenny, Fine Gael's leader, became taoiseach in coalition with Labour. Wales's National Assembly, which had been granted limited law-making powers in 2006, gained enhanced powers after a March 2011 referendum, meaning that it could pass laws on devolved matters without consulting the UK parliament or secretary of state for Wales. In Wales's May election, Labour increased its seats to just one short of a majority, so

Carwyn Jones opted to form a minority government rather than continue the coalition with Plaid. In Northern Ireland's election, both the DUP and Sinn Féin increased their number of seats. In Scotland, Salmond's SNP won the first majority since the opening of Holyrood, a remarkable feat since the additional member system – combining first-past-the-post seats with 'top-up' members elected by region – was designed to prevent any party achieving an overall majority. The SNP manifesto repeated its commitment to an independence referendum.[14]

Riots took place in cities and towns across England in August 2011, causing five deaths, attributed to factors including racial and class tensions, economic decline and unemployment. Two giant pandas called Tian Tian and Yang Guang arrived at Edinburgh Zoo from China in December 2011 to huge fanfare in what became known as 'panda diplomacy'. The UK became gripped by eight failed attempts to enable the pandas to produce cubs by artificial insemination before they were returned to China in 2023. The Scottish parliament gained more powers in 2012, including the ability to raise or lower income tax by up to 10 pence in the pound (up from 3 pence) and borrow more money. Cameron's UK government offered to legislate to provide the Scottish parliament with the powers to hold an independence referendum, providing it was 'fair, legal and decisive', which led to the vote being set for September 2014. In Wales, an act giving the Welsh and English languages equal status in the Welsh Assembly was the first law passed in the nation for more than 600 years.[15]

Belfast's last working linen factory, Copeland Linens, based in the Shankill area, closed in 2013; it was a long decline from the end of the nineteenth century when almost 100,000 people worked in the trade, making it the city's largest employer. In Ireland, a report into Magdalene asylums or laundries, institutions that operated from the eighteenth to the late twentieth centuries to house 'fallen women', found state collusion in the admission of thousands to the institutions, where they were abused and worked for nothing in conditions of slavery. Taoiseach Kenny delivered an emotional apology on the state's behalf, and 800 to 1,000 surviving Magdalene women were told that a compensation scheme would be set up. In Scotland, Glasgow School of Art, designed by Charles Rennie Mackintosh, was severely damaged in a fire in May 2014; the building was destroyed by a second fire four years later, with only the burnt-out shell remaining.[16]

In Scotland's referendum, Salmond was the leading figure in the Yes Scotland campaign. The Better Together campaign was headed by Alistair Darling, former chancellor, with support from the Conservatives, Labour and Liberal Democrats. Polls suggested from the outset that it would be an uphill battle for the pro-independence lobby, though these narrowed in the run-up to polling day. There were two televised debates between Salmond and Darling. The final result, to remain in the UK by 55.3 per cent to 44.7 per cent, represented a wider margin than polls had suggested. The 84.6 per cent turnout was high compared with a usual 56 per cent at general elections.[17]

Salmond said he accepted the 'verdict of the people' but resigned as SNP leader and first minister, saying that 'for me as leader my time is nearly over but for Scotland the campaign continues and the dream shall never die'. Cameron said he was 'delighted' with the result, adding: 'It would have broken my heart to see our United Kingdom come to an end and I know that this sentiment was shared not just by people across our country but also around the world.' Cameron later said he was 'extremely sorry and very embarrassed' for revealing Queen Elizabeth's private view by telling former New York mayor Michael Bloomberg that she 'purred down the line' when he informed her that Scotland had voted against independence. The monarch, who had urged voters to think 'very carefully' before casting their votes, had declined to take sides in public.[18]

Salmond was succeeded by Nicola Sturgeon, a former Glasgow solicitor who had been deputy first minister. The SNP enjoyed a huge surge in support after the referendum and won 56 out of 59

Scottish seats in the 2015 UK general election, replacing the Liberal Democrats as the third largest party in the Commons. Sturgeon had stated that the election was not about independence but primarily about a stronger voice for Scotland in London. She also suggested, though, that the party would hold another independence referendum if it won the next Holyrood election on a manifesto promising a second vote. Cameron won an unexpected majority of 10 seats in the general election, despite polls and commentators suggesting a second hung parliament, so the Conservatives were able to govern without the Lib Dems.[19]

In Northern Ireland, the DUP's Arlene Foster became first minister in January 2016 after Robinson stepped down. In the Irish Republic, Fine Gael lost seats in a February election, as did its coalition partner Labour. After weeks of talks, an agreement was reached in which Fianna Fáil would tolerate a Fine Gael-led minority government, and Kenny was re-elected as taoiseach. In Wales, Labour fell two seats short of a majority at that year's assembly election, but Jones eventually managed to form another minority government. Sturgeon lost her majority in the Scottish parliament but also formed a minority government.[20]

Across the UK, 2016 was dominated by a referendum on whether Britain should remain in the EU, a vote that Cameron had promised in the Conservative manifesto. He announced that he would campaign for Britain to remain within a 'reformed EU', and the UK's membership terms were revised. The option to leave became known as Brexit. Issues during the campaign included the costs and benefits of membership for the UK's economy, freedom of movement and migration. During the campaign, Jo Cox, Labour MP for Batley and Spen and a vocal campaigner for remaining in the EU, was murdered outside her constituency surgery by a man with far-right views. The UK had been a member since joining in 1973, when it was known as the European Economic Community, but membership had become increasingly divisive as integration between member states deepened. The result of the June referendum was a vote to leave the EU by 51.9 per cent to 48.1 per cent. England voted leave by 53.4 per cent and Wales by 52.5 per cent, but Scotland voted remain by 62 per cent and Northern Ireland by 55.8 per cent. Cameron announced his resignation outside 10 Downing Street and walked away humming a tune. He was succeeded by Theresa May, home secretary.[21]

Northern Ireland's executive and assembly collapsed once more in January 2017 over Foster's responsibility for the Renewable Heat Incentive scandal, a failed wood pellet burning scheme that was set to cost the public purse almost £500 million. Foster had initiated the scheme in 2012 when she was enterprise minister but failed to put adequate controls in place, so the cost spiralled. Foster refused to resign or stand aside during any investigation, saying that would be seen as admitting some culpability; she added that those calling for her to go were 'misogynists and male chauvinists'. Her refusal led Sinn Féin's McGuinness to resign in protest after 10 years as deputy first minister. Under the power-sharing arrangement, his resignation also meant that Foster was removed, causing the executive to be suspended for the next three years. McGuinness, a former IRA leader during the Troubles who became one of the main architects of the Good Friday Agreement, died in March 2017, aged 66.[22]

Theresa May, despite having supported Remain, triggered the legal process for the UK to leave the EU. She also called a snap election in June 2017, aiming to strengthen her hand in Brexit negotiations and highlight her 'strong and stable' leadership. It was a serious miscalculation and resulted in the Conservatives losing their overall majority. Former chancellor George Osborne called her a 'dead woman walking'. To prop up her government, May reached a 'confidence and supply' agreement with the DUP, whereby the party's MPs would back the government in key votes in return for various commitments and an extra £1 billion of funding for Northern Ireland, focused on health, infrastructure and education.[23]

In Ireland, Enda Kenny stepped down in 2017 and was replaced as Fine Gael leader and taoiseach by Leo Varadkar, minister for social protection. Varadkar, aged 38 and born in Dublin to a father from Mumbai and a mother from Dunvargan in County Waterford, was the youngest taoiseach in the Irish state's history and the first from an ethnic minority, as well as Ireland's first – and the world's fifth – openly gay head of government. The following year Ireland voted in a referendum to legalise abortion. Carwyn Jones stepped down as Wales's first minister in 2018 and was replaced by Mark Drakeford, finance secretary.[24]

Scotland's Alex Salmond, who had lost his Commons seat to the Conservatives in 2017, resigned from the SNP in August 2018 to fight allegations of sexual misconduct when he was first minister, which he denied. He sought a judicial review, alleging irregularities in the Scottish government's investigation of the complaints; the government conceded the review, and Salmond was awarded £512,000 in legal costs. In January 2019, Police Scotland arrested Salmond and charged him with 14 offences – two counts of attempted rape, nine of sexual assault, two of indecent assault and one of breach of the peace – against 10 women. One of the charges was later dropped. The complainants included an SNP politician, a party worker and several current and former Scottish government civil servants.[25]

May resigned in 2019 after parliament three times rejected versions of her draft EU withdrawal agreement and her party did poorly in elections for the European parliament. She was succeeded by Boris Johnson, who had earlier resigned as foreign secretary. Johnson, born in Manhattan, New York, was the first prime minister born outside British territories. He called an early election in December and won an 80-seat majority, using the slogan 'Get Brexit Done'. The result gave Johnson the mandate he sought to implement the UK's withdrawal from the EU on 31 January 2020. Jeremy Corbyn, Labour's left-wing leader, resigned and was replaced by his shadow Brexit secretary, Sir Keir Starmer.[26]

Devolved government was restored in Northern Ireland once more in January 2020, with Arlene Foster as first minister and Sinn

Féin's Michelle O'Neill as deputy, under an agreement that granted official status to both the Irish language and Ulster Scots. In the Irish Republic, after a general election in February and lengthy negotiations, Fine Gael formed a three-party coalition government with Fianna Fáil and the Green Party, which involved the Fianna Fáil and Fine Gael party leaders rotating the offices of taoiseach and tánaiste (deputy prime minister). Fianna Fáil's Micheál Martin became taoiseach for the first half of the five-year term, with Fine Gael's Varadkar returning to office in 2022.[27]

Salmond's trial in March 2020 resulted in his acquittal on all charges: not guilty on 12 counts and not proven on one of sexual assault with intent to rape. Salmond claimed the allegations were the result of a conspiracy within the Scottish government to drive him from public life. A parliamentary committee found that Nicola Sturgeon had misled parliament in recounting her knowledge of the complaints against Salmond, but an independent ethics inquiry concluded that this did not amount to a breach of the ministerial code. Salmond continued to pursue legal action against the Scottish government until his death in 2024. He served as leader of the nationalist Alba Party from 2021.[28]

The Covid-19 pandemic affected the UK from early 2020, when the virus arrived primarily from travel elsewhere in Europe, leading to high levels of infection in four waves over two years. The UK government and each of the three devolved governments introduced a varying mix of public health and economic measures, with the first national lockdown imposed between March and June 2020. Restrictions were finally lifted by March 2022. One thing that cheered a distressed UK was comedian Janey Godley's spoof voiceovers of Sturgeon's Covid briefings. There was criticism of the UK government's response to the pandemic, in particular the timeliness of public health measures. 'Partygate', a scandal about gatherings of government and Conservative Party staff at a time when public health restrictions prohibited most gatherings, contributed to Johnson's eventual downfall as prime minister.

Brexit meanwhile caused further tensions, particularly the Northern Ireland Protocol, part of the withdrawal agreement. Northern Ireland, but not the rest of the UK, remained in the EU single market for goods trade, allowing an open border to be maintained with the Republic, which instead created a de facto customs border in the Irish Sea between Northern Ireland and Great Britain. Foster launched a judicial review of the protocol, saying it had driven 'a coach and horses' through the Act of Union and the Northern Ireland Act 1998, which gave legislative effect to the Good Friday Agreement, but the High Court in Belfast ruled the protocol to be lawful. After a revolt by her own party in April 2021 over her handling of the issue, Foster resigned and was replaced by Edwin Poots as DUP leader and Paul Givan as first minister. Poots resigned shortly after and was replaced by Sir Jeffrey Donaldson. Givan resigned in February 2022 in protest against the protocol as it came into effect, leading the executive to collapse again. No agreement on power-sharing was made after the 2022 assembly election, so until February 2024 Northern Ireland was again governed by the civil service.[29]

In London, the Partygate scandal mounted as it was revealed that numerous parties had been held in 10 Downing Street during the pandemic. Johnson himself was issued with a fixed penalty notice. He survived a vote of confidence but resigned in July 2022 when there was a mass resignation of ministers over revelations that he had appointed Chris Pincher as Tory deputy chief whip while knowing of allegations of sexual misconduct against him. He was succeeded as prime minister by Liz Truss, foreign secretary. She resigned after just 45 days in office, making her the shortest-serving prime minister in UK history, when large-scale tax cuts funded by borrowing caused instability in financial markets. She was replaced by Rishi Sunak, former chancellor and the UK's first non-white prime minister.[30]

Queen Elizabeth II died in September 2022, having ruled for 70 years and 214 days, the longest reign of any British monarch, the second-longest in any sovereign state after France's Louis XIV and the longest of any reigning queen in history. She faced problems during her reign – particularly after the breakdowns of her children's marriages, including her 'annus horribilis' in 1992 and the death of former daughter-in-law Diana in 1997 – but her own popularity remained consistently high. She died at Balmoral in Aberdeenshire, her Scottish residence, making her the first monarch to die in Scotland since James V in 1542. She was succeeded by her eldest son, Charles III, educated at Gordonstoun School in north-east Scotland. Support for the monarchy as an institution has declined over the past decade or so. The British Social Attitudes survey, conducted by the National Centre for Social Research in the autumn of 2023, showed that 54 per cent of people in Britain now believed that it is 'very' or 'quite important' for Britain to have a monarchy, the lowest proportion recorded since it first asked in 1983. Back then, 86 per cent said that it was important for Britain to have a monarchy.[31]

After the 2021 Scottish parliament election, Sturgeon was again short of a majority and reached a power-sharing accord with the Scottish Green Party. She proposed a second independence referendum for October 2023, but the Supreme Court ruled that the Scottish parliament did not have the power to legislate for a referendum. Her government passed a bill making it easier for trans people to change their legal gender, controversial within her own party, but the UK government blocked it. Sturgeon resigned in February 2023, saying the job 'takes its toll on you'. Health Secretary Humza Yousaf, widely seen as Sturgeon's 'continuity candidate', succeeded her. Yousaf, born to Pakistani immigrants in Glasgow, was the youngest person, first Scottish Asian and first Muslim to serve as first minister. He lasted only 13 months in office and resigned after ending the SNP's accord with the Scottish Greens as a result of changes in climate policy, which left him facing a motion of confidence. He was replaced by John Swinney, who had previously led the SNP in 2000–4.[32]

In Wales, Mark Drakeford, who had led Wales's response to the Covid pandemic and won a working majority in the 2021 Senedd election, resigned in March 2024 and was succeeded by his health minister, Vaughan Gething. Gething resigned six months later after losing a no-confidence motion: his leadership was mired in controversy after he accepted donations from a man twice convicted of environmental offences during his election campaign. He was replaced by Eluned Morgan, health and social care secretary.[33]

In Ireland, Michelle O'Neill became first minister in February 2024, the first time a nationalist had held the post. Sinn Féin had become the largest party at the 2022 assembly election, putting her in line for the position, but for two years the DUP refused to nominate a deputy first minister, citing its opposition to the protocol. Eventually Emma Little-Pengelly was appointed when the DUP's leader, Sir Jeffrey Donaldson, agreed to end the boycott after winning concessions from the UK government that smoothed the so-called Irish Sea border. Donaldson stepped down shortly afterwards, having been charged with rape and historical sexual offences. In the Irish Republic, Varadkar resigned as taoiseach in April 2024, citing personal and political reasons, and was replaced by Fine Gael's Simon Harris. He called an election for November, as a result of which Fianna Fáil's Micheál Martin returned as taoiseach in January 2025 at the head of a coalition with Fine Gael and nine independents.[34]

At the UK general election in July 2024, Labour under Sir Keir Starmer – barrister and former director of public prosecutions, who had moved his party back towards the centre after the Corbyn era – won a 174-seat majority, ending 14 years of Conservative government. Labour won the largest number of seats in England for the first time since 2005, in Scotland for the first time since 2010 and retained its status as the largest party in Wales. His government faced a difficult economic inheritance, however, and received criticism for scrapping certain winter fuel payments for about ten million pensioners. In August, it had to cope with anti-immigration riots across England and Northern Ireland after the mass stabbing of young girls in Southport. The last blast furnace at Port Talbot Steelworks in south Wales, the largest in the UK, was closed by its owner, India's Tata Steel, in September 2024 with the loss of almost 3,000 jobs.[35]

For all the stresses in recent decades, the union of England, Scotland, Wales and Northern Ireland has survived. Scotland's referendum vote in 2014 suggests that the widespread view that the Empire's collapse would lead inevitably to Scottish independence has, at least so far, proved wide of the mark. In 1937, Andrew Dewar Gibb, professor of constitutional law at the University of Glasgow, wrote in *Scottish Empire*: 'The existence of the Empire has been the most important factor in securing the relationship of Scotland and England in the last three centuries.' He implied that without Empire, the union might not last. In *The Break-Up of Britain* (1977), writer Tom Nairn, a Marxist supporter of independence, portrayed the 'slow foundering' of the United Kingdom on the rocks of imperial decline, constitutional anachronism and civic nationalism. He was still sticking to his view in 2020, a couple of years before his death at age 90: 'Within the next five years, in one form or another, break-up is likely to come about.'[36]

The 2021 census revealed that Catholics outnumbered Protestants in Northern Ireland for the first time, a landmark change in a state designed a century earlier to have a permanent Protestant majority. The results showed that 45.7 per cent of inhabitants were Catholic or from a Catholic background compared with 43.48 per cent from Protestant or other Christian backgrounds. The comparable figures in the 2011 census were 45 per cent Catholic and 48 per cent Protestant. Historian Diarmaid Ferriter said with regard to the once impregnable Protestant majority: 'It's been long coming. They have already witnessed the loss of their political supremacy. Seeing the loss of their numerical supremacy is another blow.'[37] That shift has not so far, however, resulted in a majority for unification with the Irish Republic. Opinion polls in recent years have shown 30 to 40 per cent support for a united Ireland, though some polls also suggest the figure may rise above 50 per cent in future. In Wales, opinion polls in recent years have suggested 25 to 35 per cent support for independence.

Strains have long been evident, though, both within and between the UK's nations. It has been anything but a stable picture. If the union is to continue to survive, it will need patience, flexibility, care and understanding.

REFERENCES

Chapter 1: Ancestors, Celts and Romans

1. 'Discovering the oldest human footprints in Europe', Natural History Museum, https://www.nhm.ac.uk/discover/the-oldest-human-footprints-in-europe.html
2. 'First Britons', Natural History Museum, https://www.nhm.ac.uk/discover/first-britons.html
3. 'Waverley Wood Handaxe', British Museum/BBC, https://www.bbc.co.uk/ahistoryoftheworld/objects/ppxWBc1tTcepdoM79hR5_w
4. 'The oldest people in Wales: Neanderthal teeth from Pontnewydd Cave', Museum Wales, https://museum.wales/articles/1014/The-oldest-people-in-Wales—Neanderthal-teeth-from-Pontnewydd-Cave/#:~:text=Excavations%20at%20Pontnewydd%20Cave%2C%20Denbighshire,dating%20back%20some%20230%2C000%20years.&text=19%20teeth%20%2C%20discovered%20found%20deep,an%20early%20form%20of%20Neanderthal.
5. 'Red Lady of Paviland: Should remains come back to Wales?', BBC, 14 January 2023, https://www.bbc.co.uk/news/uk-wales-64264413
6. 'Reindeer bone found in north Cork to alter understanding of Irish human history', *Irish Examiner*, 18 April 2021.
7. 'Signs of earliest Scots unearthed', 9 April 2009, http://news.bbc.co.uk/1/hi/scotland/glasgow_and_west/7992300.stm; Alistair Moffat, *Scotland: A History from the Earliest Times* (Birlinn, 2015), 13–14, 20–1.
8. 'Dramatic discovery links Stonehenge to its original site – in Wales', *Guardian*, 12 February 2021.
9. Barry Cunliffe, *Britain Begins* (Oxford University Press, 2012), 5.

231

10. Simon Schama, *A History of Britain: At the Edge of the World? 3000 BC–AD 1603* (BBC Worldwide, 2000), 26–8.
11. Schama 29–31; Moffat 37–9.
12. David Mattingly, *An Imperial Possession: Britain in the Roman Empire* (Penguin, 2007), 93.
13. John Davies, *A History of Wales* (Penguin, 2007 [1990]), 26.
14. Nicki Howarth, *Cartimandua: Queen of the Brigantes* (History Press, 2008), 56; Tacitus, *Annals*, 12.37.
15. Guy de la Bédoyère, *Roman Britain: A New History* (Thames & Hudson, 2013), 36–9.
16. R.F. Foster (ed.), *The Oxford History of Ireland* (Oxford University Press, 2001 [1989]), 2–3.
17. Tacitus, *Agricola*, 30.
18. Vindolanda Tablet 291.
19. Tablet 346.
20. Tablet 164.
21. Cassius Dio, *Roman History*, 77.11, 77.14; Patricia Southern, *Roman Britain: A New History 55 BC–AD 450* (Amberley Publishing, 2013), 249; Bédoyère 64.
22. David Shotter, *Romans and Britons in North-West England* (Centre for North-West Regional Studies, University of Lancaster, 2004 [1993]), 129–30; Alan Kidd, *The Origins of Manchester, from Roman Conquest to Industrial Revolution* (Carnegie Publishing, 2023), 11, 14.
23. Davies 40, 50–51.

Chapter 2: Shifting Kingdoms

1. Robin Fleming, *Britain after Rome: The Fall and Rise 400 to 1070* (Penguin, 2010), 50–60; Nicholas Higham and Martin Ryan, *The Anglo-Saxon World* (Yale University Press, 2013), 78–91; Stephen Leslie et al., 'The fine-scale genetic structure of the British population', *Nature*, vol. 519 (18 March 2015).
2. Foster 9–11; Schama 48; Moffat 62–3.
3. Norman Davies, *The Isles: A History* (Papermac, 2000 [1999]), 152–5; Foster 11–12, 18–21; Hugh Kearney, *The British Isles: A History of Four Nations* (Cambridge University Press, 2006), 45–6, 52, 75; David Ross, *Ireland: History of a Nation* (Waverley Books, 2019 [2002]), 80–82; Neil Heggarty, *The Story of Ireland: In Search of a New National Memory* (BBC Books, 2012), 19–25.
4. Norman Davies 155; Michael Lynch, *Scotland: A New History* (Pimlico, 1992 [1991]), 17; Moffat 81–2.
5. Lynch 12–17; Norman Davies 161–2; Kearney 54–6; Moffat 82–90.
6. John Davies 60–4, 68–9.
7. Brian Groom, *Northerners: A History, from the Ice Age to the Present Day* (HarperNorth, 2022), 21–7, 29–40.

8. *The Saxon Chronicle*, trans. James Ingram (Longman, Hurst, Rees, Orme & Brown, 1823), entry for AD 793.
9. Groom 41–53.
10. *The Penguin Illustrated History of Britain & Ireland* (Penguin, 2004), 61–5; Schama 54–7; Kearney 60–5.
11. Moffat 125–30; Lynch 42–5.
12. 'National Shrine of Saint Andrew', St Mary's Cathedral, https://www .stmaryscathedral.co.uk/standrew
13. Schama 84–5; Moffat 136–9; Lynch 49–50.
14. Foster 31–7; Kearney 60.
15. Groom 50–2.
16. Foster 37–9; Norman Davies 215, 218, 244, 255; Kearney 75–5; Ross 85–8; Hegarty 44–9.
17. *The Penguin Illustrated History*, 65; 'About Tynwald', Tynwald, https://www .tynwald.org.im/about
18. Kearney 69, 81–2.
19. John Davies 78–96; Norman Davies 223; J. Graham Jones, *The History of Wales* (University of Wales Press, 2014), 14–16; Jon Gower, *The Story of Wales* (BBC Books, 2012), 71–80.
20. John Davies 97–9; Jones 17; Gower 80–2.

Chapter 3: Silent Tongues

1. Martin Johnes, *Wales: England's Colony? The Conquest, Assimilation and Re-creation of Wales* (Parthian, 2019), 95–105.
2. Iain MacKinnon, 'Education and the colonisation of the Gàidhlig mind 2', 4 December 2019, Bella Caledonia, https://bellacaledonia.org. uk/2019/12/04/education-and-the-colonisation-of-the-gaidhlig-mind-2/; Viv Edwards, *Multilingualism in the English-Speaking World: Pedigree of Nations* (John Wiley, 2008), 97–8; Sharon Macdonald, *Reimagining Culture: Histories, Identities and the Gaelic Renaissance* (Routledge, 2020), i.
3. 'The most spoken languages worldwide in 2023', Statista, https://www.scirp .org/reference/referencespapers?referenceid=3812670; Norman Davies 654.
4. 'Unesco world atlas of languages', https://ocm.iccrom.org/documents/unesco -world-atlas-languages
5. Ireland's Central Statistics Office, 'Census of population 2022: Summary results', https://www.cso.ie/en/releasesandpublications/ep/p-cpsr /censusofpopulation2022-summaryresults/; Welsh Government, 'Welsh language in Wales (Census 2021)', https://www.gov.wales/welsh-language -wales-census-2021-html; Scottish Government, 'Gaelic language plan 2022 to 2027', https://www.gov.scot/publications/scottish-governments-gaelic -language-plan-2022-2027/; 'Breton', Minority Rights Group, https:// minorityrights.org/communities/breton/; Isle of Man Government, '2021 Isle of Man census report part 1', https://www.gov.im/media/1375604

/2021-01-27-census-report-part-i-final-2.pdf; Siarl Ferdinand, 'Implementing Cornish in Cornwall and the Isles of Scilly: Attitudes by the population', *Studia Celtica Fennica*, vol. 16 (2019), https://journal.fi/scf/article/view /79496

6. Foster 8, 36; Ross 249; 'History of the Irish language', Údarás na Gaeltachta, https://udaras.ie/en/our-language-the-gaeltacht/history-of-the-irish -language/#:~:text=Irish%20is%20one%20of%20the,magazines%20 and%20on%20the%20internet

7. David Greene, 'Celtic languages', Britannica, https://www.britannica.com /topic/Celtic-languages

8. 'The history of Irish', BBC, https://www.bbc.co.uk/voices/multilingual/irish _history.shtml; Foster 168; Hegarty 213.

9. Norman Davies 813–14.

10. 'Anglicisation and de-Anglicisation', University College Cork, https://web .archive.org/web/20091213024342/http://multitext.ucc.ie/d/Anglicisation _and_De-Anglicisation; 'The history of Irish'; Foster 186, 219–21.

11. 'The history of Irish'; 'History of Protestants and Irish language', 6 March 2019, NorthernIrelandWorld, https://www.northernirelandworld.com /news/history-of-protestants-and-irish-language-86539; Rosalind Pritchard, 'Protestants and the Irish language: Historical heritage and current attitudes in Northern Ireland', *Journal of Multilingual and Multicultural Development*, vol. 25 (2004), https://cain.ulster.ac.uk/issues/language/pritchard04.htm

12. 'Films, books, music, agus ... yeah: The Irish language's new cultural moment', *Irish Examiner*, 22 July 2023, https://www.irishexaminer.com /lifestyle/people/arid-41188543.html; 'The Quiet Girl: The Irish-language film making noise at the Oscars', *Financial Times*, 10 January 2023, https:// www.ft.com/content/4d7a2f11-f2d3-4072-a325-b6a82de22943

13. Greene, 'Celtic languages'; 'Background on the Irish language', Údarás na Gaeltachta, https://web.archive.org/web/20191224044952/http://www .udaras.ie/en/an-ghaeilge-an-ghaeltacht/stair-na-gaeilge/; Donald MacAulay, *The Celtic Languages* (Cambridge University Press, 1992), 144; Charles Withers, *Gaelic in Scotland, 1698–1981* (John Donald, 1984).

14. Withers 19–23; Lynch 76–83.

15. Lynch 241–2; Neil Oliver, *A History of Scotland* (Weidenfeld & Nicolson, 2009), 245.

16. Lynch 338; Moffat 451–2; 'Gaelic history', Highland Council, https://www .highland.gov.uk/site/gaelic-toolkit/toolkit/gaelic_history/index.html#:~:text =Settlers%20brought%20Gaelic%20to%20Scotland,majority%20of%20 the%20country's%20population.

17. 'Scots Gaelic', bbc.co.uk; Withers 115–73; 'Where is Gaelic spoken?', Visit Scotland, https://www.visitscotland.com/things-to-do/attractions/arts -culture/scottish-languages/gaelic

18. 'Gaelic history', Highland Council; 'Scots Gaelic could die out within a decade, study finds', *Guardian*, 2 July 2020, https://www.theguardian.com

/uk-news/2020/jul/02/scots-gaelic-could-die-out-within-a-decade-study
-finds

19. 'Scots speakers', Scots Language Centre, https://www.scotslanguage.com
/articles/node/id/1192; 'Languages', Scotland's Census, https://www
.scotlandscensus.gov.uk/census-results/at-a-glance/languages/

20. 'Census 2021 main statistics language tables', Northern Ireland Statistics
and Research Agency, https://www.nisra.gov.uk/publications/census-2021
-main-statistics-language-tables

21. 'Scots: an outline history', Dictionaries of the Scots Language, https://dsl
.ac.uk

22. Groom 276–82.

23. 'A Speach in Parliament: Anno 1603', in *The Workes of the Most High and
Mightie Prince Iames, by the Grace of God* (1616), 485.

24. 'Primary education: A report of the Advisory Council on Education in
Scotland', Scottish Education Department, 1946, 75.

25. 'Scots language policy', Scottish Government, 3 September 2015, https://
www.gov.scot/binaries/content/documents/govscot/publications/factsheet
/2015/09/scots-language-policy-english/documents/scots-language-policy
-english-pdf/scots-language-policy-english-pdf/govscot%3Adocument
/scots%2Blanguage%2Bpolicy%2B-%2Benglish.pdf

26. 'Manx Gaelic', Isle of Man Government, https://www.gov.im/categories
/home-and-neighbourhood/manx-gaelic/; 'Edward Maddrell', iMuseum,
https://imuseum.im/search/collections/people/mnh-agent-94876.html

27. 'Why Cornwall is resurrecting its indigenous language', BBC, 24 April
2023, https://www.bbc.co.uk/travel/article/20230423-why-cornwall-is
-resurrecting-its-indigenous-language; 'Cornish making a comeback',
Language Magazine, 22 May 2023, https://languagemagazine.com
/2023/05/22/cornish-making-a-comeback/

28. John Davies 68; 'Taliesen', 20 October 2009, https://www.bbc.co.uk/wales
/arts/sites/early-welsh-literature/pages/taliesin.shtml

29. Johnes 68–70; John Davies 228–9, 236–9.

30. John Davies 297–9, 401–4; Johnes 88–90.

31. Johnes 92–94, 143.

32. Johnes 147–8.

33. John Davies 626–7; Johnes 156–8.

34. John Davies 627–8, 656, 703–5; 'Welsh language measure receives Royal
Assent', 11 February 2011, https://web.archive.org/web/20130922140142
/http://wales.gov.uk/newsroom/welshlanguage/2011/110211welshlang/?
lang=en

35. 'Concern raised as number of Welsh language speakers falls', *South Wales
Argus*, 19 November 2023, https://www.southwalesargus.co.uk
/news/23929540.concern-raised-number-welsh-language-speakers
-falls/

Chapter 4: Wars and Medieval Cruelty

1. Katherine Holman, *The Northern Conquest: Vikings in Britain and Ireland* (Signal, 2007), 23; Higham and Ryan, *The Anglo-Saxon World*, 418; Marc Morris, *The Norman Conquest* (Hutchinson, 2012), 338.
2. Kearney 98, 100.
3. Marjorie Chibnall, trans., *The Ecclesiastical History of Orderic Vitalis* (Clarendon, 1969–83), 230–3; quoted in Morris 229.
4. Richard Huscroft, *The Norman Conquest: A New Introduction* (Pearson Longman, 2009), 147, 152; Lynch 75–6; Moffat 144–7; Oliver 72–4.
5. Keith Stringer, 'Emergence of a nation-state', in Jenny Wormald (ed.), *Scotland: A History* (Oxford University Press, 2005), 41–7; Lynch 80–3; Moffat 149–64; Oliver 76–8.
6. Norman Davies 291–4; Schama 121–50; Kearney 117–28; Foster 43–55; Ross 95–103; Hegarty 52–81.
7. Lynch 84–7; Moffat 164–76; Oliver 78–9.
8. Norman Davies 298–9, 301–5; Schama 151–65; John Davies 131–9; Oliver 80–91; Lynch 87–8; Moffat 190.
9. Dan Jackson, *The Northumbrians: North East England and Its People* (Hurst, 2019), 38.
10. Schama 184–90; *The Penguin Illustrated History*, 88; John Davies 150–53; Gower 117–19; Jones 33–4.
11. Schama 190–93; John Davies 154–7; Gower 119–20; Jones 34–5.
12. Schama 193–6; Kearney 110–11; John Davies 162–75; Jones 37–9; Gower 123–5.
13. Schama 196–7.
14. Schama 197–200; Lynch 85, 114; Moffat 200–1; Oliver 95–7.
15. Lynch 114–15; Moffat 202–5; Oliver 96–9; Schama 200–1.
16. Lynch 116–18; Norman Davies 318–19; Schama 203–5; Moffat 216–17; Oliver 100–3.
17. Norman Davies 320; Schama 205–9; Kearney 116; Moffat 208–13; Oliver 105–17; Lynch 118–20.
18. Moffat 214–20; Lynch 120–4; Oliver 119–48; Norman Davies 321–2; Schama 210–12.
19. Schama 216–17.
20. Lynch 94, 111, 125–8; Schama 218–20; Moffat 222–5; Oliver 148–60.
21. Norman Davies 345–56; Schama 220–25; Kearney 133–4; *The Penguin Illustrated History*, 96–8; Lynch 128–30; Oliver 160–61.
22. Schama 225–38; *The Penguin Illustrated History*, 104–5.
23. Schama 241–66; Norman Davies 366–74; *The Penguin Illustrated History*, 98–9; John Davies 191–200.
24. Norman Davies 374–5; Lynch 143–58; Moffat 239–53; Oliver 170–95.
25. Foster 76–82; Katharine Simms, 'Ní Chearbhaill, Mairgréag [Margaret O'Carroll] (d.1451)', *Oxford Dictionary of National Biography* (ODNB),

https://www.oxforddnb.com/display/10.1093/ref:odnb/9780198614128.001
.0001/odnb-9780198614128-e-20486

26. Alison Weir, *Lancaster and York: The Wars of the Roses* (Jonathan Cape, 1995), 415–17.

Chapter 5: Reformation and Revolution

1. Schama 380–84; Moffat 295–6; Oliver 239; John Guy, *'My Heart Is My Own': The Life of Mary Queen of Scots* (Fourth Estate, 2004), 7–9, 488; Antonia Fraser, *Mary Queen of Scots* (Weidenfeld & Nicolson, 1994 [1969]), 538–40; Alison Weir, *Mary, Queen of Scots and the Murder of Lord Darnley* (Random House, 2008 [2003]), 209; Jenny Wormald, *Mary, Queen of Scots* (George Philip, 1988), 187.
2. Charles Carlton, *The Experience of the British Civil Wars* (Routledge, 1992), 211–14; 'The impact of the fighting', in J.S. Morrill (ed.), *The Impact of the English Civil War* (Collins & Brown, 1991), 20; Jack Binns, *Yorkshire in the Civil Wars: Origins, Impact and Outcome* (Blackthorn, 2004), ix; Blair Worden, *The English Civil Wars: 1640–1660* (Weidenfeld & Nicolson, 2009), 73.
3. R. Schofield, 'The geographical distribution of wealth in England 1334–1649', *Economic History Review*, vol. 18 (1965), 483–510.
4. Norman Davies 407; Kearney 171; *The Penguin Illustrated History* 118; John Davies 225–9.
5. Norman Davies 382, 408.
6. Kearney 159; Norman Davies 408.
7. Schama 321, 325.
8. 'Gráinne Mhaol, pirate queen of Connacht: Behind the legend', History Ireland, March/April 2005, https://historyireland.com/grainne-mhaol-pirate-queen-of-connacht-behind-the-legend/
9. Moffat 288–95; Oliver 220–33; Lynch 212–20.
10. G.P.V. Akrigg (ed.), *Letters of King James VI and I* (University of California Press, 1984), 3; Norman Davies 454–5; Oliver 234–9.
11. William Cobbett, *A History of the Protestant Reformation in England and Ireland* (Simpkin, Marshall, 1857; letters written 1820s), 229.
12. Moffat 317–18.
13. Simon Schama, *A History of Britain: The British Wars 1603–1776* (BBC Worldwide, 2001), 32–3.
14. Eric Musgrove, *The North of England: A History from Roman Times to the Present* (Basil Blackwell, 1990), 228–36; J.S. Morrill, 'The northern gentry and the great rebellion', *Northern History*, vol. 15 (1979), 66–87; Worden 390.
15. John Dorney, 'War and famine in Ireland 1580–1700', https://www.theirishstory.com/2012/01/03/war-and-famine-in-ireland-1580-1700/

16. N.J. Frangopulo (ed.), *Rich Inheritance: A Guide to the History of Manchester* (Manchester Education Committee, 1962), 31, 211–13.
17. Norman Davies 519–20.

Chapter 6: Kingdoms Unite

1. *Memoirs of the Life of Sir John Clerk of Penicuik, Baronet, Baron of the Exchequer* (Scottish History Society, 1892), 69, via National Library of Scotland, https://digital.nls.uk/scottish-history-society-publications/browse /archive/127715001#?c=0&m=0&s=0&cv=54
2. Schama, *A History of Britain: The British Wars* 330–36; Lynch 307–10; T.M. Devine, *Scotland's Empire: The Origins of the Global Diaspora* (Allen Lane, 2003), 44–8.
3. John Prebble, *The Darien Disaster* (Pimlico, 1968), 10–15; Douglas Watt, *The Price of Scotland: Darien, Union and the Wealth of Nations* (Luath Press, 2014), 1–11; Devine 44–6.
4. Lynch 307–10; Schama 330–36; Julie Orr, *Scotland, Darien and the Atlantic World 1698–1700* (Edinburgh University Press, 2018), 83; Devine 44–6.
5. *Sir John Clerk's Observations on the Present Circumstances in Scotland, 1730* (Miscellany of the Scottish History Society, 1965), 192, via National Library of Scotland, https://digital.nls.uk/scottish-history-society -publications/browse/archive/126695283?mode=transcription
6. Christopher A. Whatley, *The Scots and the Union* (Edinburgh University Press, 2006), 253–6; T.M. Devine, *The Scottish Nation 1700–2007* (Allen Lane, 1999), 13–14.
7. Norman Davies 528.
8. Hugh Douglas, 'Macdonald, Flora (1722–1790)', ODNB, https://www .oxforddnb.com/display/10.1093/ref:odnb/9780198614128.001.0001 /odnb-9780198614128-e-17432; Devine, *Scotland's Empire* 186.
9. Devine, *The Scottish Nation* 45–8.
10. Linda Colley, *Britons: Forging the Union 1707–1837* (Vintage, 1996 [1992]), 125; Devine, *Scotland's Empire* 311–12.
11. Devine, *The Scottish Nation* 196.
12. Smout cited in Colley 128.
13. Devine, *The Scottish Nation* 72–7; Devine, *Scotland's Empire* 175–81.
14. Norman Davies 606.
15. Theory outlined by Élie Halévy in various writings, notably the *History of the English People in the Nineteenth Century* (E. Benn, published from 1913 onwards).
16. Kearney 199–202.
17. John Davies 293–305.
18. Foster 145.
19. Cathal Póirtéir (ed.), *The Great Irish Famine* (Mercier, 1955), 53–5; 'Dancing on Ice: Recalling the Great Frost of 1740', *Irish Independent*, 4 March 2018,

https://www.independent.ie/irish-news/dancing-on-ice-recalling-the-great
-frost-of-1740/36663457.html; James Kelly, *Food Rioting in Ireland in the
Eighteenth and Nineteenth Centuries* (Four Courts, 2017), 36.
20. Foster 137.
21. Norman Davies 532; Foster 151–3.

Chapter 7: Britain Industrialises

1. Moffat 456; Ian Winstanley (ed.), *Children's Employment Commission 1842*
   (Picks Publishing, 1999), 88, http://www.cmhrc.co.uk/cms/document
   /1842_N_Lancs.pdf
2. Charles Campbell, *Memoirs of Charles Campbell, at Present Prisoner in the
   Jail of Glasgow* (1828), 23; cited in Emma Griffin, *Liberty's Dawn: A People's
   History of the Industrial Revolution* (Yale University Press, 2013), 25.
3. Paul Bairoch, 'International industrialisation levels from 1750 to 1980',
   Journal of European Economic History, vol. 11 (1982), 296, reproduced in
   Paul Kennedy, *The Rise and Fall of the Great Powers* (Vintage, 1989), 149.
4. Sven Beckert, *Empire of Cotton: A New History of Global Capitalism* (Allen
   Lane, 2014), ix.
5. Devine, *The Scottish Nation* 252.
6. Roger Osborne, *Iron, Steam & Money: The Making of the Industrial
   Revolution* (Bodley Head, 2013), 108–36.
7. 'Overdraft authorisation, 1728', https://www.natwestgroup.com/heritage
   /history-100/objects-by-theme/serving-our-customers/overdraft-authorisation
   -1728.html
8. Devine, *The Scottish Nation* 251.
9. Ian Adams, *The Making of Urban Scotland* (Croom Helm, 1978), 155;
   Devine, *The Scottish Nation* 334.
10. Emma Griffin, *A Short History of the British Industrial Revolution*
    (Palgrave Macmillan, 2010), 53–62; Joel Mokyr, *The Enlightened
    Economy: Britain and the Industrial Revolution 1700–1850* (Penguin,
    2009), 302–5; Fred Singleton, *Industrial Revolution in Yorkshire*
    (Dalesman, 1970), 45–6.
11. Sue Wilkes, *Narrow Windows, Narrow Lives: The Industrial Revolution in
    Lancashire* (Tempus, 2008), 56, 61.
12. Thomas Carlyle, *Past and Present* (Chapman & Hall, 1843), book 1,
    chapter 1.
13. Griffin, *A Short History of the British Industrial Revolution* 145.
14. Jonathan Bardon, 'Belfast at its Zenith', *History Ireland*, vol. 1, no. 4
    (Winter 1993), https://historyireland.com/a-history-of-ulster-jonathan
    -bardon-and-nine-ulster-lives-g-obrien-p-roebuck-eds-11/
15. Bardon.
16. 'The story of Guinness', https://www.guinness-storehouse.com/en/discover
    /story-of-guinness

17. Foster 162.
18. 'Ireland's industrial heritage: The past you might not know we had', *Irish Times*, 22 August 2015.
19. Brian R. Mitchell, *Abstract of British Historical Statistics* (Cambridge University Press, 1962), 20, 22.
20. John Davies 315–17.
21. John Davies 323–5.
22. John Davies 340–1.
23. John Davies 372–3.
24. John Williams, 'Thomas, Lucy (bap. 1781, d.1847)', ODNB, https://www.oxforddnb.com/display/10.1093/ref:odnb/9780198614128.001.0001/odnb-9780198614128-e-47974
25. 'Amy Dillwyn: LGBT History Month', 14 February 2018, https://companieshouse.blog.gov.uk/2018/02/14/amy-dillwyn-lgbt-history-month/
26. John Davies 387.
27. Lawrence James, *The Decline and Fall of the British Empire* (Little, Brown, 1994), 202.

Chapter 8: Empire on which the Sun Never Sets

1. Tim Jeal, *Stanley: The Impossible Life of Africa's Greatest Explorer* (Yale University Press, 2007), 25–8.
2. 'Dee, John (1527–1608)', Dictionary of Welsh Biography (DWB), https://biography.wales/article/s-DEE0-JOH-1527#?c=0&m=0&s=0&cv=0&manifest=https%3A%2F%2Fdamsssl.llgc.org.uk%2Fiiif%2F2.0%2F4673676%2Fmanifest.json&xywh=550%2C1184%2C1313%2C1060
3. Cecil Rhodes, *The Last Will and Testament of Cecil Rhodes*, ed. W.T. Stead (London 'Review of Reviews' Office, 1902), 58.
4. John M. Mackenzie and T.M. Devine (eds), *Scotland and the British Empire* (Oxford University Press, 2011).
5. 'Sir Walter Scott's India network', Edinburgh India Institute, https://india-institute.ed.ac.uk/india-in-edinburgh/leaving-and-arriving/sir-walter-scott; Devine, *Scotland's Empire* 251.
6. Devine, *The Scottish Nation* 290.
7. Schama, *A History of Britain: The Fate of Empire* 318–19, 324–9; 'James Andrew Broun Ramsay, marquess and 10th earl of Dalhousie', https://www.britannica.com/biography/James-Andrew-Broun-Ramsay-Marquess-of-Dalhousie
8. Schama, *A History of Britain: The Fate of Empire* 359, 363.
9. Devine, *The Scottish Nation* 474.
10. Matthew Lee, 'Historical context', University of Aberdeen, https://research-scotland.ac.uk/server/api/core/bitstreams/24f30e1e-78c7-42b5-b145-b21110c698ce/content

11. Agence France-Presse, 'Glasgow apologises for role in slave trade, saying its "tentacles" are in every corner of city', *Guardian*, 1 April 2022, https://www.theguardian.com/uk-news/2022/apr/01/glasgow-apologises-for-role-in-slave-trade-saying-its-tentacles-are-in-every-corner-of-city

12. Helen Heineman, 'Wright, Frances, 1795–1852', ODNB, https://www.oxforddnb.com/display/10.1093/ref:odnb/9780198614128.001.0001/odnb-9780198614128-e-7175

13. 'Incomplete notes for a history of Ireland [1869–70]'; quoted in *Field Day Anthology of Irish Writing*, vol. 2 (Field Day, 1991), vol. 2, 118–19.

14. Jane Ohlmeyer, 'Ireland has yet to come to terms with its imperial past', *Irish Times*, 29 December 2020, https://www.irishtimes.com/opinion/ireland-has-yet-to-come-to-terms-with-its-imperial-past-1.4444146

15. Niamh Gallagher, 'We need to recognise Irish participation in the British colonial story', *Irish Times*, 2 March 2021, https://www.irishtimes.com/opinion/we-need-to-recognise-irish-participation-in-the-british-colonial-story-1.4498224

16. Michael D. Higgins, 'Empire shaped Ireland's past: A century after partition, it still shapes our present', *Guardian*, 11 February 2021, https://www.theguardian.com/commentisfree/2021/feb/11/empire-ireland-century-partition-present-britain-history

17. John Davies 248.

18. John Davies 248, 326.

19. Marcus Tanner, *The Last of the Celts* (Yale University Press, 2004), 325.

20. 'David Thompson: Map maker, explorer and visionary', Ontario Ministry of Public Service and Business Delivery, https://www.archives.gov.on.ca/en/explore/online/thompson/index.aspx

21. John Davies 337.

22. 'The slave trade', BBC Bitesize, https://www.bbc.co.uk/bitesize/articles/z728mbk#zbry46

23. 'William Williams, Pantycelyn', BBC Bitesize, https://www.bbc.co.uk/bitesize/articles/z728mbk#zr43khv; E. Wyn James, 'The Longing and the Legacy: Liturgy and Life in the Hymns of William Williams of Pantycelyn', The Carmarthenshire Antiquary, vol. 55 (2019), https://orca.cardiff.ac.uk/id/eprint/132372/1/E.%20Wyn%20James%20on%20Williams%20Pantycelyn%2C%20Carmarthenshire%20Antiquary%2055%20%282019%29.pdf

24. 'Exploring the history of the Welsh relationship with India', 12 April 2024, https://nation.cymru/culture/exploring-the-history-of-the-welsh-relationship-with-india/

Chapter 9: Imperial Confidence, Irish Discomfort

1. Gerald Keegan, *Famine Diary: Journey to a New World* (Wolfhound, 1991), 14, 22, 48–9, 103

2. Robert Poole, *Peterloo: The English Uprising* (Oxford University Press, 2019), 391; Robert Tombs, *The English and Their History* (Allen Lane, 2014), 437.

3. John Davies 356–7; Kearney 249; Gower 233–5; J. Graham Jones 124.

4. John Davies 357–8; J. Graham Jones 124, 127; Gower 232–3.

5. John Davies 366–71; Kearney 240; J. Graham Jones 113–14, 127; Gower 236–8, 227–31.

6. Devine, *The Scottish Nation* 203–12; Devine, *Scotland's Empire* 146; Lynch 388–90.

7. Devine *The Scottish Nation* 226–30; Lynch 390–1, 394.

8. Foster 157–62; Kearney 235–6; Norman Davies 608; Schama, *A History of Britain: The Fate of Empire* 135–7, 139; *The Penguin Illustrated History* 206–7.

9. Foster 166–7, 175; Schama, *A History of Britain: The Fate of Empire* 295–312; 'Historical population of Ireland', Wikipedia, https://en .wikipedia.org/wiki/Historical_population_of_Ireland

10. Devine, *The Scottish Nation* 413–20; Devine, *Scotland's Empire* 342–4; Lynch 371–3; Wormald 216–19; Oliver 390–1.

11. Norman Davies 630; Christopher Hibbert, *Queen Victoria: A Personal History* (HarperCollins, 2000), 320; Tombs 442.

12. Kearney 225–9.

13. Adam Hochschild, *Bury the Chains: The British Struggle to Abolish Slavery* (Macmillan, 2005), 95–7.

14. John Davies 349–50.

15. John Davies 351–2, 363–4.

16. John Davies 378–1; Gower 184–789; J. Graham Jones 139; Johnes 95–6, 101, 109, 117–19.

17. Devine, *The Scottish Nation* 283, 285–6, 291, 372–7, 392, 426; Lynch 397–8, 400–2, 414–15.

18. Devine, *The Scottish Nation* 418–19.

19. Devine, *The Scottish Nation* 376–7.

20. Devine, *The Scottish Nation* 378–9; Lynch 365, 437.

21. Foster 159, 161–2, 167, 170–72, 181–2, 186, 192, 174; *The Penguin Illustrated History* 206, 209; Kearney 219, 224, 250, 253–4, 265–6, 269, 276; Mervyn Busteed, *The Irish in Manchester c.1750–1921: Resistance, Adaptation and Identity* (Manchester University Press, 2016), 211–18; Graham Davis, *The Irish in Britain, 1815–1914* (Gill & Macmillan, 1991), 193–5; Donald MacRaild, *The Irish Diaspora in Britain, 1750–1939* (Palgrave Macmillan, 2011), 126–7.

22. Foster 169, 174, 180; *The Penguin Illustrated History* 207; Kearney 253; Hegarty 225–6; Ross 237, 238–40.

23. Frank Callanan, 'Parnell, Charles Stewart', Dictionary of Irish Biography (DIB), https://www.dib.ie/biography/parnell-charles-stewart-a7199; Foster 180–4; Kearney 266; Norman Davies 617; Ross 238–44; Hegarty 228–37, 239–43; Margaret Ward, 'Parnell, Anna Mercer (Catherine Maria)', DIB,

https://www.dib.ie/biography/parnell-anna-mercer-catherine
-maria-a7198

24. Kearney 255–7; Foster 182–3; Ross 241–2, 244; Hegarty 237, 239, 242, 264.

25. Kearney 254–7, 259, 266–8; *The Penguin Illustrated History* 194, 207–8; Foster 182–4.

26. Foster 185–6; *The Penguin Illustrated History* 208; Kearney 268; Hegarty 244, 255–7.

27. John Davies 416–23, 433–4; J. Graham Jones 132–3; Johnes 118–23.

28. John Davies 436–40, 452–4, 460–4; J. Graham Jones 145–9, 153; Gower 239, 243–6; Johnes 122–6, 131–3.

29. Devine, *The Scottish Nation* 273, 281–2, 284, 299–303.

30. Devine, *The Scottish Nation* 234–5, 242–5, 292–4; Devine, *Scotland's Empire* 254–6; Lynch 355–7; Moffat 480–83; Norman Davies 702.

31. Margaret MacMillan, *The War That Ended Peace* (Random House, 2013), 29.

Chapter 10: Migrant Tales

1. 'The Scottish vagrant John Gray', Our Migration Story, https://www
.ourmigrationstory.org.uk/oms/the-vagrant-john-gray-of-north-yorkshire

2. Jean M. Morris, *Into the Crucible* (Lulu Press, 2018), 98–9; MacRaild 51–2.

3. Norman Davies 651.

4. Tombs 549.

5. Foster 175.

6. *The Penguin Illustrated History* 203.

7. Eric Richards, *Britannia's Children: Emigration from England, Scotland, Wales and Ireland since 1600* (Hambledon Continuum, 2004), 4.

8. Presidential visit to Ireland, June 1963, 'Irish emigration history', University College Cork, https://www.ucc.ie/en/emigre/history/

9. Scottish Government, 'The Scottish diaspora and diaspora strategy: Insights and lessons from Ireland', 29 May 2009, https://www.gov.scot/publications /scottish-diaspora-diaspora-strategy-insights-lessons-ireland/; Murray S. Leith and Duncan Sim, '"Will ye no' come back again?"': Population challenge and diaspora policy in Scotland', *Population, Space and Place*, vol. 28, no. 7 (11 April 2022), 5, https://onlinelibrary.wiley.com/doi/full /10.1002/psp.2572

10. David Olusoga, *Black and British: A Forgotten History* (Macmillan, 2016), 29; Peter Fryer, *Staying Power: The History of Black People in Britain* (Pluto, 2018 [1984]), 1.

11. Fryer 2–4.

12. 'Ireland's early multiracial history', Mixed Museum, https://mixedmuseum .org.uk/amri-exhibition/early-history/

13. Rozina Visram, *Asians in Britain: 400 Years of History* (Pluto, 2002), 2, 18–33; Olusoga 85–6; Barclay Price, *The Chinese in Britain: A History of Visitors and Settlers* (Amberley Publishing, 2019), 35.

14. 'Tiger Bay migration stories', National Library of Wales, https://www
    .library.wales/discover-learn/education/learning-resources/wales-migration
    -stories/tiger-bay-migration-stories
15. Frangopulo 113.
16. Paul O'Leary, *Immigration and Integration: the Irish in Wales, 1798–1922*
    (University of Wales Press, 2002), 302.
17. Devine, *The Scottish Nation* 487.
18. Busteed 30–31; Tristram Hunt, *The Frock-Coated Communist: The
    Revolutionary Life of Friedrich Engels* (Allen Lane, 2009), 232–3.
19. Anthony Tibbles, *Liverpool and the Slave Trade* (Liverpool University Press,
    2018), 4–5.
20. 'Is this James Johnson?', Gallery Oldham, https://hla.oldham.gov.uk/is-this
    -james-johnson/#:~:text=In%20our%20collections%20we%20
    hold,society%20one%20photograph%20stands%20out.
21. Lynch 374.
22. 'A home away from home: Stories of Scottish migration', Glasgow Women's
    Library, https://womenslibrary.org.uk/2023/03/27/a-home-away-from
    -home-foreign-women-coming-to-scotlands-shores/
23. *The Penguin Illustrated History* 204; 'The dream and the reality: English
    village immigrants to New Zealand in the 1870s', Prof. Rollo Arnold,
    address to the Otaki Historical Society, 1979, https://www.researchgate.net
    /profile/Margaret_Galt/publication/283833425_The_Dream_and_the
    _Reality_English_Village_Immigrants_to_New_Zealand_in_the_1870s
    /links/56482cac08ae451880ac842e/The-Dream-and-the-Reality-English
    -Village-Immigrants-to-New-Zealand-in-the-1870s.pdf
24. Norman Davies 806.
25. Devine, *The Scottish Nation* 496–8.
26. John Davies 562–3; Devine, *The Scottish Nation* 268.
27. Kearney 299.
28. 'Ethnic group, England and Wales: Census 2021', Office for National
    Statistics, https://www.ons.gov.uk/peoplepopulationandcommunity
    /culturalidentity/ethnicity/bulletins/ethnicgroupenglandandwales
    /census2021; 'Ethnic diversity in politics and public life', House of
    Commons Library 2023, https://commonslibrary.parliament.uk/research
    -briefings/sn01156/; 'Scotland's Census 2022: Ethnic group, national
    identity, language and religion', https://www.scotlandscensus.gov.uk
    /2022-reports/scotland-s-census-2022-ethnic-group-national-identity
    -language-and-religion/
29. Ireland's Central Statistics Office, 'Census of population 2022: Summary
    results'.
30. 'Migration to rich countries hits record high in 2023', *Financial Times*, 14
    November 2024, https://www.ft.com/content/c5f2ff4d-252d-45d6-ab25
    -44ee6bfabb96

31. 'Ireland's history with immigrants is fraught with tough experiences', *Irish Times*, 17 March 2018, https://www.irishtimes.com/culture/books/ireland-s -history-with-immigrants-is-fraught-with-tough-experiences-1.3421229

Chapter 11: Women's Fortunes

1. M.A. Elston, 'Edinburgh Seven', ODNB, https://www.oxforddnb.com /display/10.1093/ref:odnb/9780198614128.001.0001/odnb-9780198614128 -e-61136; 'The women of Scotland', Historic Environment Scotland, https://www.historicenvironment.scot/archives-and-research/online-exhibitions /the-women-of-scotland/
2. Groom 7–9.
3. Groom 39–40.
4. Ewan Macpherson, 'St Ethelthreda', in Charles Herbermann (ed.), *Catholic Encyclopedia*, vol. 5 (Robert Appleton, 1909).
5. Marios Costambeys, 'Æthelflæd [Ethelfleda]', ODNB, https://www .oxforddnb.com/display/10.1093/ref:odnb/9780198614128.001.0001 /odnb-9780198614128-e-8907
6. Lynch 75–8, 93–4; 'The women of Scotland', Historic Environment Scotland.
7. Schama, *A History of Britain: At the Edge of the World?* 116–17, 120–1, 125; *The Penguin Illustrated History* 75; David Carpenter, *Struggle for Mastery: The Penguin History of Britain 1066–1284* (Penguin, 2004), 147, 161–4, 170–3, 188.
8. '19 things done by inspirational women in English history', English Heritage, https://www.english-heritage.org.uk/visit/inspire-me/blog/articles/19-things -done-by-inspirational-women-in-english-history/; Margaret Wade Labarge and N.E. Griffiths, *A Medieval Miscellany* (McGill–Queen's Press, 1997), 48.
9. Jessica Brain, 'Princess Gwenllian and the Great Revolt', Historic UK, https://www.historic-uk.com/HistoryUK/HistoryofWales/Princess -Gwenllian/; Thomas Jones Pierce, 'Gwenllian (died 1136)', DWB, https:// biography.wales/article/s-GWEN-FER-1100
10. 'The women of Scotland', Historic Environment Scotland; 'Seven inspiring women from Scottish history', Edinburgh Live, https://www.edinburghlive .co.uk/news/edinburgh-news/gallery/seven-inspiring-women-scottish -history-15082838
11. Alsager Richard Vian, 'Dunbar, Agnes,' in Leslie Stephen (ed.), *Dictionary of National Biography*, vol. 16 (Smith, Elder, 1888), 150–51; 'That brawling boisterous Scottish wench', Weaving the Tapestry, https://weavingthetapestry .tumblr.com/post/77756706147/that-brawling-boisterous-scottish-wench -agnes
12. M.H. Brown, 'Joan [*née* Joan Beaufort]', ODNB, https://www.oxforddnb .com/display/10.1093/ref:odnb/9780198614128.001.0001/odnb

-9780198614128-e-14646#odnb-9780198614128-e-14646; John Cannon and Anne Hargreaves, 'Joan Beaufort', in *The Kings and Queens of Britain* (Oxford University Press, 2009).

13. Santha Bhattacharji, 'Julian of Norwich', ODNB, https://www.oxforddnb.com/display/10.1093/ref:odnb/9780198614128.001.0001/odnb-9780198614128-e-15163

14. Felicity Riddy, 'Kempe [née Brunham], Margery', ODNB, https://www.oxforddnb.com/display/10.1093/ref:odnb/9780198614128.001.0001/odnb-9780198614128-e-15337

15. Diana E.S. Dunn, 'Margaret [Margaret of Anjou]', ODNB, https://www.oxforddnb.com/display/10.1093/ref:odnb/9780198614128.001.0001/odnb-9780198614128-e-18049; Michael K. Jones and Malcolm G. Underwood, 'Beaufort, Margaret [known as Lady Margaret Beaufort], countess of Richmond and Derby', ODNB, https://www.oxforddnb.com/display/10.1093/ref:odnb/9780198614128.001.0001/odnb-9780198614128-e-1863; Richard Glen Eaves, 'Margaret [Margaret Tudor]', ODNB, https://www.oxforddnb.com/display/10.1093/ref:odnb/9780198614128.001.0001/odnb-9780198614128-e-18052; Trevor Royle, *The Wars of the Roses: England's First Civil War* (Little, Brown, 2009); Alison Weir, *Lancaster and York: The Wars of the Roses* (Jonathan Cape, 1995, Vintage, 2009).

16. Schama, *A History of Britain: At the Edge of the World?* 323, 337, 339, 346, 332–8, 338–41, 328–50, 361–92.

17. Elizabeth Goldring, 'Talbot [née Hardwick], Elizabeth [Bess] [called Bess of Hardwick], countess of Shrewsbury', ODNB, https://www.oxforddnb.com/display/10.1093/ref:odnb/9780198614128.001.0001/odnb-9780198614128-e-26925; Judy Barry, 'Campbell, Lady Agnes', DIB, https://www.dib.ie/biography/campbell-lady-agnes-a6945

18. Diane Purkiss, 'Witchcraft: Eight myths and misconceptions', English Heritage, https://www.english-heritage.org.uk/learn/histories/eight-witchcraft-myths/; James Sharpe, 'Introduction: The Lancashire witches in historical context', in Robert Poole (ed.), *The Lancashire Witches: Histories and Stories* (Manchester University Press, 2002), 3; Groom 105–9.

19. Lisa Cowan, 'Gwen ferch Ellis', DWB, https://biography.wales/article/s15-GWEN-FEL-1552; Niamh Boyce, 'Trial by fire: Remembering Ireland's witchcraft trials – and their victims', *Irish Examiner*, 31 October 2023, https://www.irishexaminer.com/news/spotlight/arid-41257942.html; 'The Irish woman executed for witchcraft 700 years ago', BBC, 30 October 2024, https://www.bbc.co.uk/news/articles/cx241e9d222o#:~:text=Petronella%20de%20Meath%20was%20a,at%20her%20boss%2C%20Alice%20Kyteler

20. Philip Paris, *The Last Witch of Scotland* (Black & White Publishing, 2023).

21. Deborah Jaffe, *Ingenious Women* (Sutton, 2003); 'Women in history, Margaret Cavendish', English Heritage, https://www.english-heritage.org.uk/learn/histories/women-in-history/margaret-cavendish/

22. F.E. Halliday, *A Shakespeare Companion 1564–1964* (Penguin, 1964), 347; Janet Todd, 'Behn, Aphra [Aphara]', ODNB, https://www.oxforddnb.com /display/10.1093/ref:odnb/9780198614128.001.0001/odnb-9780198614128 -e-1961; Tony Harcup, *A Dictionary of Journalism* (Oxford University Press, 2014).

23. 'Elizabeth Melville: Biography', Early Modern Women Research Network, https://c21ch.newcastle.edu.au/emwrn/melvillebio; 'The women of Scotland', Historic Environment Scotland.

24. 'The women of Scotland', Historic Environment Scotland; Mary B. Rose (ed.), *The Lancashire Cotton Industry: A History since 1700* (Lancashire County Books, 1996), 14, 123–30.

25. 'The women of Scotland', Historic Environment Scotland.

26. 'Peg Plunkett: Brothel madam', Women's Museum of Ireland, https://www .womensmuseumofireland.ie/exhibits/peg-plunkett; '25 fearless women who helped shape today's Ireland', *Irish Times*, 3 March 2018, https://www.irishtimes .com/life-and-style/people/25-fearless-women-who-helped-shape-today -s-ireland-1.3406499; 'Five daring women from Irish history', History Press, https://thehistorypress.co.uk/article/five-daring-women-from-irish-history/

27. 'Discover the influence of women in Welsh history', Cadw, Welsh Government Historic Environment Service, https://cadw.gov.wales/about -us/news/discover-influence-women-welsh-history

28. 'British women who changed the world', Sky History, https://www.history .co.uk/article/british-women-who-changed-the-world#:~:text=Mary%20 Anning%20(1799%20–%201847)&text=Although%20ineligible%20 to%20join%20the,the%20history%20of%20the%20Earth; 'Mary Seacole', BBC, https://www.bbc.co.uk/teach/school-radio/articles/zbphxyc; Gwyneth Tyson Roberts, 'David, Elizabeth (Betsi Cadwaladr)', DWB, https:// biography.wales/article/s12-DAVI-ELI-1789#?c=0&m=0&s=0&cv=9&man ifest=https%3A%2F%2Fdamsssl.llgc.org. uk%2Fiiif%2F2.0%2F5538658%2Fmanifest. json&xywh=421%2C818%2C1492%2C1288; Sheila Lunney, 'Moore, Georgina (Sister Mary Clare)', DIB, https://www.dib.ie/biography/moore -georgina-sister-mary-clare-a5932

29. Helen Mathers, *Patron Saint of Prostitutes: Josephine Butler and a Victorian Scandal* (History Press, 2014), 109–10; M.A. Elston, 'Anderson, Elizabeth Garrett', ODNB, https://www.oxforddnb.com/display/10.1093 /ref:odnb/9780198614128.001.0001/odnb-9780198614128-e-30406; Betty Alexandra Toole, 'Byron, (Augusta) Ada [married name (Augusta) Ada King, countess of Lovelace]', ODNB, https://www.oxforddnb.com/display /10.1093/ref:odnb/9780198614128.001.0001/odnb-9780198614128 -e-37253; Groom 240–42; Rosemary Ashton, 'Evans, Marian [pseud. George Eliot]', ODNB, https://www.oxforddnb.com/display/10.1093 /ref:odnb/9780198614128.001.0001/odnb-9780198614128-e-6794; Moira Ferguson, 'Prince [married name James], Mary', ODNB, https://

www.oxforddnb.com/display/10.1093/ref:odnb/9780198614128.001.0001
/odnb-9780198614128-e-54341; Janet Howarth, 'Fawcett, Dame Millicent
Garrett [née Millicent Garrett]', ODNB, https://www.oxforddnb
.com/display/10.1093/ref:odnb/9780198614128.001.0001/odnb
-9780198614128-e-33096; Anne Taylor, 'Besant [née Wood], Annie',
ODNB, https://www.oxforddnb.com/display/10.1093/ref:odnb
/9780198614128.001.0001/odnb-9780198614128-e-30735

30. Elizabeth L. Ewan et al. (eds), *The Biographical Dictionary of Scottish Women
From the Earliest Times* (Edinburgh University Press, 2006), 376; 'The
women of Scotland', Historic Environment Scotland; 'Phoebe Anna
Traquair', National Galleries Scotland, https://www.nationalgalleries.org
/art-and-artists/features/phoebe-anna-traquair; 'Williamina Fleming',
Undiscovered Scotland, https://www.undiscoveredscotland.co.uk/usbiography
/f/williaminafleming.html

31. Basil Walsh, 'Hayes, Catherine', DIB, https://www.dib.ie/contributor
/walsh-basil; '25 fearless women who helped shape today's Ireland'; H.P.
Hollis, revised by M.T. Brück, 'Clerke, Agnes Mary', ODNB, https://www
.oxforddnb.com/display/10.1093/ref:odnb/9780198614128.001.0001
/odnb-9780198614128-e-32444?docPos=45; 'Cashman, Ellen', Dictionary
of Canadian Biography, https://www.biographi.ca/en/bio/cashman
_ellen_15E.html#:~:text=CASHMAN%2C%20ELLEN%20(Nellie%20
Pioche%2C,Nellie)%20–%20Dictionary%20of%20Canadian%20
Biography&text=CASHMAN%2C%20ELLEN%20(also%20known%20
as,daughter%20of%20Fanny%20Cashman%3B%20d; James L. Pethica,
'Gregory [née Persse], (Isabella) Augusta, Lady Gregory', ODNB, https://
www.oxforddnb.com/display/10.1093/ref:odnb/9780198614128.001.0001
/odnb-9780198614128-e-33554

32. Angela V. John and Thomas Herbert Parry-Williams, 'Guest (Schreiber),
Lady Charlotte Elizabeth Berties', DWB, https://bywgraffiadur.cymru
/article/c-GUES-ELI-1812#?c=0&m=0&s=0&cv=0&manifest=https%3A
%2F%2Fdamsssl.llgc.org.uk%2Fiiif%2F2.0%2F4674585%2Fmanifest
.json&xywh=2285%2C1762%2C2101%2C1695; Angela V. John,
'Crawshay [née Yeates], Rose Mary', ODNB, https://www.oxforddnb
.com/display/10.1093/ref:odnb/9780198614128.001.0001/odnb
-9780198614128-e-53008; William Llewelyn Davies, 'Rees, Sarah Jane',
DWB, https://biography.wales/article/s-REES-JAN-1839#?c=0&m=0&s=0&cv
=0&manifest=https%3A%2F%2Fdamsssl.llgc.org.uk%2Fiiif%2F2.0
%2F1124576%2Fmanifest.json&xywh=1186%2C889%2C1364%2C1100;
Beth R. Jenkins, 'Hoggan [née Morgan], Frances Elizabeth', DWB,
https://biography.wales/article/s11-HOGG-ELI-1843; Beth Jenkins,
'Mackenzie [née Hughes], (Hettie) Millicent', ODNB, https://www
.oxforddnb.com/display/10.1093/odnb/9780198614128.001.0001/odnb
-9780198614128-e-56242?mediaType=Image

33. June Purvis, 'Pankhurst [*née* Goulden], Emmeline', ODNB, https://www
.oxforddnb.com/display/10.1093/ref:odnb/9780198614128.001.0001
/odnb-9780198614128-e-35376; 'The women of Scotland', Historic
Environment Scotland.

34. Krista Cowman, 'Drummond [née Gibson; other married name Simpson],
Flora McKinnon', ODNB, https://www.oxforddnb.com/display/10.1093
/ref:odnb/9780198614128.001.0001/odnb-9780198614128-e-39177#
odnb-9780198614128-e-39177

35. Angela V. John, 'Thomas, Margaret Haig, 2nd Viscountess Rhondda',
DWB, https://biography.wales/article/s12-THOM-HAI-1883

36. Maria Luddy, 'Skeffington, (Johanna) Hanna Sheehy-', DIB, https://www.dib
.ie/biography/skeffington-johanna-hanna-sheehy-a8106; Senia Paseta,
'Markievicz, Constance Georgine', DIB, https://www.dib.ie/contributor
/paseta-senia

37. 'The female war medic who refused to "go home and sit still"', BBC, 26
November 2017, bbc.co.uk; 'Marie Stopes', BBC, https://www.bbc.co.uk
/news/uk-scotland-42096350#:~:text=When%20Elsie%20Inglis%20
asked%20the,women's%20health%2C%20did%20the%20opposite;
'Victoria Drummond', Undiscovered Scotland, https://www
.undiscoveredscotland.co.uk/usbiography/d/victoriadrummond.html

38. Lyndall Gordon, 'Woolf [*née* Stephen], (Adeline) Virginia', ODNB, https://
www.oxforddnb.com/display/10.1093/ref:odnb/9780198614128.001.0001
/odnb-9780198614128-e-37018; Janet Morgan, 'Christie [née Miller; other
married name Mallowan], Dame Agatha Mary Clarissa', ODNB, https://
www.oxforddnb.com/display/10.1093/ref:odnb/9780198614128.001.0001
/odnb-9780198614128-e-30926

39. Martin Pugh, 'Astor [née Langhorne], Nancy Witcher, Viscountess Astor',
https://www.oxforddnb.com/display/10.1093/ref:odnb/9780198614128.001
.0001/odnb-9780198614128-e-30489; 'Theresa May under fire after
unveiling statue of "Nazi-sympathising" MP', *Metro*, 29 November 2019,
https://metro.co.uk/2019/11/29/theresa-may-fire-unveiling-statue-nazi
-sympathising-mp-11242921/; 'Megan Lloyd George: A true heir', BBC, 30
May 2013, https://www.bbc.co.uk/webarchive/https%3A%2F%2Fwww
.bbc.co.uk%2Fblogs%2Fwales%2Fentries%2F0eebc9ea-6017-3d50-afd9
-54b6a44e8c06; 'The duchess who helped save thousands of children', BBC,
1 December 2023, https://www.bbc.co.uk/news/uk-scotland-67576617
#:~:text=Kitty%20Murray's%20support%20for%20the,nickname%20
%22the%20Red%20Duchess%22

40. Robin Higham, revised by Anne Locker, 'Johnson [married name Mollison],
Amy', ODNB, https://www.oxforddnb.com/display/10.1093/ref:odnb
/9780198614128.001.0001/odnb-9780198614128-e-34200

41. 'Rosalind Franklin's Life', Rosalind Franklin Institute, https://www.rfi.ac.uk
/discover-learn/rosalind-franklins-life/; 'Dorothy Hodgkin FRS', Royal

Society, https://royalsociety.org/about-us/who-we-are/diversity-inclusion /case-studies/scientists-with-disabilities/dorothy-hodgkin/

42. Groom xi, 248, 249, 303, 310–11, 317.

43. David Cannadine, 'Thatcher [née Roberts], Margaret Hilda, Baroness Thatcher', ODNB, https://www.oxforddnb.com/display/10.1093 /ref:odnb/9780198614128.001.0001/odnb-9780198614128-e-106415

44. 'Mary Robinson', UCD Business Alumni, https://www.ucd.ie /businessalumni/news/inprofile/maryrobinson/; '10 years later, still no peace for Veronica Guerin', *Guardian*, 9 April 2006, https://www.theguardian .com/world/2006/apr/09/ireland

45. 'Obituary: Dame Muriel Spark', *Guardian*, 17 April 2006, https://www .theguardian.com/news/2006/apr/17/guardianobituaries.booksobituaries

46. 'SNP political icon Winnie Ewing dies aged 93', BBC, 22 June 2023, https://www.bbc.co.uk/news/uk-scotland-65988094; 'Nicola Sturgeon and Peter Murrell to end marriage', BBC, 13 January 2025, https://www.bbc .co.uk/news/articles/cvgpl37lez7o

47. 'How one woman became the guardian of Snowdonia', Wales Online, 22 November 2014, https://www.walesonline.co.uk/whats-on/arts-culture -news/how-one-woman-became-guardian-8144942; '12 Welsh women who shaped your life that you need to know about', Wales Online, 8 March 2020, https://www.walesonline.co.uk/news/wales-news/12-welsh-women -who-shaped-17858828; 'Grey Thompson confirms retirement', BBC, 28 February 2007, http://news.bbc.co.uk/player/sol/newsid_6400000/newsid _6404100/6404177.stm?bw=bb&mp=rm

48. 'Helen Sharman on STEM careers and space travel', Royal Society, 7 July 2023, https://royalsociety.org/science-events-and-lectures/2023/07/helen -sharman/#:~:text=Helen%20Sharman%20has%20dedicated%20herself, role%20model%20for%20young%20people

Chapter 12: Small Islands

1. Sarah Goodwins, *A Brief History of the Isle of Man* (Loaghtan Books, 2017), 5–50; Matthew Richardson, *The Isle of Man: Stone Age to Swinging Sixties* (Pen & Sword, 2020), 1–22; G.V.C. Young, *The History of the Isle of Man under the Norse or Now through a Glass Darkly* (Mansk-Svenska, 1981); David W. Moore, *The Other British Isles: A History of Shetland, Orkney, the Hebrides, Isle of Man, Anglesey, Scilly, Isle of Wight and the Channel Isles* (McFarland, 2005), 93–104.

2. Goodwins 51–114; Richardson 22–39; Moore 104–11.

3. Goodwins 114–27; Richardson 40–73; Moore 111–17.

4. Goodwins 127–40; Richardson 74–94; Moore 117–25.

5. 'New research conducted at late Neanderthal site', *Archaeology Magazine*, 18 October 2013, https://archaeology.org/news/2013/10/18/131018-jersey -neanderthal-la-cotte-de-st-brelade/; Moore 211–17; *Balleine's History of*

Jersey, revised and enlarged by Marguerite Syvret and Joan Stevens (Phillimore & Co., 1998), 1–17; Kevin Whelan, *Guernsey: A History* (Writer's Block, 2023), 5–18; Peter Johnston, *A Short History of Guernsey* (Guernsey Press, 1987), 1–27.

6. Moore 217–25; *Balleine* 18–100; Whelan 18–94; Johnston 27–43.
7. Moore 225–31; *Balleine* 101–231; Whelan 95–115; Johnston 44–68.
8. Moore 231–5; *Balleine* 231–63; Whelan 115–39; Johnston 68–82.
9. Moore 235–41; *Balleine* 264–78; Whelan 146–208; Johnston 86–7.
10. Therese Steiner, 'Louisa Mary Gould née Le Druillenec', Frank Fall Archive, https://www.frankfallaarchive.org/people/louisa-mary-gould/
11. Moore 241–7; Balleine 278–92; Whelan 209–22; Johnston 87–90.
12. 'Where are the windiest parts of the UK?', Met Office, https://weather. metoffice.gov.uk/learn-about/weather/types-of-weather/wind/windiest -place-in-uk
13. William P.L. Thomson, *The New History of Orkney* (Birlinn, 2008 [1987]), 1–23; Moore 30–40
14. Thomson 24–219; Moore 40–5.
15. Thomson 220–314; Moore 46–8.
16. Douglas MacKay, *The Honourable Company: A History of The Hudson's Bay Company* (Cassell, 1937), quoted in Thomson 372.
17. Thomson 315–415; Moore 48–51.
18. Thomson 416–50; Moore 51–5.
19. Moore 20–1, 24–6.
20. Moore 26–7.
21. Moore 57–67.
22. Moore 67–79.
23. Moore 79–91.

Chapter 13: Leisure Blooms

1. 'How a generation of stars bombed in Glasgow's notorious comics graveyard', *Daily Record*, 1 July 2012, https://www.dailyrecord.co.uk/news/uk-world -news/how-a-generation-of-stars-bombed-in-glasgows-1001410; 'Remembering Glasgow's "comic's graveyard" where audiences famously "shot down" acts', 8 February 2022, Glasgow Live, https://www.glasgowlive .co.uk/news/history/remembering-glasgows-comics-graveyard-audiences -23009695#
2. Devine, *The Scottish Nation* 357.
3. *The North Wales Chronicle and Advertiser for the Principality*, 2 November 1861, 11.
4. Paul Maloney, 'Scottish music hall and variety', University of Glasgow, https://www.gla.ac.uk/myglasgow/library/files/special/collections/STA /articles/music_hall/index.html; 'Cardiff remembered: How music halls like the Coliseum and theatres like the Empire were the centre of city life', 20

May 2015, Wales Online, https://www.walesonline.co.uk/lifestyle/nostalgia /cardiff-remembered-how-music-halls-9350558; 'The Albert Hall, Cradock Street, Swansea', 'The Olympia Theatre, Dame Street, Dublin', 'Theatres and Halls in Belfast', http://www.arthurlloyd.co.uk/SwanseaTheatres.htm; http://www.arthurlloyd.co.uk/Dublin/OlympiaTheatreDublin.htm; http:// www.arthurlloyd.co.uk/BelfastTheatres.htm

5. Richard Anthony Baker, *British Music Hall: An Illustrated History* (Pen & Sword, 2014), 123–5.

6. Maloney; 'How Harry Lauder went from poverty to becoming the world's first superstar', *Mirror*, 9 August 2020, https://www.mirror.co.uk/news /uk-news/how-harry-lauder-went-poverty-22494135; Denine 360.

7. Lee Jackson, *Palaces of Pleasure: From Music Halls to the Seaside to Football, How the Victorians Invented Mass Entertainment* (Yale University Press, 2019), 87–8, 90; Devine, *The Scottish Nation* 360.

8. 'From stalls to malls: A brief history of the high street', English Heritage, https://www.english-heritage.org.uk/visit/ inspire-me/a-brief-history-of-the-high-street/#:~:text=Stalls%20become%20 shops&text=The%20first%20fixed%20shops%20of,shops%20 somewhere%20near%20the%20marketplace; 'W.H. Smith: The 225-year-old chain through the ages', 15 November 2017, RetailWeek, https://www .retail-week.com/general-merchandise/whsmith-the-225-year-old-chain -through-the-ages/7027091.article

9. Devine, The Scottish Nation, 356.

10. 'Sheffield FC: Over 150 years of history', 24 October 2007, https://web .archive.org/web/20160303175319/https://www.fifa.com/world-match -centre/news/newsid/621/801/; 'One letter, two meetings and 12 teams: The birth of league football', BBC, 26 February 2013, https://www.bbc.co .uk/sport/football/21492352

11. 'Acts of parliament banning golf', National Library of Scotland, https:// digital.nls.uk/golf-in-scotland/banned/1457-act.html; Devine, *The Scottish Nation* 361–2.

12. 'Hayes Hotel & The GAA history', https://hayeshotel.ie/hayes-hotel-the-gaa/; David Smith and Gareth Williams, *Fields of Praise: Official History of the Welsh Rugby Union, 1881–1981* (University of Wales Press, 1980), 22, 24; 'Match report: The first England v Wales rugby international', Open University, https://www.open.edu/openlearn/health-sports-psychology /health/sport-and-fitness/sport/match-report-the-first-england-v-wales -rugby-international

13. Devine, *The Scottish Nation* 359; Alan Kidd, *Manchester: A History* (Carnegie, 2006 [1993]), 179–80; Alan Kidd and Terry Wyke (eds), *Manchester: Making the Modern City* (Liverpool University Press, 2016), 197; Michael Herbert, 'Women's history walk around radical Manchester', *HerStoria* (Autumn 2010), 38; Deborah Woodman, *The Story of Manchester* (Phillimore & Co., 2017), 137.

14. Judith Bowers, *Stan Laurel and Other Stars of the Panopticon: The Story of the Britannia Music Hall* (Birlinn, 2007), 143–7.

15. Kieron Casey, 'The mystery of Louis Le Prince, the father of cinematography', National Science and Media Museum, https://blog .scienceandmediamuseum.org.uk/louis-le-prince-created-the-first-ever -moving-pictures/; 'William Friese Greene', Who's Who of Victorian Cinema, https://www.victorian-cinema.net/whoswho; 'UK feature films produced 1912–2003', British Film Institute, http://www.screenonline.org .uk/film/facts/fact2.html; Suemedha Sood, 'The evolution of Irish cinema', BBC 22 June 2012, https://www.bbc.com/travel/article/20120621 -travelwise-the-evolution-of-irish-cinema ; 'Game changer: How the film industry came of age in Northern Ireland', BBC, 28 November 2014, https://www.bbc.co.uk/programmes/articles/1Td0ndWmy1WMmyxMp8hrjrT /game-changer-how-the-film-industry-came-of-age-in-northern-ireland; '52 Welsh film facts', BBC, 5 March 2010, https://www.bbc.co.uk/wales/arts /sites/film/pages/52-facts-05.shtml; 'How Green Was My Valley', 4 May 2021, Jay's Classic Movie Blog, https://www.jaysclassicmovieblog.com /post/55-how-green-was-my-valley-1941

16. 'A look at the history of dance halls: Wedding bells and questionable morals', British Newspaper Archive, 15 October 2019, https://blog .britishnewspaperarchive.co.uk/2019/10/15/a-look-at-the-history-of -dance-halls/

17. 'BBC begins daily transmissions from 2LO Station', BBC, 29 September 2014, https://www.bbc.co.uk/programmes/p027ls87; '2LO calling: The birth of British public radio', Science Museum, 30 October 2018, https:// www.sciencemuseum.org.uk/objects-and-stories/2lo-calling-birth-british -public-radio; Ian McIntyre, 'Reith, John Charles Walsham, first Baron Reith (1889–1971)', ODNB, https://www.oxforddnb.com/display/10.1093 /ref:odnb/9780198614128.001.0001/odnb-9780198614128-e-31596; Burton Paulu, *Television and Radio in the United Kingdom* (Palgrave Macmillan, 1981), 135.

18. 'What's the story? 100 years of the BBC in Scotland', BBC, 6 March 2003, https://www.bbc.co.uk/news/uk-scotland-64835319; 'Tuning in: The day Ireland got its own radio station', *Irish Examiner*, 7 August 2023, https:// www.irishexaminer.com/lifestyle/people/arid-41196799.html; 'BBC celebrates 100 years in Northern Ireland', BBC, 15 September 2024, https://www.bbc.co.uk/news/articles/

19. 'History of the BBC', BBC, https://www.bbc.co.u/historyofthebbc; Christopher H. Sterling, *Encyclopedia of Radio: 3-Volume Set* (Routledge, 2004), 524.

20. 'Hark! The herald Enya sings in historic Cork chapel', *Irish Examiner*, 23 November 2026, https://www.irishexaminer.com/news/arid-20431919 .html#:~:text=Hark!-,The%20herald%20Enya%20sings%20in%20 historic%20Cork%20chapel,Irish%20TV%20in%20a%20decade

Chapter 14: Shared Yet Separate Cultures

1. 'Dylan Thomas and the Kardomah set', *Independent*, 11 February 2006, https://www.independent.co.uk/arts-entertainment/books/features/dylan-thomas-and-the-kardomah-set-6109407.html
2. John Davies et al., *The Welsh Academy Encyclopaedia of Wales* (University of Wales Press, 2008), 861–6; Meic Stephens (ed.), *The New Companion to the Literature of Wales* (University of Wales Press, 1998), 710–12.
3. Roderick Watson, 'Grieve, Christopher Murray [*pseud.* Hugh MacDiarmid] (1892–1978)', ODNB, https://www.oxforddnb.com/display/10.1093/ref:odnb/9780198614128.001.0001/odnb-9780198614128-e-31174
4. Gina Sigillito, *The Daughters of Maeve: 50 Irish Women Who Changed the World* (Kensington Publishing, 2012), 235.
5. John Milton, 'To the parliament of England', in *The Doctrine and Discipline of Divorce* (n.p., 1643).
6. 'The Irish influence: English words and phrases that come from Ireland', *Irish Post*, 1 April 2022, https://www.irishpost.com/life-style/the-irish-influence-english-words-and-phrases-that-come-from-ireland-232423
7. R.F. Foster, 'Yeats, William Butler (1865–1939)', ODNB, https://www.oxforddnb.com/display/10.1093/ref:odnb/9780198614128.001.0001/odnb-9780198614128-e-37061
8. 'Nobel Prize in Literature 1925: George Bernard Shaw', https://www.nobelprize.org/prizes/literature/1925/summary/#:~:text=George%20Bernard%20Shaw,-Prize%20share%3A%201&text=According%20to%20the%20Nobel%20Foundation's,one%20year%20later%2C%20in%201926; Stanley Weintraub, 'Shaw, George Bernard (1856–1950)', ODNB, https://www.oxforddnb.com/display/10.1093/ref:odnb/9780198614128.001.0001/odnb-9780198614128-e-36047
9. Bruce Stewart, 'Joyce, James Augustine Aloysius (1882–1941)', ODNB, https://www.oxforddnb.com/display/10.1093/ref:odnb/9780198614128.001.0001/odnb-9780198614128-e-34247; Rachel Potter, 'Ulysses at 100: Why it was banned for being obscene', The Conversation, 1 February 2022, https://theconversation.com/ulysses-at-100-why-it-was-banned-for-being-obscene-176086
10. 'Nobel Prize in Literature 1969: Samuel Beckett', https://www.nobelprize.org/prizes/literature/1969/summary/; James Knowlson, 'Beckett, Samuel Barclay (1906–1989)', ODNB, https://www.oxforddnb.com/display/10.1093/ref:odnb/9780198614128.001.0001/odnb-9780198614128-e-40453
11. 'Nobel Prize in Literature 1995: Seamus Heaney', https://www.nobelprize.org/prizes/literature/1995/summary/; Gerald Dawe, 'Heaney, Seamus Justin (1939–2013)', ODNB, https://www.oxforddnb.com/display/10.1093/ref:odnb/9780198614128.001.0001/odnb-9780198614128-e-109270

12. James Hyman, 'Bacon, Francis (1909–1992)', ODNB, https://www
.oxforddnb.com/display/10.1093/ref:odnb/9780198614128.001.0001
/odnb-9780198614128-e-50800

13. Breandán Ó Madagáin, 'Carolan, Turlough [Toirdhealbhach Ó
Cearbhalláin] (1670–1738)', ODNB, https://www.oxforddnb.com
/display/10.1093/ref:odnb/9780198614128.001.0001/odnb-9780198614128
-e-20484

14. 'William Shakespeare's life & times: James I', Spark Notes, https://www
.sparknotes.com/shakespeare/life-and-times/historical-context/political
/james-i/

15. 'The famous Scottish tales that are actually Irish', Old Moore's Almanac,
https://oldmooresalmanac.com/famous-scottish-tales-actually-irish/

16. Robert Crawford, 'Burns, Robert (1759–1796)', ODNB, https://www
.oxforddnb.com/display/10.1093/ref:odnb/9780198614128.001.0001
/odnb-9780198614128-e-4093

17. David Hewitt, 'Scott, Sir Walter (1771–1832)', ODNB, https://www
.oxforddnb.com/display/10.1093/ref:odnb/9780198614128.001.0001
/odnb-9780198614128-e-24928

18. Davies et al. 23, 336, 426, 516, 525–6, 637, 851–2; Stephens 13, 279, 387,
456–7, 473–4, 551–2, 613, 701–2.

19. Davies et al. 458–9; Stephens 433–5.

20. Davies et al. 768; Stephens 647–9.

21. Davies et al. 228, 366, 671, 908; Stephens 315–16, 754–5, 192–3, 583–4.

22. Davies et al. 203–4, 268–9, 420; Stephens 228, 169–70, 370–1.

23. Davies et al. 200, 202, 513–14, 863; Stephens 159–60, 165–6, 452–3,
716–17.

24. Davies et al. 415–16, 957–8, 965–6; Stephens 365, 799, 812–13.

Chapter 15: War, Nationalism and Imperial Decline

1. *The Times of India*, 22 June 1911, quoted in Norman Davies 733–4.

2. Schama, *A History of Britain: The Fate of Empire* 428–32; John Davies
477–80; Tom Hazeldine, *The Northern Question: A History of a Divided
Country* (Verso, 2020), 87; Hegarty 259–62.

3. 'The Fallen: Military strength and deaths in combat', UK parliament, https://
www.parliament.uk/business/publications/research/olympic-britain/crime
-and-defence/the-fallen/; 'Statistics of the military effort of the British
Empire during the Great War, 1914–1920', War Office report (1922), 339.

4. 'How many Scots died in World War One?', BBC, 8 November 2018,
https://www.bbc.co.uk/news/uk-scotland-46124327

5. John Davies 497.

6. Foster 197–203; Hegarty 271–9; Ross 330–32.

7. Foster 206–11; Hegarty 279–84; Ross 332–3.

8. Foster 212–15; Hegarty 284–7; Ross 334.
9. Speech in Wolverhampton, 24 November 1918.
10. Charles Loch Mowat, *Britain between the Wars 1918–1940* (Methuen, 1955), 176.
11. John Davies 533.
12. *The Penguin Illustrated History* 238.
13. *The Penguin Illustrated History* 238.

Chapter 16:

1. Schama, *A History of Britain: The Fate of Empire* 509
2. 'The Fallen: Military strength and deaths in combat', UK parliament.
3. John Davies 585–91; J. Graham Jones 161–2; Johnes 144–6.
4. David Kynaston, *Austerity Britain 1945–51* (Bloomsbury, 2007), 536–7.
5. Devine, *The Scottish Nation* 551–5.
6. John Davies 597–600; J. Graham Jones 162–3; Gower 276–80; Johnes 146–50.
7. Speech at Bedford, 20 July 1957; Dominic Sandbrook, *Never Had It So Good: A History of Britain from Suez to the Beatles* (Little, Brown, 2005), 80.
8. 'Kenneth Roy Thomson', 6 July 2006, https://pressgazette.co.uk/archive-content/kenneth-roy-thomson/
9. Devine, *The Scottish Nation* 565–71; Lynch 442–3; Moffat 578–84.
10. John Davies 606–7; J. Graham Jones 163–4; Gower 280–85; Johnes 150–55.
11. J.J. Lee, *Ireland, 1912–1985: Politics and Society* (Cambridge University Press, 1989), 315, 359; Foster 225–6; Kearney 313; Hegarty 309–15; Ross 342–5.
12. Devine, *The Scottish Nation* 574–5; Lynch 444–5; Moffat 589, 595; John Davies 640, 642, 646; J. Graham Jones 170–2; Gower 286–95; Johnes 156–8.
13. Foster 226–9; Hegarty 306–9; Ross 347–8.
14. Foster 226–9; Hegarty 316–22; Ross 349–51.
15. Devine, *The Scottish Nation* 584–6; Lynch 445–6; Moffat 591–3, 600.
16. Devine, *The Scottish Nation* 586–90; Lynch 446–7; Moffat 600–4; John Davies 648–52; Johnes 159–61.
17. Devine, *The Scottish Nation* 591–4; Moffat 604–7.
18. John Davies 656–7; Johnes 161–2; Devine, *The Scottish Nation* 594–9.
19. Devine, *The Scottish Nation* 601–13; Lynch 448–9; Moffat 607–13; John Davies 657–63.
20. John Davies 663–6; Devine, *The Scottish Nation* 613–14; Moffat 615.
21. Devine, *The Scottish Nation* 606–16; Moffat 616, 620–2.
22. Devin, *The Scottish Nation* 616–17; John Davies 671–5.
23. John Davies 678–9; Gower 319–24; Johnes 162–3; Devine, *The Scottish Nation* 631; Moffat 622–4.
24. Moffat 624–5.

Chapter 17: The Break-Up That Didn't Happen

1. 'A brief history of Stormont suspensions', *Belfast Telegraph*, 11 January 2017, https://www.belfasttelegraph.co.uk/news/northern-ireland/a-brief-history-of-stormont-suspensions/35358410.html; 'Rhodri Morgan obituary', *Guardian*, 18 May 2017, https://www.theguardian.com/politics/2017/may/18/rhodri-morgan-obituary; '2000: Ken Livingstone voted London mayor', BBC, http://news.bbc.co.uk/onthisday/hi/dates/stories/may/4/newsid_2503000/2503809.stm

2. Devine, *The Scottish Nation* 634–9.

3. 'Prescott sees red', BBC, 17 May 2001, http://news.bbc.co.uk/news/vote2001/low/english/newsid_1335000/1335033.stm; Devine, *The Scottish Nation* 638–41; 'Scotland's last deep coal mine closes after flooding', *Independent*, 30 March 2002, https://www.independent.co.uk/news/uk/home-news/scotland-s-last-deep-coal-mine-closes-after-flooding-9218155.html; 'Tower: The last colliery', BBC, 25 January 2008, https://web.archive.org/web/20100104150035/http://www.bbc.co.uk/wales/southeast/sites/rct/pages/towercolliery.shtml

4. Lawrence Goldman, 'Elizabeth [*née* Lady Elizabeth Angela Marguerite Bowes-Lyon] (1900–2002)', ODNB, https://www.oxforddnb.com/display/10.1093/ref:odnb/9780198614128.001.0001/odnb-9780198614128-e-76927

5. 'Ahern's winning streak', *Guardian*, 20 May 2002, https://www.theguardian.com/politics/2002/may/20/eu.ireland; 'A brief history of Stormont suspensions', *Belfast Telegraph*, 11 January 2017; 'Denis Donaldson: Family attacks Irish government after inquest delay', BBC, 12 December 2023, https://www.bbc.co.uk/news/uk-northern-ireland-67696773

6. 'Blair secures historic third term', BBC, 6 May 2005, http://news.bbc.co.uk/1/hi/uk_politics/vote_2005/frontpage/4519863.stm; 'The Charles Kennedy story', BBC, 2 June 2015, https://www.bbc.co.uk/news/uk-politics-32972470

7. 'Blair resigns as prime minister', BBC, 27 June 2007, http://news.bbc.co.uk/1/hi/uk_politics/6243558.stm; 'Brown is the UK's new prime minister', BBC, 27 June 2007, http://news.bbc.co.uk/1/hi/6245682.stm; 'Timeline: Blair vs Brown', BBC, 7 September 2006, http://news.bbc.co.uk/1/hi/uk_politics/5322946.stm

8. David C. Shiels, 'Paisley, Ian Richard Kyle, Baron Bannside (1926–2014)', ODNB, https://www.oxforddnb.com/display/10.1093/odnb/9780198614128.001.0001/odnb-9780198614128-e-108503; 'Historic Labour–Plaid deal agreed', BBC, 27 June 2007, http://news.bbc.co.uk/1/hi/wales/6245040.stm

9. 'Salmond elected first minister', *Guardian*, 16 May 2007, https://www.theguardian.com/politics/2007/may/16/scotland.devolution

10. 'Scotland's economy: Ten years on from the financial crisis', Fraser of Allender Institute, 24 October 2018, https://fraserofallander.org/scotlands-economy-ten-years-on-from-the-financial-crisis/ ; 'Fears over 1,100 Welsh

steel jobs', BBC, 26 January 2009, http://news.bbc.co.uk/1/hi/wales/7850113
.stm; '300 jobs to go as Hoover ends manufacturing at site', *Irish
Independent*, 6 March 2009, https://www.independent.ie/world-news
/europe/300-jobs-to-go-as-hoover-ends-manufacturing-at-site/26518873.
html#:~:text=Electrical%20goods%20company%20Hoover%20is,will%20
end%20on%20March%2014; '302 jobs lost as factory closes', BBC, 4 June
2009, http://news.bbc.co.uk/1/hi/wales/north_east/8081186.stm#:~:text
=A%20washing%20machine%20plant%20is,plans%20were%20rejected
%20during%20consultation; 'UK unemployment increases to 2.62m', BBC,
16 November 2011, https://www.bbc.co.uk/news/business-15747103 k

11. 'Republic of Ireland confirms EU financial rescue deal', BBC, 22 November
2010, https://www.bbc.co.uk/news/business-11807730; 'Was it for this?',
Irish Times, 18 November 2010, https://www.irishtimes.com/opinion
/was-it-for-this-1.678424

12. 'Johnson beats Livingstone to become mayor of London', *Guardian*, 3 May
2008, https://www.theguardian.com/politics/2008/may/02/london08.
london; 'Northern Ireland: Robinson becomes first minister', *Guardian*, 5
June 2008, https://www.theguardian.com/politics/2008/may/02/london08.
london; 'Antonine Wall joins pyramids as a world heritage site', *Herald*, 8
July 2008, https://www.heraldscotland.com/default_content/12469562
.antonine-wall-joins-pyramids-world-heritage-site/; 'McIlroy's rise continues
as he holds off Rose for first title', *Guardian*, 1 February 2009, https://www
.theguardian.com/sport/2009/feb/01/rory-mcilroy-dubai-desert-classic
-justin-rose

13. 'Election 2010: David Cameron becomes new UK prime minister', BBC,
12 May 2010, https://www.bbc.co.uk/news/newsbeat-10109774

14. 'New taoiseach Enda Kenny foresees "darkness before dawn" in Ireland', 9
March 2011, *Guardian*, https://www.theguardian.com/world/2011/mar/09
/ireland-enda-kenny-elected-taoiseach; 'Welsh referendum: Voters give
emphatic Yes on powers', BBC, 4 March 2011, https://www.bbc.co.uk
/news/uk-wales-politics-12648649; 'Analysis: Martin Shipton on Labour's
decision to form minority government', Wales Online, 22 March 2013,
https://www.walesonline.co.uk/news/wales-news/analysis-martin-shipton
-labours-decision-1832676; 'Scottish election: SNP majority for second
term', BBC, 7 May 2011, https://www.bbc.co.uk/news/uk-scotland-13319936

15. 'Looking back at the 2011 London riots: What sparked the violence and
disorder that time?', *London Standard*, 5 August 2024, https://www
.standard.co.uk/news/uk/london-riots-2011-cause-what-happened-mark
-duggan-racism-b1174748.html; 'Edinburgh pandas spend last day in the
spotlight', BBC, 30 November 2023, https://www.bbc.co.uk/news
/uk-scotland-edinburgh-east-fife-67566112#:~:text=Edinburgh%20
Zoo%20visitors%20have%20been,extended%20due%20to%20the%20
pandemic; 'Devolution of tax powers to the Scottish parliament: The
Scotland Act 2012', House of Commons Library, 23 January 2015, https://

commonslibrary.parliament.uk/research-briefings/sn05984/; 'Scottish independence: Cameron and Salmond strike referendum deal', BBC, 15 October 2012, https://www.bbc.co.uk/news/uk-scotland-scotland -politics-19942638; 'Welsh assembly passes its first bill', *Guardian*, 12 November 2012, https://www.theguardian.com/politics/2012/nov/12 /welsh-national-assembly-bill-law

16. 'Copeland Linens, Belfast's last working linen factory closes', BBC, 25 January 2013, https://www.bbc.co.uk/news/uk-northern-ireland-21192216; 'Magdalene laundries report to be raised in Irish parliament', BBC, 6 February 2013, https://www.bbc.co.uk/news/world-europe-21348473; 'Cause of fire that destroyed Glasgow School of Art "will never be known"', *Guardian*, 25 January 2022, https://www.theguardian.com/artanddesign /2022/jan/25/cause-of-fire-that-destroyed-glasgow-school-of-art-will-never -be-known#:~:text=The%20report%20stated%20that%2C%20after,cause %20of%20the%20fire%20has

17. 'Scottish referendum: Scotland votes "No" to independence', BBC, 19 September 2014, https://www.bbc.co.uk/news/uk-scotland-29270441

18. 'Scottish referendum: Salmond to quit after Scots vote No', BBC, 19 September 2014, https://www.bbc.co.uk/news/uk-scotland-29277527; 'In full: David Cameron statement on the UK's future', BBC, 19 September 2014, https://www.bbc.co.uk/news/uk-politics-29271765; 'David Cameron "embarrassed and sorry" for saying queen purred', *Guardian*, 28 September 2014, https://www.theguardian.com/politics/2014/sep/28/david-cameron -sorry-queen-purred

19. 'How a historic tide of political change swept all before it in this election', *Guardian*, 9 May 2015, https://www.theguardian.com/politics/2015 /may/09/election-2015-how-historic-tide-political-change-swept-all -sturgeon; 'Fate of second Scottish independence referendum "in hands of the people"', *Guardian*, 15 October 2015, https://www.theguardian.com /politics/2015/oct/15/second-scottish-independence-referendum-hands -people-nicola-sturgeon-snp

20. 'Arlene Foster: DUP leader becomes new NI first minister', BBC, 11 January 2016, https://www.bbc.co.uk/news/uk-northern-ireland -politics-35260201; 'Taoiseach Enda Kenny re-elected as Irish prime minister after 70-day wait', BBC, 6 May 2016, https://www.bbc.co.uk /news/world-europe-36228773; 'Carwyn Jones reappointed first minister after Labour–Plaid deal', BBC, 18 May 2016, https://www.bbc.co.uk/news /uk-wales-politics-36312517; 'Nicola Sturgeon rules out Holyrood coalition after falling short of majority', *Guardian*, 6 May 2016, https://www .theguardian.com/politics/2016/may/06/nicola-sturgeon-rules-out -holyrood-coalition-snp-falls-short-majority

21. 'UK votes to leave EU after dramatic night divides nation', *Guardian*, 24 June 2016, https://www.theguardian.com/politics/2016/jun/24/britain -votes-for-brexit-eu-referendum-david-cameron; 'David Cameron hums a

merry tune as he hands over to Theresa May', *Guardian*, 11 July 2016, https://www.theguardian.com/politics/2016/jul/12/david-cameron-hums-a-merry-tune-as-he-hands-over-to-theresa-may

22. 'Martin McGuinness resigns as NI deputy first minister', BBC, 10 January 2017, https://www.bbc.co.uk/news/uk-northern-ireland-38561507; Chria Ryder, 'McGuinness, (James) Martin Pacelli (1950–2017)', ODNB, https://www.oxforddnb.com/display/10.1093/ref:odnb/9780198614128.001.0001/odnb-9780198614128-e-90000380305

23. 'Theresa May: 10 reasons why the PM blew her majority', BBC, 14 June 2017, https://www.bbc.co.uk/news/election-2017-40237833; 'Theresa May is "dead woman walking": Osborne', Politico, 11 June 2017, https://www.politico.eu/article/theresa-may-dead-woman-walking-george-osborne-boris-johnson-always-leadership-campaign/; 'Conservatives agree pact with DUP to support May government', BBC, 26 June 2017, https://www.bbc.co.uk/news/uk-politics-40403434

24. 'Leo Varadkar becomes Republic of Ireland's taoiseach', BBC, 14 June 2017, https://www.bbc.co.uk/news/world-europe-40266513; 'Irish abortion referendum: Ireland overturns abortion ban', BBC, 26 May 2018, https://www.bbc.co.uk/news/world-europe-44256152; 'Mark Drakeford confirmed as new Welsh first minister', BBC, 12 December 2018, https://www.bbc.co.uk/news/uk-wales-politics-46537794

25. 'Alex Salmond charged with two attempted rapes and nine sexual assaults', Sky News, 24 January 2019, https://news.sky.com/story/alex-salmond-former-snp-leader-arrested-and-charged-11616043

26. 'Election results 2019: Boris Johnson hails "new dawn" after historic victory', BBC, 13 December 2019, https://www.bbc.co.uk/news/election-2019-50776671

27. 'Stormont deal: Arlene Foster and Michelle O'Neill new top NI ministers', BBC, 12 January 2020, https://www.bbc.co.uk/news/uk-northern-ireland-51077397; 'Micheál Martin becomes new Irish PM after historic coalition deal', BBC, 27 June 2020, https://www.bbc.co.uk/news/world-europe-53201346; 'Senedd Cymru: Why has the National Assembly for Wales changed its name?', House of Commons Library, 6 May 2020, https://commonslibrary.parliament.uk/senedd-cymru-why-has-the-national-assembly-for-wales-changed-its-name/

28. 'Alex Salmond cleared of all sexual assault charges', BBC, 23 March 2020, https://www.bbc.co.uk/news/uk-scotland-52004285; 'Nicola Sturgeon cleared of breaching ministerial code over Alex Salmond saga', BBC, 22 March 2021, https://www.bbc.co.uk/news/uk-scotland-scotland-politics-56482878; 'Alex Salmond obituary: A man and a politician of contradictions', BBC, 12 October 2024, https://www.bbc.co.uk/news/articles/cd13102l9g5o

29. 'Paul Givan: Northern Ireland First Minister resigns ending "privilege of my lifetime"', Sky News, 3 February 2022, https://news.sky.com/story/paul-givan-northern-ireland-first-minister-preparing-to-resign-12531664

30. 'Boris Johnson resigns as prime minister, saying "No one is remotely indispensable"', Sky News, 8 July 2022, https://news.sky.com/story/boris -johnson-resigns-as-prime-minister-12647466; 'Liz Truss resigns: PM's exit kicks off another Tory leadership race', BBC, 20 October 2022, https:// www.bbc.co.uk/news/uk-politics-63332037

31. 'Obituary: Queen Elizabeth II', BBC, 8 September 2022, https://www.bbc .co.uk/news/uk-61605149; 'British Social Attitudes: Support for monarchy falls to new low', National Centre for Social Research, 29 April 2024, https://natcen.ac.uk/news/british-social-attitudes-support-monarchy-falls -new-low

32. 'Why did Nicola Sturgeon resign as first minister?', BBC, 16 February 2023, https://www.bbc.co.uk/news/uk-scotland-scotland-politics-64661974 ; 'Humza Yousaf quits as Scotland's first minister', BBC, 30 April 2024, https://www.bbc.co.uk/news/uk-scotland-scotland-politics-68918151; 'Swinney wins Holyrood vote to be Scotland's first minister', BBC, 7 May 2024, https://www.bbc.co.uk/news/articles/c0de2ke9vjdo

33. 'Peter Murrell charged with embezzlement in SNP finance probe', BBC, 18 April 2024, https://www.bbc.co.uk/news/uk-scotland-68850088; 'Nicola Sturgeon and Peter Murrell to end marriage', BBC, 13 January 2025, https://www.bbc.co.uk/news/articles/cvgpl37lez7o

34. 'Stormont: Michelle O'Neill makes history as nationalist first minister', BBC, 3 February 2024, https://www.bbc.co.uk/news/uk-northern-ireland -politics-68180505; 'Micheál Martin elected taoiseach after chaos subsides', BBC, 23 January 2025, https://www.bbc.co.uk/news/articles/c05l794gze6o

35. 'Keir Starmer hails "sunlight of hope" as Britain wakes up to Labour landslide', Guardian, 5 July 2024, https://www.theguardian.com/politics /article/2024/jul/05/time-for-us-to-deliver-says-starmer-as-labour-heads -for-landslide; 'Winter fuel payments scrapped for millions', BBC, 29 July 2024, https://www.bbc.co.uk/news/articles/cx02zdd92zdo; 'Traditional steelmaking in Port Talbot ends', BBC, 29 September 2024, https://www .bbc.co.uk/news/articles/c70zxjldqnxo

36. Devine, The Scottish Nation 618–19; 'Tom Nairn, 1932–2023: "Britain will break up in the next 5 years"', openDemocracy, 11 December 2020, https:// www.opendemocracy.net/en/opendemocracyuk/its-time-to-break-up -britain/

37. 'Catholics outnumber Protestants in Northern Ireland for first time', Guardian, 22 September 2022, https://www.theguardian.com/world/2022 /sep/22/catholics-outnumber-protestants-northern-ireland-census

SELECT BIBLIOGRAPHY

Adams, Ian, *The Making of Urban Scotland* (Croom Helm, 1978)

Akrigg, G.P.V. (ed.), *Letters of King James VI and I* (University of California Press, 1984)

Baker, Richard Anthony, *British Music Hall: an Illustrated History* (Pen & Sword, 2014)

Balleine's History of Jersey, revised and enlarged by Marguerite Syvret and Joan Stevens (Phillimore & Co., 1998)

Beckert, Sven, *Empire of Cotton: A New History of Global Capitalism* (Allen Lane, 2014)

Bédoyère, Guy de la, *Roman Britain: A New History* (Thames & Hudson, 2013)

Binns, Jack, *Yorkshire in the Civil Wars: Origins, Impact and Outcome* (Blackthorn, 2004)

Bowers, Judith, *Stan Laurel and Other Stars of the Panopticon: The Story of the Britannia Music Hall* (Birlinn, 2007)

Bull, Stephen, *'A General Plague of Madness': The Civil Wars in Lancashire, 1640–1660* (Carnegie Publishing, 2009)

Busteed, Mervyn, *The Irish in Manchester c.1750–1921: Resistance, Adaptation and Identity* (Manchester University Press, 2016)

Carlton, Charles, *The Experience of the British Civil Wars* (Routledge, 1992)

Carlyle, Thomas, *Past and Present* (Chapman & Hall, 1843)

Carpenter, David, *Struggle for Mastery: The Penguin History of Britain 1066–1284* (Penguin, 2004)

Cobbett, William, *A History of the Protestant Reformation in England and Ireland* (Simpkin, Marshall, 1857)

Colley, Linda, *Britons: Forging the Union 1707–1837* (Vintage, 1996 [1992])

Cunliffe, Barry, *Britain Begins* (Oxford University Press, 2012)

Davies, John, *A History of Wales* (Penguin 2007 [1990])

Davies, John, Nigel Jenkins, Menna Baines and Peredur I. Lynch (eds), *The Welsh Academy Encyclopaedia of Wales* (University of Wales Press, 2008)

Davies, Norman, *The Isles: A History* (Papermac, 2000 [1999])

Davis, Graham, *The Irish in Britain, 1815–1914* (Gill & Macmillan, 1991)

Devine, T.M. *Scotland's Empire: The Origins of the Global Diaspora* (Allen Lane, 2003)

—— *The Scottish Nation 1700–2007* (Allen Lane, 1999)

Edwards, Viv, *Multilingualism in the English-Speaking World: Pedigree of Nations* (John Wiley, 2008)

Ewan, Elizabeth L., Sue Innes, Sian Reynolds et al. (eds) *The Biographical Dictionary of Scottish Women from the Earliest Times* (Edinburgh University Press, 2006)

Fleming, Robin, *Britain after Rome: The Fall and Rise 400 to 1070* (Penguin, 2010)

Foster, R.F. (ed.), *The Oxford History of Ireland* (Oxford University Press, 2001 [1989])

Frangopulo, N.J. (ed.), *Rich Inheritance: A Guide to the History of Manchester* (Manchester Education Committee, 1962)

Fraser, Antonia, *Mary Queen of Scots* (Weidenfeld & Nicolson, 1994 [1969])

Fryer, Peter, *Staying Power: The History of Black People in Britain* (Pluto, 2018 [1984])

Goodwins, Sarah, *A Brief History of the Isle of Man* (Loaghtan, 2017)

Gower, Jon, *The Story of Wales* (BBC Books, 2012)

Griffin, Emma, *A Short History of the British Industrial Revolution* (Palgrave Macmillan, 2010)

Griffin, Emma, *Liberty's Dawn: A People's History of the Industrial Revolution* (Yale University Press, 2013)

Groom, Brian, *Northerners: A History, from the Ice Age to the Present Day* (HarperNorth, 2022)

Guy, John, *'My Heart Is my Own': The Life of Mary Queen of Scots* (Fourth Estate, 2004)

Halliday, F.E., *A Shakespeare Companion 1564–1964* (Penguin, 1964)

Hazeldine, Tom, *The Northern Question: A History of a Divided Country* (Verso, 2020)

Heggarty, Neil, *The Story of Ireland: In Search of a New National Memory* (BBC Books, 2012)

Hibbert, Christopher, *Queen Victoria: A Personal History* (HarperCollins, 2000)

Higham, Nicholas and Martin Ryan, *The Anglo-Saxon World* (Yale University Press, 2013)

Hochschild, Adam, *Bury the Chains: The British Struggle to Abolish Slavery* (Macmillan, 2005)

Holman, Katherine, *The Northern Conquest: Vikings in Britain and Ireland* (Signal, 2007)

Howarth, Nicki, *Cartimandua: Queen of the Brigantes* (History Press, 2008)

Hunt, Tristram, *The Frock-Coated Communist: The Revolutionary Life of Friedrich Engels* (Allen Lane, 2009)

Huscroft, Richard, *The Norman Conquest: A New Introduction* (Pearson Longman, 2009)

Jackson, Lee, *Palaces of Pleasure: From Music Halls to the Seaside to Football, How the Victorians Invented Mass Entertainment* (Yale University Press, 2019)

Jaffe, Deborah, *Ingenious Women* (Sutton, 2003)

James, Lawrence, *The Decline and Fall of the British Empire* (Little, Brown, 1994)

Jeal, Tim, *Stanley: The Impossible Life of Africa's Greatest Explorer* (Yale University Press, 2007)

Johnes, Martin, *Wales: England's Colony? The Conquest, Assimilation and Re-creation of Wales* (Parthian, 2019)

Johnston, Peter *A Short History of Guernsey* (Guernsey Press, 1987)

Jones, J. Graham, *The History of Wales* (University of Wales Press, 2014)

Kearney, Hugh, *The British Isles: A History of Four Nations* (Cambridge University Press, 2006)

Keegan, Gerald, *Famine Diary: Journey to a New World* (Wolfhound, 1991)

Kelly, James, *Food Rioting in Ireland in the Eighteenth and Nineteenth Centuries* (Four Courts, 2017)

Kidd, Alan, *Manchester: A History* (Carnegie Publishing, 2006 [1993])

—— *The Origins of Manchester, from Roman Conquest to Industrial Revolution* (Carnegie Publishing, 2023)

Kidd, Alan and Terry Wyke (eds), *Manchester: Making the Modern City* (Liverpool University Press, 2016)

Kynaston, David, *Austerity Britain 1945–51* (Bloomsbury, 2007)

Labarge, Margaret Wade and N.E. Griffiths, *A Medieval Miscellany* (McGill–Queen's Press, 1997)

Lee, J.J., *Ireland, 1912–1985: Politics and Society* (Cambridge University Press, 1989)

Lynch, Michael, *Scotland: A New History* (Pimlico, 1992 [1991])

MacAulay, Donald, *The Celtic Languages* (Cambridge University Press, 1992)

Macdonald, Sharon, *Reimagining Culture: Histories, Identities and the Gaelic Renaissance* (Routledge, 2020)

Mackenzie John M. and T.M. Devine (eds), *Scotland and the British Empire* (Oxford University Press, 2011)

MacMillan, Margaret, *The War That Ended Peace* (Random House, 2013)

MacRaild, Donald, *The Irish Diaspora in Britain, 1750–1939* (Palgrave Macmillan, 2011)

Mathers, Helen, *Patron Saint of Prostitutes: Josephine Butler and a Victorian Scandal* (History Press, 2014)

Mitchell, Brian R., *Abstract of British Historical Statistics* (Cambridge University Press, 1962)

Mattingly, David, *An Imperial Possession: Britain in the Roman Empire* (Penguin, 2007)

Moffat, Alistair, *Scotland: A History from the Earliest Times* (Birlinn, 2015)

Mokyr, Joel, *The Enlightened Economy: Britain and the Industrial Revolution 1700–1850* (Penguin, 2009)

Moore, David W., *The Other British Isles: A History of Shetland, Orkney, the Hebrides, Isle of Man, Anglesey, Scilly, Isle of Wight and the Channel Isles* (McFarland, 2005)

Morrill, J.S. (ed), *The Impact of the English Civil War* (Collins & Brown, 1991)

Morris, Jean M., *Into the Crucible* (Lulu Press, 2028)

Morris, Marc, *The Norman Conquest* (Hutchinson, 2012)

Mowat, Charles Loch, *Britain between the Wars 1918–1940* (Methuen, 1955)

Musgrove, Eric, *The North of England: A History from Roman Times to the Present* (Basil Blackwell, 1990)

O'Leary, Paul, *Immigration and Integration: The Irish in Wales, 1798–1922* (University of Wales Press, 2002)

Oliver, Neil, *A History of Scotland* (Weidenfeld & Nicolson, 2009)

Olusoga, David, *Black and British: A Forgotten History* (Macmillan, 2016)

Orr, Julie, *Scotland, Darien and the Atlantic World 1698–1700* (Edinburgh University Press, 2018)

Osborne, Roger, *Iron, Steam & Money: The Making of the Industrial Revolution* (Bodley Head, 2013)

Paulu, Burton, *Television and Radio in the United Kingdom* (Palgrave Macmillan, 1981)

The Penguin Illustrated History of Britain & Ireland (Penguin, 2004)

Póirtéir, Cathal (ed.), *The Great Irish Famine* (Mercier, 1955)

Poole, Robert (ed.), *The Lancashire Witches: Histories and Stories* (Manchester University Press, 2002)

—— *Peterloo: The English Uprising* (Oxford University Press, 2019)

Prebble, John, *The Darien Disaster* (Pimlico, 1968)

Price, Barclay, *The Chinese in Britain: A History of Visitors and Settlers* (Amberley Publishing, 2019)

Rhodes, Cecil, *The Last Will and Testament of Cecil Rhodes*, ed. W.T. Stead (London 'Review of Reviews' Office, 1902)

Richards, Eric, *Britannia's Children: Emigration from England, Scotland, Wales and Ireland since 1600* (A&C Black, 2004)

Richardson, Matthew, *The Isle of Man: Stone Age to Swinging Sixties* (Pen & Sword, 2020)

Rose, Mary B. (ed.), *The Lancashire Cotton Industry: A History since 1700* (Lancashire County Books, 1996)

Ross, David, *Ireland: History of a Nation* (Waverley Books, 2019 [2002])

Sandbrook, Dominic, *Never Had It So Good: A History of Britain from Suez to the Beatles* (Little, Brown, 2005)

Schama, Simon, *A History of Britain: At the Edge of the World? 3000 BC–AD 1603* (BBC Worldwide, 2000)

—— *A History of Britain: The British Wars 1603–1776* (BBC Worldwide, 2001)

Shotter, David, *Romans and Britons in North-West England* (Centre for North-West Regional Studies, University of Lancaster, 2004 [1993])

Sigillito, Gina, *The Daughters of Maeve: 50 Irish Women Who Changed the World* (Kensington Publishing, 2012)

Singleton, Fred, *Industrial Revolution in Yorkshire* (Dalesman, 1970)

Southern, Patricia, *Roman Britain: A New History 55 BC–AD 450* (Amberley Publishing, 2013)

Stephens, Meic (ed.), *The New Companion to the Literature of Wales* (University of Wales Press, 1998)

Sterling, Christopher H., *Encyclopedia of Radio 3-Volume Set* (Routledge, 2004)

Tanner, Marcus, *The Last of the Celts* (Yale University Press, 2004)

Thomson, William P.L., *The New History of Orkney* (Birlinn, 2008 [1987])

Tibbles, Anthony, *Liverpool and the Slave Trade* (Liverpool University Press, 2018)

Tombs, Robert, *The English and Their History* (Allen Lane, 2014)

Visram, Rozina, *Asians in Britain: 400 Years of History* (Pluto, 2002)

Watt, Douglas *The Price of Scotland: Darien, Union and the Wealth of Nations* (Luath Press, 2014)

Weir, Alison, *Lancaster and York: The Wars of the Roses* (Jonathan Cape, 1995)

—— *Mary, Queen of Scots and the Murder of Lord Darnley* (Random House, 2008 [2003])

Whatley, Christopher A., *The Scots and the Union* (Edinburgh University Press, 2006)

Whelan, Kevin, *Guernsey: A History* (Writer's Block 2023)

Wilkes, Sue, *Narrow Windows, Narrow Lives: The Industrial Revolution in Lancashire* (Tempus, 2008)

Winstanley, Ian (ed.), *Children's Employment Commission 1842* (Picks Publishing, 1999)

Withers, Charles, *Gaelic in Scotland, 1698–1981* (John Donald, 1984)

Woodman, Deborah, *The Story of Manchester* (Phillimore & Co., 2017)

Worden, Blair, *The English Civil Wars: 1640–1660* (Weidenfeld & Nicolson, 2009)

Wormald, Jenny, *Mary, Queen of Scots* (George Philip, 1988)

—— (ed.), *Scotland: A History* (Oxford University Press, 2005)

Young, G.V.C., *The History of the Isle of Man under the Norse or Now through a Glass Darkly* (Mansk-Svenska, 1981)

ACKNOWLEDGEMENTS

I am profoundly grateful to all those who read and commented on my first two books, *Northerners: A History, from the Ice Age to the Present Day* and *Made in Manchester: A People's History of the City that Shaped the Modern World*. Your support, and that of all the booksellers who got behind it, and the societies and festivals that invited me to speak, has given me immense encouragement.

Massive thanks are due again to the brilliant team at HarperNorth, who have done so much to boost the publishing scene outside London since it was founded in 2020. Particular credit goes to Jonathan de Peyer, editorial director for non-fiction, who has guided me expertly through the publishing processes. Genevieve, Alice, Megan, Taslima, Hilary and their colleagues have been tremendously supportive – thoughtful, constructive, kind and encouraging. My agent Andrew Lownie, a prolific historian and biographer, has been a rock.

Above all, I thank my wife Carola for her advice and for casting her novelist's eye over each chapter. I could not have done it without her. Thank you to all my family and friends who have been patient with me while I grappled with this project.

INDEX

TK

For more unmissable reads,
sign up to the HarperNorth newsletter at
www.harpernorth.co.uk

or find us on socials at
@HarperNorthUK

**Harper
North**